Afe Adogame, Magnus Echtler,
Ulf Vierke (eds.)

Unpacking the New

Beiträge zur Afrikaforschung

ISSN 0938–7285

Herausgegeben vom Institut für Afrika-Studien

in Verbindung mit dem
Kulturwissenschaftlichen Forschungskolleg SFB/FK 560
„Lokales Handeln in Afrika im Kontext globaler Einflüsse“
der Universität Bayreuth

Band

36

LIT

Unpacking the New

Critical Perspectives
on Cultural Syncretization
in Africa and Beyond

edited by

Afe Adogame, Magnus Echtler
and Ulf Vierke

LIT

Gedruckt mit Unterstützung der Deutschen Forschungsgemeinschaft

Bibliographic information published by the Deutsche Nationalbibliothek
The Deutsche Nationalbibliothek lists this publication in the Deutsche Nationalbibliografie; detailed bibliographic data are available in the Internet at http://dnb.d-nb.de.

ISBN 978-3-03735-934-1 (Schweiz)
ISBN 978-3-8258-0719-1 (Deutschland)

A catalogue record for this book is available from the British Library

Dufourstr. 31
CH-8008 Zürich
Tel. +41 (0) 44-251 75 05
Fax +41 (0) 44-251 75 06
e-Mail: zuerich@lit-verlag.ch
http://www.lit-verlag.ch

LIT VERLAG Dr. W. Hopf
Berlin 2008
Auslieferung/Verlagskontakt:
Fresnostr. 2
D-48159 Münster
Tel. +49 (0)251–62 03 20
Fax +49 (0)251–23 19 72
e-Mail: lit@lit-verlag.de
http://www.lit-verlag.de

Auslieferung:

Schweiz/Österreich: Medienlogistik Pichler-ÖBZ GmbH & Co KG
IZ-NÖ, Süd, Straße 1, Objekt 34, A-2355 Wiener Neudorf
Tel. +43 (0) 2236/63 535 - 290, Fax +43 (0) 2236/63 535 - 243, e-Mail: mlo@medien-logistik.at

Deutschland: LIT Verlag Fresnostr. 2, D-48159 Münster
Tel. +49 (0) 2 51/620 32 - 22, Fax +49 (0) 2 51/922 60 99, e-Mail: vertrieb@lit-verlag.de

Distributed in the UK by: Global Book Marketing, 99B Wallis Rd, London, E9 5LN
Phone: +44 (0) 20 8533 5800 – Fax: +44 (0) 1600 775 663
http://www.centralbooks.co.uk/acatalog/search.html

Acknowledgements

This book has grown from the international and interdisciplinary conference, *Questioning the New: Explorations in Processes of Cultural Syncretization in Africa and Beyond*, convened by the Humanities Collaborative Research Centre (SFB and FK 560 - Local Action in Africa in the Context of Global Influences) at the University of Bayreuth in October 2004. Our gratitude goes to the *Deutsche Forschungsgemeinschaft* (German Research Foundation) for funding the conference and the publication. Many thanks to our colleagues of the SFB/FK 560 and all those who contributed in one way or another to making this publication a reality. The inputs of Maike Birzle, Sarah Böllinger, Verena Kremling, Peter Probst, Sonja Ruff and Christine Scherer deserve mention. Special thanks to Jim Spickard, whose significant critical reflection of the entire conference was invaluable in structuring the book.

Contents

Introduction
Unpacking the New: Critical Perspectives on Cultural Syncretization in Africa and Beyond

Afe Adogame, Magnus Echtler, Ulf Vierke

In a world supposedly characterized by the production of new differences and cultural permutations resulting from the twin processes of globalization and cultural syncretization, hardly anything has remained as obscure and theoretically under-theorized as the very notion of the 'new' itself. An inherent relativity accompanies any contemplation of what is new or old, a fuzziness regarding the point at which a phenomenon transcends an old state to become new. This state can be likened to the uneasiness that is associated with the complex semantic history of syncretism, including its adoption and re-semantization in academic discourse. Syncretism as both process and description hinges largely on the assumption and premise that what is observed has appropriately or inappropriately mixed categories – culture, religion, language – that are intrinsically alien to each other. Such a syncretic constellation is bound to result in something that may be considered new. Any definition of 'syncretism', the syncretization process and the appropriation of the notion of the 'new' as useful heuristic tools must indeed be located within specific local contexts, as such terms are unlikely to serve as adequate descriptions of homogenous sets of phenomena. Syncretism as a process is intertwined with processes of contextualization. Against this backdrop, the aim of this book is to unravel and demystify the ideology of the new on the basis of concrete case studies from various regions across Africa and beyond.

The contributions in this book have been selected and peer-reviewed and draw on papers originally presented at the international and interdisciplinary conference, *Questioning the New: Explorations in Processes of Cultural Syncretization in Africa and Beyond*, hosted by the Humanities Collaborative Research Centre (SFB and FK 560 - Local Action in Africa in the Context of Global Influences) at the University of Bayreuth in October 2004. The contributions are organized into three main sections, carefully chosen in view of thematic coherence and the way in which the conference presentations actually probed the question of the 'new'. With contributions confronting the politics of the new – strategies of concealing and revealing the historical processes of mixing, legitimizing or discrediting the new – the first section focuses on issues of power and control. By considering issues of epistemology and transactions of art and performance as ways of testing what is possible and what is not, the second section engages with questions of negotiation and exploration. Finally, by investigating the realm of experience and belief as crucial cultural domains for the expansion and dispersal of the new, the third section tackles issues of persuasion and success. *Unpacking the New* thus illuminates the intricately intertwined processes of cultural syncretization just as these modes of entanglement reveal the manifold ways in which the new is socially realized and put into practice.

The various authors share a common theoretical perspective as they test the analytical utility of the syncretization concept within their respective case studies. The term 'syncretism' seems rather old-fashioned, as it was initially employed within the fields of theology and religious studies to discuss the mixing of the heterogeneous roots of religious traditions for more than a century, a long and varied history of scientific enquiries (Leopold and Jensen eds. 2004). From the second half of the twentieth century onward, the concept has been increasingly criticized for two reasons: for its normative connotations, based on the implicit or even explicit judgement of pure vs. impure religious traditions; and for its analytical emptiness, based on the fact that all religious traditions can be described as culturally mixed in terms of their historical origin (see Baird 1991: 63, 69; Lincoln 2001: 454). If everything is syncretistic, does it make sense to say that nothing is syncretistic? Otherwise, how useful is the metaphor for particular things if it thus applies to all things? Or is it simply based on degree or intensity? Are these metaphors not simply languages of power or who decides what is syncretic – self or the Other?

These issues are controversial because different hermeneutical communities or individuals attach different meanings to what is going on or being observed. Partially as a reaction to these criticisms, other disciplines in the social sciences and linguistics have developed different concepts and terminologies such as creolization, hybridity, bricolage and *métissage* or *mestizaje*. While the concepts differ with regard to their specific approach, which is often coloured by the history of their particular disciplines, they share a common interest in innovations under conditions of culture contact, and they all try to come to terms with the 'conundrum of mixing' (Coombes and Brah 2000). In actual fact, the recourse to alternative concepts and terminologies does not render the syncretism concept anathema within the social sciences and linguistics. Recent works show how scholars have continued to explore the concept in order to unravel its heuristic value and how it may or may not serve as a useful analytical device. The Special Issue of *Social Compass* edited by McGuire and Maduro (2005) brought together experts from the social sciences and the history of religion to explore further the concepts 'syncretism' and 'hybridity'. In another interesting piece on 'syncretism' in the *World History Connected,* the social historian Lindenfeld viewed it as 'an umbrella-like term, covering a wide variety of strategies and processes by which cultures with differing beliefs and practices adapt to one another' (Lindenfeld 2006:1). He distinguishes between 'syncretism from above' and 'syncretism from below'. Eric Maroney's *The SCM Core Text: Religious Syncretism* (2006) attempts to present a more nuanced view of the Abrahamic religions – Judaism, Christianity and Islam – as compelling examples of religious syncretism. Using some forms of the Abrahamic religions, he illustrates 'contrasting views on the nature of religion in order to show the diversity of responses to changing circumstances that people have had in these three faiths, and how people have moulded the religions to suit the times in which they were living, the social and political circumstances by which they were surrounded, and cultural crises they were facing, and above all, the unique needs of their different communities of believers' (Maroney 2006: xiii). As Maroney demonstrates throughout his book, syncretism is often the opposite of fundamentalism (cf. Droogers' contribution in this volume). Linguists have also appropriated the concept of syncretism in a variety of interesting ways, the works of Stump (2001) and Baerman, Brown and Corbett (2005) being prominent examples. Stump proposed a typology distinguishing four types, namely unidirectional, bidirectional, unstipulated and symmetrical syncretism. Baerman et al. explore syncretism – where a single form serves two or more morphosyntactic functions – as a persistent problem at the syntax-morphology interface.

On the conceptual level, we suggest integrating the perspectives of the other approaches, but expressing this through the notion of syncretization rather than syncretism. Scientific studies of processes of mixing are of basic importance for understanding the dynamics of the contemporary world, even though historical research has shown that mixing has been part of every culture and society in the past. Concepts of mixing remain central to the interpretation of heterogeneity on all levels of social and cultural analysis, as a challenge to views of modernization or globalization as homogenizing, teleological processes (see, for instance, Appadurai 1996, Eisenstadt 2000, Loimeier, Neubert and Weißköppel 2005, Meyer and Geschiere 1999, Probst and Spittler 2004).

On the level of terminology, the terms under consideration are not restricted to scientific usage, but form part of wider discourses. They all carry negative and positive connotations and all imply the mixing of at least two distinct entities, usually connected with some notions of pure and impure units. In considering all such related concepts as creolization, hybridity, bricolage and *métissage* or *mestizaje*, syncretism is the only term that does not draw its source as a metaphor from the field of biology. While this conceptual link with constructions of race and colour and associated relations of power is of critical value in some contexts, it does not apply to all instances of mixing. Because the concept of syncretism is cultural rather than biological and therefore better suited for use in diverse contexts, it retains some value for analysing how mixing the multi-stranded flows of heterogeneous origins creates new social and cultural formations. However, in order to develop this argument further, it is necessary to return to the histories of its usage.

Historicizing the Concept of Syncretism

Prior to its academic usage, Plutarch employed syncretism to refer to the unity of the Cretans in the face of an outside foe, although they fought against each other at other times (see Rudolph 2004: 68f.). He employed the term in a positive sense, advocating unity through the merging of similar but antagonistic units. In the syncretistic strife of sixteenth- and seventeenth-century post-Reformation Europe, the term 'syncretism' was used to promote unity among Christian denominations, as well as to criticize these very attempts to unify competing groups (ibid.: 69f.). In this second meaning, based on the theological notion of the revealed religion, syncretism denounced the illegitimate mixing of 'pure' units.

Scholars in religious studies in the nineteenth century applied the label 'syncretism' primarily to Hellenistic religion. Interpreted within Hegelian notions of historical process, Greek syncretism formed a transitional stage in the teleological movement towards Christianity. This first scientific concept of syncretism was not detached from wider discourses and implied a historical or evolutionary superiority of the 'own' in relation to the mixed 'other' (see Shaw and Stewart 1994: 4f.; Droge 2001; Leopold and Jensen 2004: 20f.). By the turn of the twentieth century, the concept of syncretism was being used to interpret Christianity itself. Again the term marked a relation of difference, but this time it referred to the superior position, the vitality of early Christianity, based on the mixing of the Judaic and Hellenistic traditions, as contrasted with the supposedly 'barren' and law-centred tradition of Judaism. Again, the scientific concept of syncretism was not restricted to disinterested scholarly dispute, but formed part of wider cultural struggles over the role of religion in the modern world (Kippenberg 2004).

In spite of these rather contradictory usages, 'syncretism' retained its negative meaning, at least in the African context, where it was used in missiology in the middle of the twentieth century. Faced with the emergence of the African Initiated Churches, and burdened by the divergent interests of theology and the study of religions, as well as by the close historical connections between Christian missions and colonial regimes, missiologists interpreted the mixing of African and European religious traditions as syncretism, and saw these 'syncretic religions' as dangerous developments leading away from Christianity, as bridges back to 'heathenism', 'tradition' or 'nativism' (Sundkler 1961: 297; Oosthuizen 1968: xi). In these studies, descriptions of processes of mixing were explicitly merged with the theological critique of syncretism, a normative judgment refuted by other scholars (Peel 1968; Adogame 1999: 208-14; Berner 2001; see also Adogame and Kuponu, this volume). As Adogame aptly remarks:

> Syncretism is a very problematic and contentious term which has transcended historical transformations in meaning. [...] While recognising that the concept of syncretism might even be defined in a 'good', 'positive' conceptual analysis, it remains to be seen to what extent this effort will go to 'undress' new religious initiatives, such as the Celestial Church of Christ (and in fact African churches), of the old, obnoxious 'cloak' with which they have been dressed or tagged. [...] Syncretism is a concept applied to a religion by those who stand outside its circle of faith and hence fail to see or to experience its inner unity. Scholars must show restraint in using the epithet 'syncretism' for rituals or practices [they do] not really understand. While we recognise its universal application in the historical sense on the one hand, it poses [...] a barrier to authentic religio-historical understanding in its theological sense (Adogame 1999: 208ff.).

Given the history of this term, which is often coloured by theological considerations, the study of religion or *Religionswissenschaft* has embarked on a critical re-evaluation of the concept (see Colpe 1975, Pye 1971, Wießner 1978, Berner 1978, Baird 1991, Rudolph 2004). In this vein, Berner distinguished syncretism on the level of elements from syncretism on the level of systems, as well as introducing a complex terminology to differentiate between numerous types of mixing (Berner 1978, 2004). But despite the theoretical work invested in the development of the concept, its analytical value remains challenged within the field of religious studies, and there is only agreement on the problematic nature of the term (see Cassidy 2001, Leopold and Jensen eds. 2004).

Outside religious studies, some anthropologists have used the term 'syncretism' in their interpretations of African and African-American cultures. Pioneered by Herskovits (1941), this endeavour to establish the scientific significance of African-American culture and history defined syncretism as the reintegration of cultural traits of various origins within a process of acculturation. Besides reconstructing the more or less 'pure' African roots of African-American cultures, Herskovits emphasized their vitality and power to survive, thus striving to repossess the African heritage of African-American culture and to promote its importance within the melting-pot ideology of the United States (Apter 1991: 160; Shaw and Stewart 1994: 5). Herskovits' focus on the African roots of cultural traits, and therefore on their continuity, was opposed to the position of Frazier (1939), who emphasized the disruptive quality of the social structures of slavery (see Yelvington 2001: 228-33). Bastide, in his study of African-Brazilian religions, moved beyond cultural traits by taking account of the importance of structural, cultural and sociological factors in the mixing of African religions and Catholicism. He also focused on the level of collective representations, where he distinguished between religious syncretism as correspondence between the distinct religions and magical syncretism as the addition of diverse elements within one tradition (Bastide 1995: 365, 386ff.).

Also looking for underlying principles of what had been 'mixed' in African-American culture were Mintz and Price, who took up the opposition of survival vs. creation posed by Herskovits and Frazier. They conceptualized the process of mixing as one of creolization, based on the linguistic distinction between pidgin languages spoken as a second language, and creole languages employed as first language.

The concept of creolization thus posits a two-step process of survival and re-creation, taking into account the cultural content and social context of the mixing (Mintz and Price 1992: 20ff.; for linguistics, see Hymes ed. 1971; Owens, this volume). Hannerz (1987, 1997) introduced creolization to the global stage and to popular culture, emphasising the volatility of mixing by using the metaphors of cultural flows and dissolving boundaries.[1] But not all anthropologists have followed the conceptual shift to creolization. In the field of the anthropology of religion, Stewart and Shaw's *Syncretism and Antisyncretism: The Politics of Religious Synthesis* (1994) linked syncretism with agency, relations of power and strategies of resistance, and opposed syncretic processes to antisyncretisms in the varied forms of multiculturalism, authenticity, nationalism or fundamentalism, an argument taken up by Beyer and Droogers in this volume. Shaw and Stewart aptly show that problems with syncretism do not seem to lie with any substantive objections to the semantics of the term – since hardly anyone would deny that different religious traditions have amalgamated in the past, or that they continue to interact and borrow from each other today – but with the very word itself and its history of its application (Shaw and Stewart 1994: 3). As they note further, 'simply identifying a ritual or tradition as 'syncretic' tells us very little and gets us practically nowhere, since all religions have composite origins and are continually reconstructed through ongoing processes of synthesis and erasure' (ibid.: 7). Thus, instead of seeing 'syncretism' as a category, their emphasis is on 'processes of religious synthesis and discourses of syncretism'.

While the term 'creolization' implies a notion of biologically mixed descent, the questions of the construction of race and its links with power relations were made explicit in the concepts of hybridity and *métissage* or *mestizaje*. Developed in the fields of literary, cultural and postcolonial studies, and centred originally on African-American

[1] For more recent applications of the concept of creolization to the study of language, social structure, folk culture, literature and art, see Collier and Fleischmann (eds.) 2003.

and Latin-American cultures or colonial encounters, but quickly extended to the global context, these concepts were often applied to artistic expressions, while making use of their biological connotations in the deconstruction of race, gender, nation and ethnicity.[2] With the new terms established in interwoven discourses, the proponents of the two concepts soon engaged in struggles over scientific hegemony (see Brah and Coombes 2000, Duboux 1994, Nederveen Pieterse 2001, Toumson 1998).[3]

Whither Syncretism?

The conceptualization of processes of mixing in situations of culture contact has come a long way. It is possible to account for both the cultural content and the social setting of mixing, and to distinguish between elemental and systematic levels of mixing. The process is differentiated in time, with the notion of actors socialized into mixed systems of cultural significance, mixed material environments, mixed ethno- or mediascapes, and mixed forms of social organization. Against essentialist notions of race, nationalism and ethnicity, of pure and homogeneous units of culture, and the 'refusal to accept the complicity and syncretic interdependency of black and white thinkers' (Gilroy 1999: 31), there is the option to come to terms with mixing through 'the theorization of creolization, métissage, mestizaje, and hybridity. From the viewpoint of ethnic absolutism, this would be a litany of pollution and impurity.' Such is the critical value of these concepts, but Gilroy adds that '[t]hese terms are rather unsatisfactory ways of naming the processes of cultural mutation and restless (dis)continuity that exceed racial discourse and avoid capture by its

---

[2] See e.g. Audinet 2004, Bhabha 1994, De Villanova and Vermès (eds.) 2006, Kraidy 2005, Laplantine and Nouss 2001, Martínez-Echazábal 1998, Nederveen Pieterse 1994, Turgeon (ed.) 2001, Weißköppel 2005, Young 1995.

[3] Scientific discourse did not stop with hybridity and *métissage*, and the speed of the invention of 'new' concepts seems to be accelerating. For mixing in the global context, see e.g. the concept of 'transdifference', which is intended to account for both the construction and transgression of cultural differences (Allolio-Näcke and Kalscheuer and Manzeschke eds. 2005).

agents' (ibid.: 2), processes he pictures in the moving ships of the black Atlantic.

As long as one takes account of the complexity of mixing, the choice of terms is one of personal taste and theoretical nuances. Most often the authors' interests, based on their position within the scientific field, will guide the terminological choices. Unsurprisingly, the heterogeneous group of authors that make up this book do not necessarily meet on same conceptual or terminological grounds. Within the discursive framework of our interdisciplinary project (SFB and FK 560) at the University of Bayreuth, we agreed on the term 'syncretization' intending to emphasise the processual concept of mixing and its links with mediascapes and perception, as well as with both structural and actor-based theories of power. The fact that the term was chosen in an interdisciplinary compromise points to its major strength: its wide applicability within the specific local setting. All the terms in question share the root metaphor of mixing, of the blending of distinct units. This constitutes their critical value against all kinds of proclaimed purities, but it still carries the image of somewhat purer substances being merged in the process. The past usage of all these terms was not restricted to the pure field of disinterested science, but formed part of differentiating strategies within the scientific field, and of wider discourses and conflicts. All the terms carry positive and negative connotations and all take sides, both critically and affirmatively. They all share these problems, but the terms 'creolization', '*métissage*' or '*mestizaje*' and 'hybridity' draw their metaphors from the biological context of the mixture of 'pure races' (see Stewart 1999). In the case of syncretism, the metaphor refers to the uniting or mixing of antagonistic social or cultural units, groups of Cretans and Christian denominations. By avoiding a biological source, the term 'syncretism' loses some critical nuances, but gains a wider applicability, especially for instances where cultural or social mixing does not contribute to the construction of racial difference.

There is another incentive for the reactivation of the term 'syncretism': its marginal position within the ideology of the new. Just as attention has been drawn to the ideological function of the reconstruction of cultural roots (see Apter 1991), the celebration of the creativity and vitality of mixing has been criticized as a 'new planetary ideology' or 'another kind of intellectual imperialism' (Kraidy 2005: 68, referring to Toumson 1998; Shaw and Steward 1994: 23). Hannerz exemplifies the shift in the conceptualization of mixing with quotes from W.E.B. DuBois and Salmon Rushdie. In the first case, according to Hannerz, there is a marginal man split into two, whose agency 'concerns strength in the face of adversity', while in the second case mixing is celebrated as 'a source – perhaps the most important source – of desirable cultural renewal' (Hannerz 1997: 12). It is a question of perspective, of a choice between mixing conceived as a strategy to survive and mixing as an expression of creativity. Mixing is surely both, but are migrants trying to enter 'Fortress Europe', with six hundred confirmed deaths on the passage to the Canary Islands in 2006, tricksters thriving in the borderlands?[4] Does the scientific affirmation of the empowering quality of creative mixing serve an ideological function? We suspect it does, therefore some authors will prefer to stick to the term 'syncretism'. For them, it is most closely connected with social struggles, due to its connotations of unity in the face of an outside foe, and it is least tainted with the celebration of the new, due to its unpopularity in recent discourses. If the creation of the new is pictured in the enriching intermingling of cultural flows, then it is also necessary to look at the dams that bar the flows and at the people who drown in the turbulences. As scientists we have command over a veritable amount of symbolic capital, we shape views and define what is worth acknowledging, and we are never outside the social game.

Historically, the basic elements and features that often lead to a certain kind of combination are as important as the 'syncretistic' outcome of the process of combination, fusion or mixing. The metaphors employed indicate broad models of interaction and encounter, which sometimes evoke descriptions of a static condition or state, but

---

[4] http://news.bbc.co.uk/2/hi/europe/6213495.stm [accessed 13 Feb. 07]; Hannerz 1997: 15.

also attempts to define both the condition and process. The metaphors of syncretism presuppose original, essential and axiomatic categories of cultural and religious experience, which are also exclusive, regardless of the past or present relevance of Orientalist and colonial perspectives (Stewart and Ernst 2003). The model of borrowing and influence describe transactions in which two groups or individuals are affected by each other through direct and indirect contact respectively. Borrowing suggests that one group has taken and incorporated an idea, custom or specific item from another. The implication of this model of physical exchange, as enthusiastically suggested by Stewart and Ernst, is that the borrowing group is independent, lacking in creativity and fundamentally incapable of defining itself (Stewart and Ernst 2003:2). However, this model does not adequately encompass the complex process that is perhaps better described as 'appropriation', in which the borrowed item is transformed through the process of incorporation, thus fundamentally altering both the appropriated and the appropriator (true synthesis). The same holds for the model of 'influence'. Indices of influence nearly always define the 'source' as dominant over the passive recipient, thus raising the problematic issues of derivation and authenticity. It is sometimes evident how non-adherence to the strictures of dominant cultural, religious and ideological modes of organization may evoke 'syncretism' as a language of power to concretise the initial cultural and religious categories that the interpreter presumes to be self-evident. Interrogations of processes of cultural syncretization may involve several levels, including uncovering the actual practice(s), phenomena or ideas; understanding and interpreting the practice(s), phenomena or ideas; and a level of analysis to determine the appropriateness or inappropriateness of the practice(s) and ideas under consideration. It is to this complex politics of 'confrontation', 'negotiation' and 'expansion' of the 'new', to which the contributions in this volume have been carefully structured, that we now turn.

Confronting the New

In the first section of this book, the 'new' is confronted with its social or cultural adversaries, with anti-syncretisms and fundamentalisms, with the construction of 'purities' as opposed to the mixed 'impurities'. Against this backdrop, processes of syncretization produce relations of power within social struggles; they redraw boundaries and recreate identities. The contributions in this section employ actor-centred concepts of power. Taking due cognisance of structural dispositions of power, they analyse the encounter with the new as both active appropriation and passive alienation. By distinguishing between mixing on the level of form and meaning, they confront the problem of conscious and unconscious syncretization. Finally, the problem of mixing is reflected back on to scholarly discourse itself by asking how academic battles over terminological and conceptual borders reproduce wider social conflicts.

Beyer's opening contribution introduces syncretism or hybridization as a relational concept within a global context. With specific reference to African Christianity and Hinduism, he analyses how notions of contingency and self-evidence produce categories, identities and differences in scholarly discourse and beyond, thus contributing to the construction of religious and cultural purities, which in turn legitimize access to institutionalized power. In this context, the label 'syncretization' points to the contingent history of any given purity, thus criticizing its proclaimed self-evidence. Peter Beyer aptly argues that the successful syncretisms are those that manage to be acknowledged as distinct cultural units, either despite or because of their history of mixing, as in the case of African Christianity and Hinduism. Beyer challenges scholars confronting the problem of the 'mixed new' to break with the currently unquestioned conceptual framework and to reflect on their position in the social struggles between mixtures and purities.

André Droogers explores the process of mixing in the religious field by contrasting syncretism and fundamentalism as opposite reactions to the challenges of modernization and globalization. He proposes a wider applicability of the opposition between mingling and essentialism as ambivalent concepts for the reproduction of cultural repertoires. But his main point is to reflect this conceptual distinction on to academic discourse and its disputes between the positivist and constructivist paradigms. In analysing the parallels between syncretism and constructivism, and between fundamentalism and positivism, as well as the two distinct scientific approaches to both religious and cultural syncretism and fundamentalism, Droogers addresses the question of the ideological function of postmodernist and modernist science.

Hans Peter Hahn is concerned with processes of mixing in material culture, where the global distribution of consumer goods is popularly conceived as either the destruction of local systems of significance or the creative reinterpretation of new things. With examples drawn from a village in Burkina Faso, he analyses the dialectical relationship of processes of appropriation and alienation in confronting the new. Though parallel, these processes differ in character, the difference between drowning in and creatively mixing cultural streams, as well as in degree of agency or consciousness. But, as Hahn demonstrates in the intricate intermingling of appropriation and alienation, both processes play an important part in the encounter with the new, as well as in the reconstruction of identities and differences within the local social context.

Hans-Jörg Schmid, Dymitr Ibriszimow, Karina Kopatsch and Peter Gottschligg examine cultural blending in the conceptual structure of cognitive categories and underscore the question of self-evidence earlier raised by Beyer. In comparing these concepts in Nigerian English and Hausa, both spoken by bilingual Hausa in northern Nigeria, with the corresponding concepts in the American English of native speakers, they confront the categorical consequences of processes of unconscious mixing. The authors uncover the multi-variant complexity of conceptual blending by taking into account the form and the referent for each of the concepts. They conclude that the mixed is never new because the inputs can always be traced to source concepts and cultures. As for the sources of blending, the variability of mixed concepts does not allow general conclusions to be made with regard to the importance of linguistic interference vs. cultural appropriation. But if cultural knowledge is inevitably conceptual knowledge, the conceptual shifts based on unconscious mixing have to be accounted for in the analysis of conscious processes of syncretization.

In the last contribution in this section, Jonathan Owens engages with the linguistic discourse on creolization, according to which simplification can be regarded as a distinguishing feature of creole languages, and he provides examples that challenge the general applicability of some of the parameters along which linguistic simplicity is measured. As for the wider implications of the linguistic data, Owens points out that there is no cultural correlate of linguistic simplification. He remains sceptical with regard to the interdisciplinary transfer of concepts, if only metaphorical, because of the heterogeneity of the units in question. Nevertheless, Owens' contribution confronts the 'mixed new' with the question of time-bound differentiation and complexity, and he calls for caution with regard to the ideology of the new, which – at least in the creolization variant – draws metaphorical if not conceptual inspiration from the linguistic distinction between pidgin and creole languages.

Negotiating the New

The second section of the book focuses on creativity in the complex process of mixing for the production of the new. The examples employed range from various artistic genres to religious rituals and even the practice of 'idle talking'. The authors confront the question of creativity by tackling the problem of the 'newness' of the new, especially with regard to the historical dimension or socio-economic context of processes of mixing. A commonly shared feature is their use of spatial metaphors to disentangle the production of mixed cultural expressions. The criss-crossing of boundaries of all types form one of the interpretative lenses for the negotiation of the new.

Roman Loimeier describes the predominately male practices of sitting and talking in the *baraza*, referring to both the space of the 'veranda' and the group of people sitting and talking right there in Zanzibar. He analyses these practices with regard to gender, space and time, and takes account of their variability. He points out how the 'sitting' and 'talking' connects the participants with their immediate local surroundings, their transnational social networks and current debates within the global media community. As he suggests, in this way the participants are continuously re-creating specific Swahili identities or *cosmopolitanity* through the discursive negotiation of local, national and international frameworks.

Said A.M. Khamis takes up another example from the East African coast concerned with an artistic genre, the lyrics of *taarab* songs, and focuses especially on the increasing 'fuzziness' of the genre within the last twenty years, which he links to the feature of code-mixing. Against the backdrop of traditional *taarab* – a more stable form, although itself the product of processes of cultural exchange – recent lyrics mix old and new images, creating a specific 'newness' by drawing on the jargon of modern media technology. Khamis interprets these artistic expressions within an autobiographical approach as the negotiation of the new through the blurring of boundaries.

Dana Rush is concerned with Hindu images in West African Vodun art and religion. She provides an overview of the history of the appropriation of Hindu lithographs of predominately Indian origin in West Africa and analyses the actual uses to which these images are put. The Vodun 'remix' of pictures of Hindu gods reinterprets their meaning, establishes links with the Vodun pantheon of spiritual beings and forces, and negotiates 'Self' and 'Other', especially in relation to both local and global spheres of the sea. In her analysis, Rush shows that creative merging does not produce a stable 'Vodun remix' of cultural expression, but that the meaning of even one single depiction of a Hindu god oscillates between possible interpretations within the multilayered matrix of cultural references. Finally she takes up the fluidity of the oceans in cultural remixing by tracing the spread of Hindu images in the transatlantic diasporas of Vodun.

Farouk Topan takes us back to the East African coast by discussing the ways in which the historical experience of a 'mixed' people, the Swahili, is recreated in the dramatic, poetic and narrative genres of Swahili literature. Theoretically, he employs a concept of hybridity characterised by liminality, ambivalence and mimicry. With regard to the history of the Swahili, he notes a 'double hybridity' in relation to an Arab and European 'Other', a long-standing necessity to negotiate one's own cultural space within asymmetrical relations of power. To these two identities he adds a third in the more recent form of the nation states of Kenya and Tanzania. Topan analyses how artists reflect on both the unconscious and intentional mode of 'being in-between' and on the marginalizing and empowering aspects of hybrid experience, and how this reflection is further diversified through the diasporic experience of some of the authors.

Astrid Bochow examines the changing marriage customs of urban Ghana as a context for analysing how the new is negotiated via a religio-cultural rite of passage. She identifies Pentecostal churches as one of the major providers of marriage ceremonies. She notes that these groups are especially popular among urban youths because of a certain perception that they are presenting themselves as proponents of Western modernity. Through a morally charged discourse on sexuality, purity and holiness, these churches take a fiercely anti-syncretistic stand. Yet in the actual marriage practices, the pastors cooperate with the elders representing traditional authority. Bochow analyses how various actors – the church leaders, the young couples and the elders – are constantly re-negotiating the new, as well as their social position in relation to the new, in and through the actual rites of passage connected with marriage.

Expanding the New

The contributions in the last section attempt to expand the notion of the new by linking it with sociological interpretations of modernization, by examining the social conditions for the survival of quite old 'syncretistic' rituals in modern times and by returning reconfigured concepts of syncretism to its original domain, the study of religions. By focusing on the rapidly expanding Pentecostal Christianity, the negotiation of Western and African modernities, and the contestations of 'traditional religion' in the face of social change and influences, these contributions espouse how 'mixing' and 'mingling' contribute to the expansion of the 'new', but also the continuity and resilience of the 'old'.

Elisio Macamo and Dieter Neubert explore the 'new' by linking its production to processes of modernization. In opposition to a teleological notion of modernization, they propose an interactional concept of 'multiple modernities'. Using the appropriation of diesel engines in Sudan and the implementation of medical services in Mozambique as examples, Macamo and Neubert analyse how 'the new' is based on complex interactions between 'products of modernity' and local everyday life. Based on the central theoretical concept of technical, ideological or institutional products of modernity, they argue that the innovative temptation of 'the new' in the form of the products of modernity is leading to their implementation through processes of syncretization. However, locally specific adaptations are restricted by the dynamics inherent in products of modernity. These institutional, structural or ideological side-effects, which cannot be evaded, are in part responsible for the success or failure of the new.

Afe Adogame and Selome Kuponu take the concept of syncretization back into the field of religious studies. In their analysis of two Nigerian Pentecostal churches, they interpret the trope of 'spiritual terrorism' as an adaptation of Christianity to the African cultural context, but emphasise at the same time the perspective of the actors, who justify the need for 'spiritual warfare' with biblical references and regard the Christian purity of the 'spiritual warriors' as their essential characteristic. The processes of cultural mixing are further differentiated through the mission of African Pentecostal churches in Europe, conceived as the 'dark continent of Satan' in dire need of spiritual deliverance. In their interpretation, Adogame and Kuponu caution against the normative use of the term 'syncretism' as employed in the dialectics of 'Othering', since this only serves to discredit the religious traditions of other people.

Simon Coleman expands the concept of the new through his analysis of translocal mixing, not between different purities, but within a single religion, the charismatic Faith Movement. He describes Prosperity Christianity as a cultural phenomenon that transcends any single locality but is constituted by mutual conversations and gazes, forms of mimesis, apparently shared narratives and tropes, face-to-face and virtual interactions, and material and symbolic exchanges. Despite its apparent unity and its anti-syncretistic attitude on the discursive level, Coleman argues that the Faith Movement constitutes a diffuse, syncretic and heterogeneous entity on the level of translocal practices.

In the last contribution, Ulrich Rinn expands the notion of the 'new' in what may appear to be a response to Beyer's call for a historical perspective on syncretism. The New Year's Festival of the Swahili forms the paradigm for discourses on Swahili identity and history, drawing upon African and Persian influences, whose mixing arguably contributed to the emergence of the distinct group of towns-people on the East African coast. However, Rinn does not focus on the old mixing, but analyses how the festival has survived more recently in some locations by being cut off from globalized culture flows, by merging with local strategies to revitalize Swahili culture, or by intermingling with regional politics and the tourism industry.

Bibliography

Adogame, Afe (1999): *Celestial Church of Christ: The Politics of Cultural Identity in a West African Prophetic-Charismatic Movement*. Frankfurt am Main: Peter Lang.

Allolio-Näcke, Lars, Kalscheuer, Britta and Manzeschke, Arne (eds.) (2005): *Differenzen anders denken: Bausteine zu einer Kulturtheorie der Transdifferenz*, Frankfurt: Campus.

Appadurai, Arjun (1996): *Modernity at Large: Cultural Dimensions of Globalization*, Minneapolis: University of Minnesota Press.

Apter, Andrew (1991): Herskovits's Heritage: Rethinking Syncretism in the African Diaspora, *Diaspora: A Journal of Transnational Studies* 1, 3: 235-60.

Audinet, Jacques (2004 [1999]): *The Human Face of Globalization: From Multicultural to Mestizaje*, Lanham: Rowman & Little-field.

Baird, Robert (1991): *Essays in the History of Religions*, New York: Peter Lang.

Baerman, Matthew and Brown, Dunstan and Corbett, Greville (2005): *The Syntax-Morphology Interface: A Study of Syncretism*, Cambridge: Cambridge University Press.

Bastide, Roger (1995 [1960]): *Les religions africaines au Brésil: Contribution à une sociologie des interpenetrations de civilization*, Paris: Presses Universitaires de France.

Berner, Ulrich (1978) : Heuristisches Modell der Synkretismus-Forschung, in Wiessner, Gernot (ed.), *Synkretismusforschung: Theorie und Praxis*, Wiesbaden: Otto Harrassowitz, 11-26.

Berner, Ulrich (2001): The notion of syncretism in historical and and or empirical research, *Historical Reflections / Réflexions Historiques* 27, 3: 499-509.

Berner, Ulrich (2004 [1979]): The Concept of 'Syncretism': An Instrument of Historical Insight and Discovery?, in: Leopold, Maria and Jensen, Jeppe (eds.), *Syncretism in Religion: A Reader*, London: Equinox, 295-315.

Bhabha, Homi (1994): *The Location of Culture*, London: Routledge.

Brah, Avtar and Coombes, Annie (eds.) (2000): *Hybridity and its Discontents: Politics, Science, Culture*, London: Routledge.

Cassidy, William (ed.) (2001) Retrofitting Syncretism?, *Historical Reflections / Réflexions Historiques* 27, 3.

Collier, Gordon and Fleischmann, Ulrich (eds.) (2003): *A Pepper-pot of Cultures: Aspects of Creolization in the Caribbean* (*Matatu* 27 and 28), Amsterdam: Rodopi.

Colpe, Carsten (1975): Die Vereinbarkeit historischer und struktureller Bestimmungen des Synkretismus, in: Dietrich, Albert (ed.), *Synkretismus im syrisch-persischen Kulturgebiet.* Göttingen: Vandenhoeck & Ruprecht, 15-37.

Coombes, Annie and Brah, Avtar (2000): Introduction: The Conundrum of 'mixing', in: Avtar Brah and Annie Coombes (eds.), *Hybridity and its discontents: Politics, Science, Culture*, London: Routledge, 1-16.

De Villanova, Roselyne and Vermès, Geneviève (eds.) (2006): *Le métissage interculturel : Créativité dans les relations inégalitaires*, Paris: L'Harmattan.

Droge, A.J. (2001): Retrofitting and Retiring 'Syncretism', *Historical Reflections / Réflexions Historiques* 27, 3: 375-87.

Duboux, R. (1994): *Métissage ou barbarie*, Paris: L'Harmattan.

Eisenstadt, S.N. (2000): Multiple Modernities, *Daedalus: Journal of the American Academy of Arts and Science* 129,1: 1-30.

Frazier, E. Franklin (1939): *The Negro Family in the United States*, Chicago: The University of Chicago Press.

Gilroy, P. (1993): *The Black Atlantic: Modernity and Double Consciousness*, Cambridge: Harvard University Press.

Hannerz, Ulf (1987): The World in Creolization, *Africa* 57, 4: 546-59.

Hannerz, Ulf (1997): Flows, Boundaries and Hybrids: Keywords in Transnational Anthropology, http:// www.transcomm.ox.ac.uk-/working%20papers/hannerz.pdf [16.1.2007] [Published in Portuguese: Fluxos, fronteiras, híbridos: palavras-chave da antropologia transnational, *Mana* (Rio de Janeiro) 3 (1): 7-39].

Herskovits, Melville (1941): *The Myth of the Negro Past*, New York: Harper.

Hymes, Dell (ed.) (1971): *Pidginization and Creolization of Languages*, London: Cambridge University Press.

Kippenberg, Hans (2004): In Praise of Syncretism: The Beginnings of Christianity Conceived in the Light of a Diagnosis of Modern Culture, in: Leopold, Maria and Jensen, Jeppe (eds.), *Syncretism in Religion: A Reader*, London: Equinox, 29-38.

Kraidy, Marwan (2005): *Hybridity or the Cultural Logic of Globalization*, Philadelphia: Temple University Press.

Laplantine, Francois and Nouss, Alexis (2001): *Dictionnaire des métissages*, Paris: Pauvert.

Leopold, Maria and Jensen, Jeppe (2004): Introduction to Part II, in: Leopold, Maria and Jensen, Jeppe (eds.), *Syncretism in Religion: A Reader*, London: Equinox, 14-28.

Leopold, Maria and Jensen, Jeppe (eds.) (2004): *Syncretism in Religion: A Reader*, London: Equinox.

Lincoln, Bruce (2001): Retiring syncretism, *Historical Reflections / Réflexions Historiques* 27, 3: 453-60.

Lindenfeld, David (2006): Syncretism, in: *World History Connected*, 4, 1. Online version available at: http://worldhistoryconnected.-press.uiuc.edu/4.1/index.html

Loimeier, Roman and Neubert, Dieter and Weißköppel, Cordula (eds.) (2005): *Globalisierung im lokalen Kontext: Perspektiven und Konzepte von Handeln in Afrika*, Münster: Lit.

Maroney, Eric (2006): *The SCM Core Text: Religious Syncretism*, London: SCM Press.

Martínez-Echazábal, L. (1998): Mestizaje and the Discourse on National/Cultural Identity in Latin America, *Latin American Perspectives* 25, 3: 21-42.

McGuire, Meredith B. and Maduro, Otto (eds.) 2005: *Social Compass*, 52, 4.

Meyer, Birgit and Geschiere, Peter (eds.) (1999): *Globalization and Identity: Dialetics of Flow and Closure*, Oxford: Blackwell.

Mintz, Sidney and Price, Richard (1992 [1976]): *The Birth of African-American Culture: An Anthropological Perspective*, Boston: Beacon Press.

Nederveen Pieterse, Jan (1994): Globalisation as Hybridisation, *International Sociology* 9, 2: 161-84.

Nederveen Pieterse, Jan (2001): Hybridity, So What? The Anti-hybridity Backlash and the Riddles of Recognition, *Theory, Culture, and Society* 18, 2: 219-45.

Oosthuizen, G.C. (1968): *Post-Christianity in Africa: A Theological and Anthropological Study*, London: Hurst.

Peel, J.D.Y. (1968): Syncretism and Religious Change, *Comparative Studies in Society and History* 10: 121-41.

Probst, Peter and Spittler, Gerd (eds.) (2004): *Between Resistance and Expansion: Explorations of Local Vitality in Africa*, Münster: Lit.

Pye, Michael (1971): Syncretism and Ambiguity, in: *Numen* 18: 83-93.

Rudolph, Kurt (2004[1991]): Syncretism: From Theological Invective to a Concept in the Study of Religion, in: Leopold, Maria and Jensen, Jeppe (eds.), *Syncretism in Religion: A Reader*, London: Equinox, 68-85.

Shaw, Rosalind and Stewart, Charles (1994): Introduction: problematizing syncretism, in: Charles Stewart and Rosalind Shaw (eds.), *Syncretism/Anti-syncretism: The Politics of Religious Synthesis*, London: Routledge, 1-26.

Stewart, Charles (1999): Syncretism and its Synonyms: Reflections on Cultural Mixture, in: *Diacritics* 29, 3: 40-62.

Stewart, Tony and Ernst, Carl (2003): Syncretism, in: Claus, Peter and Mills, Margaret A. (eds.) *South Asian Folklore: An Encyclopedia*, Garland Publishing Inc.

Stump, Gregory (2001): *Inflectional Morphology: A Theory of Paradigm Structure*, Cambridge: Cambridge University Press.

Sundkler, Bengt (1961[1948]): *Bantu Prophets in South Africa*, London: Oxford University Press.

Toumson, R. (1998): *Mythologie du métissage*, Paris: Presses Universitaires de France.

Turgeon, Laurier (ed.) (2001). *Regards croisés sur le métissage*, Laval: Presses de l'Univérsité de Laval.

Weißköppel, Cordula (2005): 'Hybridität': die ethnografische Annäherung an ein theoretisches Konzept, in: Loimeier, Roman and Neubert, Dieter and Weißköppel, Cordula (eds.), *Globalisierung im lokalen Kontext: Perspektiven und Konzepte von Handeln in Afrika*, Münster: Lit, 311-54.

Wießner, Gernot (ed.) (1978): *Synkretismusforschung: Theorie und Praxis*, Wiesbaden: Harrassowitz.

Yelvington, Kevin A. (2001): The Anthropology of Afro-Latin America and the Caribbean: Diasporic Dimensions, in: *Annual Review of Anthropology* 30: 227-60.

Young, Robert (1995): *Colonial Desire: Hybridity in Theory, Culture, and Race*, London: Routledge.

Concealing the New

Purity as Hybridization: Religio-Cultural Syncretisms in the Context of Globalization[1]

Peter Beyer

Some years ago, Mary Douglas published two works with titles that can serve as a good starting point for discussing syncretism. In *Purity and Danger* (1966) and 'Self-Evidence' (1975), she argued that the most important categories of understanding in any society are reflections of its underlying social structures and the concrete material situations of its members. In this context, Douglas focuses critically on the contingency of boundaries. The most fundamental distinctions by which people live become self-evident for them, yet they also carry the symptoms of their own arbitrariness and of the insecurity of the world that they call into being. Douglas draws her empirical illustrations from various small-scale societies in different parts of the world, but she implies that such relationships between categories, context and culture, while very varied, are universal to human existence. They should therefore be applicable to contemporary global society too.

Without addressing the details of her theories, their relevance here is in the nexus between the self-evident, the pure and the dangerous. The taken-for-granted categories by which we think and act are vital because they construct an ordered, meaningful world for us, but just as importantly because they mediate power in that world. Classifications matter for who has what sort of power, yet they are also contingent and therefore changeable. It is this combination that dovetails with the notions of syncretization and hybridization, process terms that highlight contingency or malleability, but in so doing point to the purpose behind them, which is to alter meaning and refashion power relations. They imply that the current classifications or reigning

---

[1] A similar version of this article was also published as Au croisement de l'identité et de la différence: les syncrétismes culturo-religieux dans le contexte de la mondialisation, Social Compass, 54 (2005): 417-429.

'purities' will not do, and that in bringing them into question, the first task is to undo their self-evidence.

Self-Evidence and Contingency in Global Society

In comparison with the sort of societies that Douglas described for her purposes, the contemporary global context is somewhat peculiar, not in the importance of classifications, categories and differences, but rather in the degree to which the self-evidence of basic categories is accompanied by a high degree of awareness and thematization of their contingency (Beck et al., eds., 1994). By this I mean that we still treat various categories of difference – for example, gender, nation, culture, race and person – as unquestionable and thus as self-evident, but at the same time we are also aware of how we constructed them and how we may change them. Symptoms of this current condition are, for instance, to be found in certain categories that we use to name the social whole, that is, overall identity in the context of which we understand these differences. Thus, for instance, the now quite popular notion of 'globalization' evokes both an ineluctable social whole – we are all involved, whether we like it or not – and a process. Globalization is both the condition under which we live and the direction in which we are supposedly headed. Until not so long ago, the concept of modernization often occupied this position, but recently it has tended more towards a category of difference, rather than identity (Eisenstadt 2001). The idea of 'development' has similar features: we are all, it seems, on the road to development or are developed but need to keep on developing. On the individual level we are the educated and the uneducated, the accomplished and those yet to fulfil their potential. On the collective level, we commonly divide the world into developed and developing countries. In both cases, constant criticism of these ideas accompanies their almost unquestioned status. Rather than constituting a negation of globalization and development, however, the criticisms are, in effect, an aspect of their self-evidence as well as their contingency. Consider, for instance, how the anti-globalization movements that have recently arisen have quickly assumed the attitude of 'alternative globalization' movements; or how the very cogent critiques of development theory of the last few decades have centered more on the failures of development, the fact that it was not happening for a great many people, but should be happening, or that development could and should take different paths. It is not that no one lives essentially outside these concepts: a great many people do, but many of them, and most of those of us who do not, generally consider them to be extremely unfortunate and their exclusion to be a severe problem that must be addressed. We are practically without exception caught in the orbit of these classifications and the distinctions they have spawned. Our awareness of their contingency expresses itself not primarily in terms of known alternatives, of a different social world, but instead rests in the conviction, the taken-for-granted belief, that this world can and should be constantly changed. Socially, that impetus expresses itself in terms of power, both the power to 'do something about it' and the dynamic – and unequal – relationships of power. Temporally, it manifests itself not only in an open future that permits such possibilities of change, but also in our sense of history as the 'real' stories out of which we have emerged. Objectively, it points to the importance of individual and collective identities, which are the subjects of those histories and the holders of or aspirants to that power. It is in the context of this nexus of power, history and identity that I wish to look more closely at the question of syncretizations – specifically, religious and cultural syncretizations.

Identities: Religions and Cultures as Global Purities

Change and contingency would not be recognizable if there were not also, at least provisionally, stable points of reference that permit comparison. In the contemporary globalized social world there are a great many of these, i.e. identities that constitute difference. Any of a number of institutional realities could serve as examples, such as families, political parties, professions, organizations, clans, nations, genders, sports, schools, armies, cities, villages, states, industries, and of course selves or individuals. For present purposes, I select two cases that illustrate nicely the combination of self-evidence and contingency, of power, history and identity, that the phenomena of syncretization and hybridization evoke, namely religions and cultures. I begin with these two, but in keeping with my own specialization, the more detailed illustrations that I will introduce later focus on religions.

Following the work of scholars such as Wilfred Cantwell Smith (1991), Michel Despland (1979), Peter Harrison (1990) and Raymond Williams (1983), Western understandings of the concepts of religion and culture underwent rather similar transformations between roughly the seventeenth and twentieth centuries. In particular, both came to be viewed as terms referring to what we now call ways of life or world-views, encompassing systems for understanding and being in the world. Accompanying this universalization or 'foundationalization', however, was a concomitant and somewhat paradoxical pluralization: concretely, religion and culture came to be seen as manifesting themselves in an inherently plural fashion. The 'wholes' appeared primarily as 'parts'. There was religion, but it appeared in real social life above all as religions, something that did not exclude continuing claims to the universal and even exclusive validity of one or another religion by its adherents. Similarly, there was culture, but as total ways of life culture realized itself primarily as cultures. A critical aspect of their foundational quality was that religions and cultures did not need to be, and indeed could not be, otherwise or externally justified. They are usually conceived as having emerged at particular times in history, but the founding myths that told such stories were themselves aspects of these very religions or cultures, not something supplied to them as a source of legitimacy from the outside, say like the narrative of historical research. The acceptance or not of a claimant to the status of a religion or a culture has therefore remained largely 'irrational', meaning that they could not be justified or legitimated by criteria formally outside of themselves. Indicative of this quality, for instance, the association of a culture with a particular political state is not a strategy for justifying the culture, here the nation. Rather, the conceptualization has been the other way around:

the state justifies itself as the necessary expression or tool of the culture. That logic has worked even, and sometimes especially, when the culture or nation actually had to be invented ('nation-building'). It is as expressions of a cultural collectivity that states have legitimated themselves in modern times, including their power over their citizens and their most often entirely arbitrary but precise and highly stable boundaries. Moreover, although the development of this understanding began historically in the West, the ideas of foundational but plural cultures and religions have expanded to the rest of the world in the process of their institutionalization. Neither is any longer a uniquely Western notion, and their appropriation or particularization by people in various other parts of the world has been an integral part of their formulation. Indeed, without this additional step, the categories could hardly have attained their present status as globalized ways of declaring collective and individual identity and therefore difference, that is to say, the status of distinct actors in global society (Beyer 2006).

This global and solid institutionalization of plural religions and cultures does not in any way remove their contingency and the thematization or awareness of that contingency. Therefore, while generally accepting the legitimacy and incontrovertibility of cultures and religions, globalized discourse allows and even encourages their contestation, in at least two basic ways: we contest what will count as a religion or a culture; and we disagree about what does and does not belong to a religion or a culture that is already recognized. Although there exist various terms to express these contestations, such as heresy or cult in the domain of religion, for both religions and cultures, syncretism is among the more common. Like heresy, but perhaps in a less pejorative way, syncretism or syncretization signals a manifestation that is somehow both included in already recognized instances of the category of identity in view, and yet also in important ways outside it. Syncretisms in this sense are mixtures of purities and therefore either negatively judged as 'impure' or positively judged as potential 'new purities'. We can apply a similar understanding to the ideas of hybrid and hybridization. Both word-sets point in essence to mixture, to métissage. Moreover, they often carry an additional connotation, namely that what they apply to is somehow marginal. This leads the discussion to the question of power.

Religions and Cultures as Loci of Power

As is the case with all important social classifications, these incontrovertible but nonetheless contingent categories of identity in global society bear a relation to the construction and distribution of social power. By power, I refer in a broad way to forms of social influence, and not just, for instance, to political, military or economic power. Religion and culture in today's global society also designate distinct forms of power, such as the power of ecstatic religious communication, the power of religious authority or the power of culturally identified artistic expression. While these are not among the more dominant modes of social power in comparison with the others just mentioned, they are nevertheless not to be underestimated. In the present context, however, it is not religion and culture as direct forms of power that I wish to emphasise. Rather, it is the role that these categories play in constructing claims for access to other, not culturally or religiously specific forms of power. One can illustrate this possibility through various discourses and documents, such as declarations of rights or independence, state constitutions and public legitimations of the rights and dignity of people and individuals. These are all by now very globally present and intimately tied up with globalized values of equality, inclusion, progress and sustainability. An individual or collectivity can, according to this understanding, claim the 'right' to inclusion in the form of access to various power modalities ranging from the political and economic to the artistic and educational. Exclusion from these can be and is put forward as a 'violation' of those 'rights', as unjust, as a problem that has to be fixed. The legitimacy or incontrovertibility of a culture, of a religion, or other such identity categories (race, nation, gender, etc.) thus turns these qualities into resources for making claims to power. Syncretizations, therefore, are not just ways of forming and seeking to legitimate new or different instances of cultures and religions, they are also critical elements in the quest for inclusion in the power benefits of various globalized systems of social power. To succeed in establishing the legitimacy and social efficacy of a new or different identity is to build a base and a set of critical resources for the claims and aspirations to inclusion in the major power modalities of global society.

Another way of understanding this role of religions and cultures is to think in terms of the often used distinctions between the global and the local, or, in Robertsonian language, between the universal and the particular (see Robertson 1992). Briefly, religion and culture are two instances of categories which refer to recognized and distinct platforms for the localization of global structures and processes, or the particularization of globalized universals. The capitalist economy and the modern sovereign state, with its typical educational or legal institutions, are, for instance, globalized social structures with their own recursive logics and institutional rationalities (Meyer et al. 1997, Wallerstein 1979). Yet, following the discourse of different legitimated identities, these should all be appropriated in particular ways among particular individuals and collectivities so as to express and reflect their particular identities. And this notion means more than simply that certain individuals or members of certain collectivities ought to have the power associated with these globalized institutions. It means, much more basically, that these institutions ought to be, as it were, 'formed in the likeness' of their particular identities, that they be, for example, Japanified capitalism, the Islamicized state, Africanized medicine or Hinduized education. The critical relation to power of syncretizations, therefore, is that they will allow their carriers to make such claims, to become meaningful and therefore more or less powerful actors on the world stage precisely as different people who are nevertheless and therefore included. The recognition of exclusivity is a basis for inclusion.

Religions and Cultures as History

The historical or temporal dimension of these identities has two aspects, one relating more directly to the unquestionable status that they attain or to which they aspire, the other highlighting much more their recognizable contingency. In each case of an entity that we accept as 'one of the religions' or as 'one of the cultures', a critical part of their construction is rooted in their incontrovertibility in foundational histories, whether in linear historical time or in mythic time. Plural cultures are the cultures of peoples, each of whom has a history which is a vital ingredient of their identity, a formative aspect of their self-descriptions. These histories are often mythical in the sense that they consist of selective narratives whose purpose is precisely to profile what are deemed to be essential features of the people's culture, or their identity as a people, and only as a function of that purpose to present what 'may actually have happened'. Such histories recall great heroes, great battles, epic migrations, critical institutional foundations, divine interventions and so forth; but they do this as an exercise in removing that history from critical (that is, relativizing) or outside scrutiny and thus from questionability. They help ground the cultural identity's self-evidence. Nonetheless, just because these narratives take the form of history, they are also open to reflective scrutiny in a society with a high, institutionally supported awareness of its own contingency. Accordingly, in a great many cases, we do in fact re-examine the historical conditions of the emergence of a cultural or religious identity, a process that not infrequently results in a questioning of the mythic narrative or in the temporal relocation of an identity's formation. Given the social importance of the perceived non-contingency of these identities and their supporting historical narratives, such activity is frequently not without controversy. Indeed, what is perhaps remarkable is the degree to which such reflexive questioning – whether by insiders or outsiders – can take place without the cultural or religious identities in question suffering seriously in terms of their self-evidence and legitimacy.

The significance of syncretisms in this context is perhaps obvious. To judge a phenomenon as the outcome of syncretism is to profile its contingency and to be aware of or highlight the historical conditions of its emergence. A hybrid can thus be deemed inauthentic and questionable, and the older uses of the word 'syncretism' carry this sense. Yet in a social context such as our contemporary global one, with its institutionalized reflexivity, that need not be the outcome at all. The opposite may in fact be the case. In this light, what a focus on syncretizations allows and even encourages is the 'normalization' of syncretization, not its exceptional or suspect character. From this perspective, the established and taken-for-granted identities are revealed as themselves but previous, or 'successful', syncretizations, the only difference between them and those we still call by that name being their level of legitimation, not their degree of visible construction. In this regard there does seem to be a very rough correlation between how long an identity is deemed to have existed and its acceptance – or at least, those identities with a more recent historical origin have greater difficulty attaining self-evidence. Indeed, one of the more common tactics for seeking to undermine self-evidence is to try to debunk the historical depth of the identity. Somehow, when it comes to these foundational differences, what people invented 2,000 years ago impresses us as more authentic than what arose only 150 years ago.

Two Religious Illustrations

These general observations could be illustrated through an examination of an exceedingly wide variety of phenomena in our contemporary world. Above, I have already limited the purview of the discussion to religions and cultures. In passing now to empirical illustrations, space limitations lead me to restrict myself even more to two religious examples. My aim with each of them is to show the close dialogical relation between the self-evidence of these identities and their nonetheless visible contingency, and to set this very much in its historical and global context.

Syncretization as Particularization in African Christianity

The historical transplantation of Christianity to sub-Saharan Africa may on the surface appear to be a straightforward case of a historically pre-existing Christian identity – or better, pre-existing identities – which European missionaries attempted to implant among Africans, against which new versions then actually developed in Africa can be compared. That would be too shortsighted a view, however, and this from at least two perspectives. First, the Christianities that the Europeans were seeking to spread were themselves but previously 'purified' syncretizations. Secondly, the 'syncretized' Christianities that the Africans then adopted can just as easily be regarded as 'purifications' if one adopts the point of view of the African Christians. Today, when African Christians are seeking to 'return the favour' by treating Western Europe and North America, the regions from which the original missionaries came, as mission fields, this latter aspect is perhaps much easier to see than it was before (Adogame 2000, Bennetta 1997, Lanternari 1998, Ter Haar 1998).

Instead of looking at the development of Christianity in sub-Saharan Africa over the last century and a half as a question of the adaptation of this religion in new cultural contexts, for present purposes it is more instructive to analyse this process as one of 'recognizing' and then 'undoing' European and North American syncretizations (or self-evidences) so as to enable the construction of new, more Africa-adapted Christian identities, ones that for African Christians are in fact 'truer' to 'original Christianity'. It is by now a commonplace in literature on African Christianity to point out the degree to which the outside missionaries brought a Christianity loaded with European cultural baggage so that, for the most part, they did not seem capable of distinguishing 'becoming Christian' from 'becoming European' (Isichei 1995, Peterson 2002). Although there is a tendency to be rather judgemental about this, it begs the question of how it could possibly have been otherwise. The European missionaries could hardly be expected to have arrived with an already formed idea of what about their Christianity was 'essential' and what was secondary and thus changeable, since this would have required the isolation of an abstract sense of Christian 'purity' that could only have arisen in the context of a comparison with an African Christianity which did not at that time exist. Only as African Christians engaged in the gradual process of syncretization over a fairly long period of time would that sort of exercise have any meaning. Even then, a 'pure' or 'essential'

Christianity could not, as it were, precipitate out of the process except analytically and invariably without much chance of agreement, since there exists no concrete outside standard that is not itself just another syncretized variation. Another way of putting this is to say that the Europeans sought to propagate and the Africans adopted the universal Christian identity, but each could do so only in its own particular form. There could be no concrete universal on the basis of which either particularism could be judged.

Evidence of this lack of a 'middle term' can be seen in various aspects of how Christianity historically became African. First, we note that, although the European and North American missionaries had already succeeded in establishing their churches in Africa in the course of the nineteenth century (and to a limited extent well before this time), the 'take-off' period of the twentieth century occurred only when African Christian converts themselves took over the task of propagating the religion among Africans. This outcome is easy to understand. On the one hand, for the African converts, the European syncretizations had not achieved and indeed could not attain the kind of self-evidence that they had for the outside missionaries: to question or undo them was for them comparatively straightforward and unavoidable. On the other hand, the same African converts had their own self-evidences which we can call African culture or even African traditional religion, although it must be stressed that these quantities also did not simply exist and had to be imagined for the sake of creating a narrative about what was going on. Thus, for instance, the European stress on features like particular styles of clothing and housing, spatial and temporal organization, particular forms of bodily discipline and hygienic practice and family relationships – notably monogamy – could be seen as what they also were: accretions, syncretic elements that the Europeans had grafted into their Christianity. By contrast, such ideas as that religious belief and practices should have practical, this-worldly benefits, especially in the form of healing; that therefore the 'miracles' recorded in the Christian Bible should be just as possible today as they were during the apostolic period; that a world of (evil) spirits, and above all therefore the Christian Holy

Spirit, were an obvious part of everyday reality; that polygamy was both natural and biblical; these were not only possible, they were for many African Christians more or less self-evident and clear aspects of what Christian religion 'originally' had been.

The history of the formation and eventual broad legitimization of African Independent or African Instituted Churches gives a clear illustration of various aspects of this process, as well as pointing directly to the question of power and power relations. Whether we are speaking of the Aladura Churches of West Africa, the Kimbanguist churches of Central Africa or the Zionist churches of Southern Africa – and these seem to be the most commonly discussed and cited examples (Clarke 1986, Maboia 1994, Mnende 1998, Olupona ed. 1991, Ositelu 2002) – it is not always the case that these were simply deliberate schismatic movements resulting from frustration at working within the confines of the missionary churches. More often, one might say, they were at least as much, and probably more, spontaneous outgrowths of prophetic impulses on the part of indigenous Christian Africans like Simon Kimbangu, William Wade Harris and Isaiah Shembe, leaders who styled their Christianity in ways that were quite self-evident and thus resonant for themselves and their African followers, but often, therefore, in ways that disturbed the Europeans, who were just as understandably looking at the situation with different Christian eyes. What both helped spawn these independent movements and allowed them at times to be treated as syncretic 'heresies' were the asymmetric power relations between the Europeans and North Americans on the one hand and the Africans on the other. The former, with the effective social power in the colonial circumstances of the time, were the ones who got to judge what was 'pure' and therefore 'true' Christianity and what was, by contrast 'hybrid' or 'syncretic' and therefore 'false' Christianity. Two developments changed and to some degree reversed this assessment. First, and probably of lesser importance, these AICs survived and in many cases thrived, thus giving them the legitimacy of longevity. Secondly, and undoubtedly of far greater importance, the end of the colonial era shifted a good measure of social power to Africans, a shift that acquired legitimacy in the eyes of the erstwhile missionary and colonial powers. As a result, the Christianities of these Africans appeared as more authentic, as expressions of the identity of Africans, to which they had a right like other nations. Thus today, not only are the AICs recognized as legitimate Christianities in the African countries that are their homes, they have for the most part received parallel recognition in the larger Christian world, for instance, by becoming accepted members of the World Council of Churches (Pobee 2002). In the light of their gain in social power, the identities of Africans could more easily be recognized as 'purities' and no longer as syncretizations.

The Invention of Hinduism: From Self-Evidence to Syncretization

It is today a commonplace in the literature on Hinduism to point out, to insist, and often to lament how the very idea of this religion is a modern, recent invention, attributable in large part to the selective imaginations and understandings of eighteenth- and nineteenth-century British colonialists, along with a small elite of local Brahmans who came under their influence (Balagangadhara 1994, Fitzgerald 1990, Frykenberg 1989, Thapar 1989). While many aspects of these perspectives on Hinduism allow renewed insight into modern South Asian religious realities, our brief look at aspects of the reconstruction of African Christianity should warn us that this sort of analysis is at least as much about the legitimacy of certain historical developments as about the nature of the developments themselves. The issue concerns Hinduism's character as a modern instance of syncretization and hybridization, as opposed to its self-evident identity or purity, implicitly in comparison with often only assumed and presumed notions of pre-existing or underlying South Asian purities.

The confluence of issues of identity, power and history is so clearly present in this example that it is somewhat surprising that few if any observers use the notions of syncretization or hybridization to refer to it. The reasons, I would suggest, have to do with how power relations enter the picture. As I noted above, syncretization and its cognate terms tend to be reserved for quests for identity recognition by the marginalized and subaltern, not for the categories of the dominant. That the modern construction of Hinduism has become such a consistent and contested issue is due to the status of certain driving and visible forces behind the construction of modern Hinduism, by and large, as already suggested, representatives of the colonialist imperial power and indigenous elites, which is to say segments of the power elite in South Asia from the eighteenth to twentieth centuries. Moreover, and perhaps less obviously, it has to do with the rising influence in the late twentieth century of certain 'fundamentalist' (very much in quotation marks!) movements in India which have sought to claim the category of Hindu as a central mobilizing resource. This is a case of the 'wrong' people appropriating an unquestioned category of identity.

When British orientalists and segments of the Bengali Brahman elite began to imagine a single and singular Hindu religion after the latter part of the eighteenth century, they did so necessarily in highly selective ways. In all the variations that people as diverse as H.H. Wilson and Rammuhon Roy put together, there was a clear separation between those elements that were to be considered 'truly' Hindu and those that were regarded as illegitimate and unfortunate accretions. The orientalists and the reformers both had to construct an image of a 'pure' Hinduism that could then be compared to the then present reality, which would in turn be found wanting and in need of restoration to the original or reform to the genuine. The Vedas, for instance, were the core sacred scriptures, but for many the Puranas were at least a little suspect. The true Hindu religion was at root monotheistic: all the polytheism was to be explained as error or compromise for the sake of the spiritually less advanced. In various bold and syncretic moves, Hinduism was to be understood as a religion like the others, especially Christianity or Islam. It had to have an origin or at least an original pure version as revealed in mythic narrative; it had to have at least the equivalent of a foundational 'revelation'; it had to be somehow monotheistic. And lest we think that it was only the orientalists and reformers who engaged in such imaginative hybridizations, those who reacted to and against these notions – people such as fellow early nineteenth-century Bengalis Mrytyunjay Vidyalankar or Radhakant Deb– engaged in a parallel selective exercise in isolating what they defended as Hindu orthodoxy or Sanatana Dharma. Like the Christianity of Roman Catholic missionaries in Africa, this orthodox purity had to be imagined and defended for these historical circumstances. In the process, elements such as the four-fold varna system and 'idol worship' came to take on a heightened symbolic importance because they clearly differentiated these versions from their competition. This too was an exercise in hybridization.

Although much contested and still largely a phenomenon of the urban and middle- to upper-class Indian elites, such visions of a reconstructed and single Hinduism have become more or less solidly institutionalized in the South Asian subcontinent and among diaspora communities around the world, and this for quite some time already. However, the explicit and thematized awareness of the syncretic and hybrid nature of this religious identity has only come to the fore rather more recently. Another way of putting this is to say that, while both outside observers and internal professed adherents to this single Hinduism have from the beginning been entirely aware of the different versions – that is to say, of a Hindu internal diversity parallel to the internal diversity of other religions – effective voices that sought to deconstruct and discredit the very idea of this category of religious identity for the most part date from the mid-1980s at the earliest. Thus, while one might think that this critical discourse would have its roots in a post-colonial situation paralleling Indian independence from the British colonial yoke after 1947, it does not really become prevalent until roughly forty years later. Only then do Western and Indian authors alike come together in a seeming chorus of objection, pointing out how the idea of Hinduism is an inappropriate, inauthentic, even illusory chimera of the colonial and comprador elites, a syncretic aberration that cannot escape its own contingency by appealing to a trans-historical mythic reality. The reasons for this timing are complex and probably symptomatic of that broader rise of post-colonial awareness, assertion and discourse that is so characteristic of many regions in the last decades of the twentieth century. A particular factor that is also involved in the case of Hinduism, however, is the rise to power of what is often labelled Hindu nationalism or Hindu fundamentalism.

The issue of 'communalism', or identity politics on the basis of religious distinctions, has a much older history in India than just the last forty years (Pandey 1992). Virtually from the foundation of the nationalist Congress movement in the nineteenth century, the issue of a pan-Indian identity has been both critical and contested. Historically, in the first half of the twentieth century, three perspectives emerged as the dominant and persistent ones: the eventually dominant Congress view that India was to be a tolerant, 'secular' country in which no religion defined the nation; that represented by the Muslim League, which distrusted the Congress vision as a disguised Hindu vision; and the Hindu nationalist one, hovering at the edges of the Congress movement and represented by such organizations as the Hindu Mahasabha and the Rashtriya Swayamsevak Sangh. In 1947, the irreconcilability of the two most powerful visions, those of Congress and the Muslim League, helped bring about a bipartite political structure in the form of two independent states, Pakistan and India. In post-independence India, 'communalism' came to be institutionalized for some time as a dangerous source of strife and disunity, a tendency to be discouraged and, if necessary, violently suppressed. After the death of Nehru and the troubled regime of Indira Gandhi, however, the political climate changed and allowed the already present but marginalized Hindu nationalist option an opening of which its movements and organizations took full advantage. The latter portion of the 1980s marked the beginning of the Hindu nationalist rise to power, with the Bharatiya Janata Party eventually forming the national government by the end of the 1990s. This period in India's political history coincides more or less exactly with the rediscovery of Hinduism's hybridized and historical construction as a single religion. My suggestion is that this cannot have been a coincidence: the relegation of the category of Hinduism to a syncretic and far from self-evident 'pure' status has been part of a strategy to discredit Hindu nationalism, and this in the context of ongoing attempts to revision the history and identity of the subcontinent in efforts to overcome its colonial past.

Conclusions

To speak of syncretisms, whether in the domain of religion or culture, is to problematize and thematize important aspects of social change and social formation. A phenomenon can only be understood as syncretic or hybrid in terms of the other side of such forms, which in this presentation, borrowing from Mary Douglas, I have called purities. One can analyse this reciprocal relation between purity and syncretism according to three dimensions: the objective dimension of identity, the social dimension of power, and the temporaral dimension of history. Whenever we wish to examine a social form as an instance of syncretism, there are these three basic questions: What are the identities in terms of which this syncretism can be recognized, and when does the syncretism become a new pure form in its turn? What possible narratives are there to describe the development of this syncretism, given that its identity can only arise in time and with reference to the past, present and future? Finally, what are the social conditions of its arising, a context that can always be described in terms of power sought, power produced and power relations changed? A main purpose of adopting such a tripartite approach to syncretisms is that they offer a way of understanding such phenomena from a perspective that is not enmeshed in the historical process that is the object of inquiry. To look at, for instance, the formation of Afro-Brazilian religions like Candomblé strictly in terms of how much they conform, modify or deviate from originally African traditions requires that we assume the identity of those African traditions. A better understanding, I would suggest, is available if we can incorporate into the analysis the contemporary construction of such an African purity that is part and parcel of the ability to recognize and discuss Candomblé as syncretism. Those African purities are in no sense simply and straightforwardly 'out there', available for relatively unambiguous observation. We, the observers, must first imagine them as purities, give them a name and select from a variety of possibilities which elements will belong to them, which will be deemed authentic and which will be excluded and thereby classified as inauthentic. Adopting a perspective which views syncretism as the obverse of an historical process for which purities act as the reverse allows both the syncretisms and their supposed components to float as terms in an analysis that need not assume either one as given.

The examples I have used to illustrate this dialogical relation of syncretism and purity, namely African Christianity and modern Hinduism, were chosen to show that 'questioning the new', as indicated in the title of this volume, is but a moment in observing the contingency and selectivity of the old. The distinction between the old and the new is itself an operation within this process. What today is syncretism and hybridity is purity and self-evidence from another perspective or in another time, whether past or future. The single greatest difference of the global context in which we find ourselves today is that the global condition has, as it were, conspired to make that relationship itself something close to self-evident.

Bibliography

Adogame, Afe (2000): Mission from Africa: The Case of the Celestial Church of Christ in Europe, *Zeitschrift für Missionswissenschaft und Religionswissenschaft*, 84: 29-44.

Balagangadhara, S.N. (1994): *The Heathen in His Blindness: Asia, the West, and the Dynamic of Religion*, Leiden: Brill.

Beck, Ulrich; Giddens, Anthony; Lash, Scott (1994): *Reflexive Modernization: Politics, Tradition, and Aesthetics in the Modern Social Order*, Stanford: Stanford University Press.

Bennetta, Jules-Rossete (1997): Prophetic Movements and Independent Churches in Central and Southern Africa, *Archives de sciences sociales des religions* 99: 153-67.

Beyer, Peter (2006): *Religions in Global Society*. London: Routledge.

Clarke, Peter B. (1986): *West Africa and Christianity*. London: Routledge.

Despland, Michel (1979): *La religion en occident: évolution des idées et du vécu,* Montreal: Fides.

Douglas, Mary (1966): *Purity and Danger: An Analysis of the Concepts of Pollution and Taboo*. New York: Praeger.

Douglas, Mary (1975): Self-Evidence, in Douglas, Mary: *Implicit Meanings: Essays in Anthropology*'. London: Routledge & Kegan Paul: 276-318.

Eisenstadt, S.N. (2001): The Vision of the Modern and Contemporary Society, in: Ben-Rafael, Eliezer and Sternberg, Yitzhak (eds.): *Identity, Culture and Globalization*, Leiden: Brill: 25-47.

Fitzgerald, Timothy (1990): Hinduism and the World Religion Fallacy, *Religion* 20: 101-18.

Frykenberg, Robert Eric (1989): The Emergence of Modern 'Hinduism' as a Concept and as an Institution: A Reappraisal with Special Reference to South India, in: Sontheimer, Günther and Kulke, Hermann (eds.): *Hinduism Reconsidered*, Delhi: Manohar, 29-49.

Harrison, Peter (1990): *'Religion' and the Religions in the English Enlightenment*, Cambridge: Cambridge University Press.

Isichei, Elizabeth Allo (1995): *A History of Christianity in Africa: From Antiquity to the Present*, Grand Rapids MI & Lawrenceville NJ: Eerdmans & Africa World Press.

Lanternari, Vittorio (1998): From Africa to Italy: The Exorcistic-Therapeutic Cult of Emmanuel Milingo, in: Peter Clarke (ed.): *New Trends and Developments in African Religions*, Westport: Greenwood, 263-83.

Maboia, S.I. (1994): Causes for the Proliferation of the African Independent Churches, in: Oosthuizen, G.; Kitshoff, M. and Dube, S. (eds.): *Afro-Christianity at the Grass-Roots: Its Dynamics and Strategies*, Leiden: Brill, 122-36.

Meyer, John; Ramirez, Francisco et al. (1997): World Society and the Nation-State, *American Journal of Sociology*, 103, 1: 144-81.

Mndende, Nokuzola (1998): From Underground Praxis to Recognized Religion: Challenges Facing African Religions, *Journal for the Study of Religion*, 11, 2: 115-24.

Olupona, Jacob K. (ed.) (1991): *African Traditional Religions in Contemporary Society*, New York: Paragon House.

Ositelu, Rufus (2002): *African Instituted Churches: Diversities, Growth, Spirituality, and Ecumenical Understanding of African Instituted Churches*, Münster: Lit.

Pandey, Gyanendra (1992): *The Construction of Communalism in Colonial North India*, New York: Oxford University Press.

Peterson, Derek (2002): Gambling with God: Rethinking Religion in Colonial Central Kenya, in: Peterson, Derek and Walhof, Darren (eds.): *The Invention of Religion: Rethinking Belief and Politics in History*, New Brunswick: Rutgers University Press: 37-58.

Pobee, John (2002): *African Instituted (Independent) Churches*, Geneva: World Council of Churches.

Robertson, Roland (1992): *Globalization: Social Theory and Global Culture*, London: Routledge.

Smith, Wilfred Cantwell (1991): *The Meaning and End of Religion*, Minneapolis: Fortress Press.

Ter Haar, Gerrie (1998): The African Diaspora in the Netherlands, in: Clarke, Peter: *New Trends and Developments in African Religions*, Westport: Greenwood: 245-62.

Thapar, Romila (1989): Imagined Religious Communities? Ancient History and the Modern Search for a Hindu Identity, in: *Modern Asian Studies*, 23: 209-31.

Wallerstein, Immanuel (1979): *The Capitalist World-Economy* Cambridge: Cambridge University Press.

Williams, Raymond (1983): *Culture and Society, 1780-1950*, New York: Columbia University Press.

Syncretists, Fundamentalists and Scholars Compared

André Droogers

Introduction[1]

In this volume, a definition of syncretism is used that widens the field from the usual religious interpenetration to forms of cultural mixing in a broad and general way. The concept thus takes on meanings that are similar to those that define creolization (e.g. Hannerz 1992: 264ff.) or hybridization (e.g. Canclini 1995). The advantage of such a broadened approach to syncretism is that it can be shown that processes in the religious field, through which elements from different sources are mixed, may also be encountered in other domains. Mixing is not the privilege of religions alone. Broad concepts make similarities visible. The disadvantage is that a broader concept always is less precise when it is used for descriptive, classificatory or analytical purposes: the specifics of a particular field, such as religion, become less relevant.

Consolation can be found in the relativism that is inherent in the art of defining phenomena. As long as the map of the different options is readable to all, any definition of syncretism, narrow or broad, contributes to the appraisal of the field that is covered.

So, respecting the options made by the organizers of the Bayreuth conference and by the editors of this book in combining a broad and a narrow concept, I will focus on a particular field of cultural syncretism, namely religious syncretism. Yet, my treatment of religious syncretism includes a broadening in three respects. First, I will include a comparison between syncretism and fundamentalism,

---

[1] This article is a rewritten and extended version of an article that was published in a special issue of *Social Compass* (Droogers 2005). That article in turn was based on a paper originally presented at the conference on which this volume is based.

looking especially for differences. Secondly, I will compare believers and academics, focusing on similarities in mind frames. Thirdly, in passing I will examine the relevance of my approach to religious syncretism for the study of cultural syncretism.

The article starts with a justification of the comparisons I make. I then give a brief review of the concepts of syncretism and fundamentalism, which I will use subsequently as the basis for the comparison of the two phenomena. In order to elaborate on the power mechanisms in syncretism and fundamentalism, a three-dimensional model will be presented. In the section that follows, I then apply the model to syncretism and fundamentalism. In the last section I make comparisons of the frames of mind behind syncretism and constructivism, and fundamentalism and positivism, respectively.

Inappropriate comparisons?

With regard to the first comparison, that between syncretism and fundamentalism, a preliminary observation must be made. Making a comparison between syncretism and fundamentalism might seem inappropriate or even impossible, because syncretism and fundamentalism are not really commensurate. Though both concepts are part of the vocabulary of the student of religion, they are rarely discussed in connection with each other. Am I comparing apples and pears? Much depends on the characteristics that are steering the comparison. Though syncretism and fundamentalism are much older than the processes of modernization and globalization, in the current world situation they can both be viewed as opposite reactions to these processes, which is my main reason for drawing fundamentalism into the syncretism debate. When I focus on syncretism and fundamentalism as distinct modes of religious reflection on globalization, there is sufficient ground for comparison. By contrasting the positions taken, such a comparison may sharpen our understanding of each of the two phenomena. These two modes of religious construction and reproduction make very different use of the same religious repertoires.

This approach will also allow me to address an aspect that is proper to the theme of this book: the unpacking and questioning of the new. If religions with many centuries of history and tradition are exposed to such recent processes as modernization and globalization, one may ask what happens to them and how tradition and innovation are related. What happens if these processes put believers and their religions on to a worldwide information and media market, growing with migration, where competition and expansion are organizing principles? Syncretists and fundamentalists make opposite choices when confronted with alternatives and with challenges to the accepted beliefs and practices of daily life: the former appear to embrace the new with enthusiasm, whereas the latter seem to question it.

As I will show, in both cases the dimension of power and control that is the subject of this part of the book is an important aspect of the comparison between syncretism and fundamentalism. The framework for the comparison of these two modes of being religious is therefore found in a three-dimensional model of the power relations that occur in any religious context and that are used strategically by the participants in that religious setting. The three-dimensional model allows me to take stock of internal and external factors that may play a role in the rise of fundamentalism or syncretism, without losing sight of the specific nature of religious praxis. Syncretism and fundamentalism, as contrasting ways of using religious repertoires, express power relations and do have implications for them. The three-dimensional model may also help us understand the conditions under which each of the two phenomena flourishes or may change.

An appraisal of the role of fundamentalism and syncretism in the current cultural context of globalization points to a perhaps unexpected and inappropriate parallel with the scholarly paradigmatic debate between positivist and constructivist approaches. This relates to the second way of widening my scope, drawing into my argument the comparison of competing scientific paradigms. I will argue that there are striking similarities between fundamentalists and positivists on the one hand, and between constructivists and syncretists at the other. Obviously both positivism and constructivism can be applied to the scholarly study of fundamentalism and syncretism, but what is more important here is that, as specific forms of reflection, they show remarkable similarities with the world-views under study.

This may seem far-fetched: where syncretism and fundamentalism could already be viewed as incommensurate and too different to be compared, this would even more be the case for a comparison – with more emphasis on the commonness than on the obvious differences – between syncretism and constructivism on the one hand, and fundamentalism and positivism on the other. Religion and science are commonly considered opposite institutions, and sometimes they appear to combat each other. Especially secular scholars will frown upon any comparison between science and religion, at least if common elements are detected – the differences are quite obvious to them. Common elements have usually been overlooked, a blind spot that is explored in this article.

In short, I will suggest that, although with opposite results, both syncretism and fundamentalism are creative ways of being religious under changing conditions. More specifically, I hope to contribute to the discussion of the question of the power constellations under which these phenomena come about. In addition, I expect to contribute to the debate on the relationship between science and religion by exploring a side that has been underexposed so far: the commonness in ways of thinking between believers and scholars. Another spin-off of this discussion is to show the relevance of this argument for the study of cultural syncretism.

Defining Syncretism and Fundamentalism

Various efforts have been made to define syncretism and fundamentalism. Depending on the discipline, the theoretical preference and the selected illustrative example, the two phenomena have been defined in a variety of ways. The usual difficulties that accompany any effort at defining a concept have led to predictable suggestions, such as to distinguish between various types of syncretism or fundamentalism, sometimes in the plural (Lawrence 1998, Marty and Appleby 1991), or to abandon the term altogether (Baird 1971: 142-52). Another recommendation has been to stress the dynamic nature of these phenomena and to avoid any definition that merely represents a state of affairs.

With regard to syncretism, my own contribution to the debate has been influenced by my view as an anthropologist with a special interest in religion as a way of producing meaning in a cultural context that is marked by power mechanisms. In a collective interdisciplinary volume produced in 1989 under the auspices of the religious studies department of my university (Gort, 1989), I defined syncretism as 'religious interpenetration, either taken for granted or subject to debate' (Droogers 1989: 20, 21) and suggested that the power aspect should be prominent in the study of syncretism (Droogers 1989: 16-18; see also Greenfield and Droogers 2001). Other anthropologists have also stressed the importance of the political dimension (e.g. Stewart and Shaw 1994). In preparation of my effort to compare syncretism and fundamentalism, I will summarily discuss, using family resemblances, the defining characteristics that might be included when describing the two phenomena.

Fundamentalism

I start with fundamentalism. Though finding its origin, as an emic term, in American Protestantism, it has been recognized in other world religions. One common characteristic often mentioned is that it is a critical reaction to the process of modernization. I treat modernization as the process by which the results of science and technology influence the set-up of societies. Fundamentalists often take an anti-modernist stance, which does not prevent them from using the technological means of communication and transport that modernization has made abundantly available in the remotest corners of the world. In fundamentalism's anti-modernism, social and moral aspects predominate. In general the new is interpreted from the perspective of the old. This happens in such ways that, forgetting the modern challenge to which it is an answer, people are unaware of the innovation and modernity involved in the fundamentalist position. Through globalization – the process by which the world is experienced as one place – both modernity and fundamentalism have become part of the world as we know it today. The mass media have played a decisive role in this, especially after 9/11. One might even say that the media and politics have hijacked the definition of fundamentalism from academia and produced their own definition, with a strong emphasis on Islam, terrorism and the use of violence – to the point that the Christian origin of the term sometimes seems to have been forgotten.

Another defining characteristic of fundamentalists that should be mentioned is their activist, exclusive and assertive position. Their anti-modernist programme reflects a dualist way of thinking, dividing the world in two camps. Military metaphors are sometimes turned into real military, or at least militant activity. In terms of power, charismatic leaders may play a leading role in fundamentalist circles, reinforcing the attractiveness of the message by their own personalities. In the public appearance of fundamentalists, markers can be used regarding the body, such as beards, or the clothes that cover the body, making the adherents' identity recognizable and reinforcing their visibility. When sacred texts are available, these are often read in a literal manner as undisputable truth and as historical reports. Religion is taken in what anthropologists would call an essentialist way. Similarly there is a rather legalistic way of handling ethical matters. Finally, male dominance must be mentioned as a frequent characteristic, often connected with the literal reading of sacred texts that privilege men in taking power positions.

In sum, the following 'family resemblances' of fundamentalism can be mentioned:

- Anti-modernist
- Assertive, activist
- Dualist, 'enemy'-thinking
- Led by charismatic leaders
- Sacred text taken literally and as history
- Moral consciousness, laws
- Identity reinforced by external characteristics
- Male dominance

One final question can now be raised. Can the concept of fundamentalism be given a much wider connotation, just as the editors of this book have in mind with regard to syncretism? If the term syncretism lends itself to such an amplified use, could the concept of fundamentalism be submitted to a parallel extension? If syncretism in the ample sense, applicable to the whole of culture, corresponds to notions such as hybridization and creolization, fundamentalism would then refer to the opposite process, i.e. as a return to essentialist cultural patterns in reaction to modernist influences, perhaps for political reasons. Giving such a new meaning to the concept would remind one of the metaphorical use of the term 'fundamentalism' by selecting one or more characteristics, possibly corresponding to some that have been listed above. Thus regional separatist movements could be labelled 'cultural fundamentalism'. This broadening of the term 'fundamentalism' may appear less convincing than the extension of the concept of syncretism, but it follows similar lines of reasoning.

Syncretism

Turning now to an equally brief and incomplete characterization of syncretism, a first aspect that presents itself, of course, is that elements from different religious sources are in some way brought together in a new constellation. The degree to which elements are mixed can be observed to vary, and accordingly types of syncretism have been distinguished, with e.g. forms of symbiosis at one end of the spectrum and complete fusion at the other. The two or more religious sources that provide elements for the syncretistic process do not necessarily occupy an equal position. One may be dominant, thus coloring and redefining the elements taken from the other religion. Depending on the focus a scholar prefers –and this would fit the wider perspective adopted in this volume – non-religious elements are viewed as part of the process, especially where the religious sphere, in a holistic manner, influences other areas of life or is influenced by them.

Much syncretism seems to occur in a non-reflected manner, as a natural or more accurately a cultural routine process. As a consequence, and in contrast to fundamentalists, people who mix varied religious elements need not do so in a self-conscious manner and would not defend or propagate their behaviour, let alone raise the banner of syncretism or any other term. This is reinforced by the practical drive for syncretism as a way of solving existential problems. If one religion disappoints as a problem-solver, another may offer compensation. This also means that situations of affliction, abundantly present when modernization processes fail to bring wealth and health, may stimulate people to appeal to forms of syncretization.

Another aspect that can be mentioned here is that phenomenological or other similarities between religions may promote syncretism. Similarity may facilitate mingling, as when pantheons are structured in the same way, or when extra-sensory experiences are common to both religions. But not only do similarities stimulate syncretism, complementarities may also create an ambiance for syncretization, e.g. when one religion helps out where the other fails, or when one religion has a strong concept of a high god that is lacking in the other.

A further characteristic to be mentioned is that the actors in syncretization often are lay believers, predominantly women, who have withdrawed from the control of the (usually male) religious specialists. Here the power dimension of syncretism and anti-syncretism becomes visible in terms of both gender and religious organization.

The term 'syncretism', whether used by religious leaders or by scholars, is a product of the surprising event that seemingly separate elements from different orders are brought together. In that sense, scholars and religious leaders react surprised because both think in similar rather essentialist ways, presupposing as the normal situation that more or less closed, autonomous systems exist that syncretists perforate and perturb. Whereas religious leaders condemn this as heresy, scholars jump to the opportunity to study this unexpected matter out of order.

In sum, syncretism may have all or most of the following characteristics:

- Syncretism occurs as a reaction to contact between religions
- Modernization and globalization create opportunities for mingling
- Syncretists rarely act in a self-conscious manner
- Syncretists are focused on everyday life and view religions as problem-solvers
- Affliction, e.g. because of modernization, stimulates mingling
- Common characteristics facilitate mingling
- Complementary differences facilitate mingling
- Laity is active, especially women
- Religious leadership is critical

As in the case of fundamentalism, reference can now be made to the broad definition of syncretism that is adopted in this volume, raising the question of which of the defining characteristics just mentioned can be transferred, either metaphorically or literally, from the religious to the broader cultural domain. It seems that there are in fact similarities that make the comparison between religious and cultural syncretism instructive, just as my own –perhaps equally unexpected – comparison between the concepts of syncretism and fundamentalism brings new insights. Yet, some characteristics cannot be included in the extension from the religious to the general cultural field. In cultural syncretism contact is not primarily between religions, and a society's leaders do not necessarily opinionate. A further difference may affect the gender dimension, since cultural syncretists are not predominantly women. But the other items on my list do apply to cultural syncretism as well and may help increase our understanding of processes of hybridization.

Syncretism and Fundamentalism Compared

Turning now to a comparison of the two processes, not all the characteristics just mentioned can be retaken. The two lists of characteristics cannot simply be arranged in a parallel way, with a clear correspondence between individual items. In a similar vein, I do not want to suggest that fundamentalism and syncretism necessarily go together in all religious situations, as two sides of the same coin. Moreover, my comparison will stress the contrasts, leaving aside the common characteristics.

Distinguishing between the emic and the etic uses of the terms, both terms can be said to have been used originally at the emic level, long before becoming part of the scholarly vocabulary (Droogers 2001). In its more ancient emic meanings, syncretism did not have the negative connotation that later religious leaders came to give it in condemning it. One example is Erasmus of Rotterdam, who recommended syncretism as a positive and productive way of reconciling differences in Christian theology. The more recent emic use of syncretism concerns the vocabulary leaders use in condemning the mingling of Christian with non-Christian elements that takes place among ordinary believers. The leaders usually view this practice as impure and offensive, even as heretical, partly because, in terms of the religion's power structure, it threatens the monopoly of the clergy over the production of religion. Accordingly those same leaders may identify with fundamentalism. Yet, when tolerance towards other religions is a basic value in their religion, leaders may be more lenient. This tolerance may change, as when leaders in Hinduism, for a long time considered a very tolerant religion, adopt fundamentalist attitudes in the course of competition with other world religions. Furthering the comparison, it can be observed that whereas fundamentalists, especially certain Christian Americans, may proudly label themselves as such, syncretists hardly ever adopt that particular banner and often do not even know the term. Another difference at the emic level is that fundamentalists see the whole world as their setting, whereas syncretists usually have a local perspective.

Including the etic level, it has already been observed that both the emic and the academic applications of these terms start from a rather essentialist presupposition. This is the deeper reason why syncretism commands our attention. Similarly, though at the other extreme, the exclusiveness of fundamentalism has drawn attention because it represented the most outspoken defence of essentialism in religion.

Apart from the emic and etic uses of the terms, the phenomena themselves show some striking differences. An obvious and basic contrast between the two processes is that fundamentalists opt for one exclusive religious source, with one version and interpretation, whereas syncretists see no problem in using more sources and feel free to interpret them as they like, notwithstanding orthodox intentions or safeguards. In using one source only, fundamentalists make use of a limited number of metaphors, or even just one key metaphor that becomes codified and sacrosanct, whereas syncretists explore the usefulness of many metaphors, especially when they consider them complementary to each other and effective in practical use.

Another contrast is that fundamentalists seek institutionalization, whereas syncretists operate in a much more informal sphere. Religious (and sometimes political) authorities officially stimulate fundamentalism and commonly condemn syncretism. Fundamentalists and syncretists, though both popular in their expressions and success, thus differ in their appraisal of religious authority.

In the long run, syncretists may adopt some form of fundamentalism. When syncretism attains the status of an official religion, as in some Japanese and Brazilian religions, it may develop into a single-perspective religion and even adopt fundamentalist characteristics in some of its manifestations. Similarly, fundamentalism may in the long run be eroded through syncretistic tendencies.

In terms of gender, and corresponding to the distinction between official and popular religion, fundamentalists – including women – accept male dominance, whereas active syncretists are often women. The latter's way of producing religion may serve as a form of unconscious and unreflected resistance against male dominance. Women may use the exclusive informality of their own religious sector, separate from male dominance, to develop syncretistic ideas and practices.

Syncretism and fundamentalism can also be compared in terms of repertoire use. This may help us understand them as ways of 'unpacking or questioning the new'. In using the repertoire metaphor for the way culture, society and religion are managed and lived, a number of the characteristics of cultural, social and religious processes can be clarified. Just like cultures, societies and religions, a repertoire will show change, almost by definition, while maintaining continuity to a certain degree. Elements are added and discarded. Innovation, revival and reform may occur. Repertoires contain many latent elements that are only activated when the situation or the context demands it. In their history, the cultures, societies and religions of the world bear the traces of this process. In the case of the world religions, for example, different schools and movements make their own selection from the general repertoire. Power relations, in the case of religions legitimated by an appeal to the sacred, regulate access to repertoires and the right to change or maintain them. The control of repertoires is part of the power play that takes place in any culture, society or religion. Since repertoires are used contextually, they may contain inconsistencies, especially in their popular use, despite efforts by the leadership to maintain a particular logic or system, and despite their possible emphasis on orthodoxy and orthopraxis.

The processes of syncretism and fundamentalism can be understood as contrasting ways of dealing with cultural and more specifically religious repertoires, within the context of modernization and globalization. Whereas fundamentalists centripetally focus on one exclusive repertoire that is defended against threats to basic, i.e. fundamental principles, syncretists make a centrifugal use of as many repertoires as are needed to solve their existential or practical questions and problems. Both modernization and globalization represent processes that expand the range of available repertoires, while at the same time creating situations in which the need for repertoires is stimulated. This leads to either centripetal or centrifugal reactions. In sum, and more schematically:

SYNCRETISM	FUNDAMENTALISM
Etic term, more than emic	Etic and emic term
Tolerant	Intolerant
More sources, more versions	One source, one version
Experiment with metaphors and metonymies	Codification of one central metaphor
Condemned by religious leaders	Applauded by religious leaders
Hardly institutionalized	Institutionalized
Experimenting with many repertoires	Loyal to one repertoire

The Three-Dimensional Model

The three-dimensional model presented here focuses on power and may therefore be helpful in making sense of the power mechanisms at work in both syncretism and fundamentalism. The three dimensions that are distinguished are the external, internal and supernatural dimensions. In each of these dimensions, categories of actors who are involved in some power relationship can be distinguished. Depending on their relationship, the modes of religious construction differ. In schematic form, the model is as follows:

DIMENSION	Actors	Mode of religious construction
INTERNAL	Believers/Believers Lay believers/Religious specialists	Horizontal vs. Vertical
EXTERNAL	Believers/Non-believers Believers and Believers of other worldviews	Hostile vs. Tolerant
SUPERNATURAL	Believers/God, gods, spirits, saints	Manipulative vs. Submissive

In this model, I bring together the power relations that prevail at the three levels of the religious group: the internal, external and supernatural or transcendental levels. The units to which the model can be applied could be as small as an African clan or a cell group in a local Pentecostal church, or as large as the Muslim Brotherhood or the worldwide Catholic Church. While the external and internal levels refer primarily to the social structural aspects, the supernatural dimension is more cultural in nature, or reflects, more specifically, the religious world-view.

I take power to mean the capacity to influence other people's behaviour. At the internal level power relations exist between believers, but also, and more visibly, between religious leaders and the laity. At the external level there is a power relationship between believers on the one hand and non-believers on the other, or, perhaps more importantly, believers of other religious preferences. At the supernatural level, there is a power relationship between believers and their god, gods, spirits and whatever other forms the sacred might take. Usually the repertoires for behaviour, reflection and perception that are constructed and activated at each of the three levels are interconnected and influence each other.

Having defined the three levels, I would now like to suggest that the power relationships at each of the three levels move along a spectrum between extremes and may change in the course of time and depending on the case. Thus at the internal level, when there is a clear leader, his or her position may be strong, influencing the thinking and behaviour of the ordinary believers. In other cases, at the other end of the spectrum, there may be a preference for rather horizontal relations between members, but also between leaders and members. In the course of time changes may take place, as occurs in reformations. Within the internal dimension, one might thus distinguish between the poles of a vertical, hierarchical and a horizontal, inclusive mode of power relations and religious construction, with many variations in between.

Moving on to the external dimension, power relations may take the form of an effort to influence outsiders in their behaviour, for example by converting them or by imposing ethical rules. In the course of history, for example, Christianity and Islam became known for their proselytism and for their influence on legislation. At the other end of the spectrum, this tendency may be fully absent. On the contrary, the believers may easily adopt values and behavioural models that are normal in the surrounding society, the direction of the power mechanisms being in fact inverted. Liberal Protestants and

Reform Jews, for example, have sought ways to reconcile religion and science. Consequently, at this level we may distinguish between an exclusive or even hostile pole and an inclusive, tolerant pole. Religious groups may, in the course of their history, move from tolerance to intolerance, through all positions in between (see e.g. Yinger 1970: 256 ff.).

At the transcendental or supernatural level, power relations are equally given expression, even though believers may not like to think of their religious experience as involving power, or prefer to think of power in a unilateral way, as when praising the power of their God. In terms of influence on the other's behaviour, believers accept the influence of the sacred in their lives and may submit to it. On the other hand, believers may seek to take part in the power of the sacred and to influence the sacred to their advantage. Religions know all forms of sacrifice and prayer. One of the possible meanings of the term 'magic' points to the manipulation of sacred power for the believer's purposes. We may label the poles of the spectrum of power relations at this level as respectively submissive and manipulative. Here too believers may in the course of time, and depending on the context they find themselves in, change their views on the sacred and move along the spectrum.

Power Relations in Fundamentalism and Syncretism

The three-dimensional model can now be applied to the phenomena under comparison, namely fundamentalism and syncretism. The model proves helpful when the question is under what power relations the conditions are propitious for either syncretism or fundamentalism. Though the model does not include all the factors that may be relevant, it may show under which mode of religious construction fundamentalism or syncretism respectively may occur.

When we thus consider fundamentalism, it seems to me that, in terms of its characteristics as summarized above, it usually comes with an emphasis in the internal dimension on vertical and hierarchical power relations, with a clergy that is there to guard the fundamentalist heritage. Because of the emphasis on the purity of its doctrine and praxis, a vertical structure that guarantees discipline is implied and even necessary. If we then look at the external dimension, it becomes clear that, as a consequence of their exclusive view of the truth, fundamentalists protect their group boundaries and adopt a rather hostile attitude towards non-believers and believers in other religious expressions. Though the methods may vary, the rest of the world is meant to adopt the basic fundamentalist position. On the supernatural level, the fundamentalist position seems to tend towards a submissive rather than manipulative position. The strictness of the position matches a view of the sacred as dominant, demanding full surrender in all areas of life. It should be noted that the modes of religious production adopted at the three levels reinforce each other, thus forming in this case a triangle, with vertical, hostile and submissive modes of religious construction at its corners.

As far as syncretism is concerned, on the internal dimension it works best when believers are able to avoid control by religious leaders or when such control is simply absent because of the rather horizontal power relations. One might even think of the rare case of leaders stimulating a mingling of elements from a variety of religions. At the external level, syncretism, by its very nature, is open to external influences and thus adopts an open and tolerant attitude towards other believers and their religions. Turning to the supernatural level, the practical approach of syncretists points to a more manipulative than submissive attitude. Though the power of the sacred is acknowledged, precisely for that reason it is a potential resource for the solution of problems. As soon as other religious sources are adopted, the number of sacred powers available for such use increases. Again, the constellation of positions and attitudes at the three levels may serve to reinforce the net result. The triangle in this case is composed of the corners of horizontal, tolerant and manipulative modes of religious construction.

Thinking of the wider view of syncretism that is the starting point for this book, one may ask what the three-dimensional model has to offer to those interested in the broader definition of syncretism, more specifically to the understanding of cultural hybridization. The model was developed for the study of religious groups (e.g. Droogers 2003), but some of its ingredients may stimulate understanding of cultural syncretism (or for that matter cultural fundamentalism, if that term is to be included in the vocabulary). The supernatural dimension that is proper to the religious field could be reformulated as a cultural dimension, including repertoires of more general values and convictions, the other two dimensions containing repertoires of a social nature, ruling the internal and external relationships of a group or society. The degree of cultural syncretism – or resistance to such syncretism – could be studied as the constellation of the three dimensions and the interaction between the repertoires that are characteristic of each. Even though this may not lead to such neat triangles as suggested above, the mixing of cultural elements may then prove to obey mechanisms that are similar to those that predict either religious syncretism or religious fundamentalism.

Positivism and Fundamentalism, Constructivism and Syncretism

In order to complete this exercise, let us now explore possible resemblances between fundamentalism and positivism on the one hand, and syncretism and constructivism on the other. First of all, the two modes of doing science must be discussed. Following Guba (1990), a distinction can be made between paradigms – paradigm defined as 'a basic set of beliefs that guides action' (ibid.: 17) – that rule scientific activity. Though Guba mentions four, for the purpose of this paper I restrict myself to the two extreme types, the positivist and the constructivist paradigms, leaving what he calls the post-positivist approach and critical theory out of this discussion.

The positivist position, as summarized by Guba (ibid.: 20), presupposes a reality out there that is driven by natural laws. The scientist's task is to discover these laws and to produce generalizations. Many of these laws refer to relations of cause and effect. There is only one reality and only one main story involved. Also, the researcher should not intervene in the reality studied: his or her preferences or values should not influence the outcome. The positivist methodology requires hypotheses that can be subjected to empirical tests, to be held under carefully controlled conditions. The natural sciences are the preferred example of this paradigm.

At the other end of the spectrum, the constructivist position adopts an ontology that presupposes the existence of more realities, as multiple mental constructions that are thought of by scholars of different leanings. There are fragments of stories to be told about an unlimited number of realities. These realities are socially and experientially based, local and specific in nature, and depend for their form and content on the person who holds them. Findings emerge in the interaction between the inquirer and the inquired, and also in the debate between inquirers. Accordingly the method adopted is dialectic and hermeneutic. In this model of science, the ambition to reach 'the' scientific truth is absent or at the least made relative. Constructivists emphasise that the study of human beings demands its own model of science.

Adopting the manner of the positivist tradition, fundamentalism and syncretism will be studied for their objective general characteristics, the type of aspects that would help to define the phenomenon. In view of the rule-driven nature of social reality, it will be considered possible to make general predictions about the conditions under which fundamentalism and syncretism emerge. For example, whether the fundamentalism is Christian or Muslim or Jewish, common traits and mechanisms will be looked for. Causes and consequences can be identified, and general structures will become visible. In fact, my three-dimensional model serves just such a purpose: my affirmations can be tested as a hypothesis for research.

What I have tried to do is to isolate a limited number of factors, especially related to the power constellation.

On the other hand, if we followed a constructivist interaction approach, the focus would switch from the conditions as defined by a positivist approach to what the syncretistic or fundamentalist actors do with these conditions and how each of them constructs his or her religious reality and identity. Through interaction with the people studied, the researcher will try to come as close as possible to this process of constructing a meaningful world. But at the same time the researcher is constructing a meaningful world as well. In both cases, the social and experiential basis for the construction of these identities and worlds depends on the consensus that can be reached on a particular view. The suggestion that we speak of fundamentalisms, in the plural, is an example of recognizing the variety of forms, and ultimately the plurality of realities, as experienced and constructed. In using the three-dimensional model to draw attention to the power mechanisms at work in syncretism and fundamentalism, I have brought the actors and their strategies into the discussion, not only those of the religious leaders, but also of the ordinary believers.

Depending on the science paradigm that is adopted, a different image is given of the phenomena under study, and different aspects are selected as typical. In addition, the two models differ markedly in the degree of generalization. They also differ in their handling of variables, the positivist model seeking to control them, the constructivist approach treating them as the raw material for the ongoing process of identity and reality construction. The positivist paradigm will help to make the structural givens of power mechanisms visible, whereas the constructivist approach will show the processes in which actors do something with these structures. Positivists will emphasise rules and generalities, constructivists exceptions and the particularities.

Having compared the two perspectives and their application to the study of syncretism and fundamentalism, it appears to me that somewhat more can be said on the science models and the two religious phenomena that interest us here. Guba's definition of a paradigm, quoted above, with its explicit reference to beliefs that guide action, appears to facilitate such a comparison. There seems to be a certain kinship in the type of reflection or frame of mind, on the one hand between positivism and fundamentalism, and on the other between syncretism and constructivism. If we take as an important difference between positivists and constructivists that the term 'reality' is used in either the singular or the plural as well, then there is a parallel with the fundamentalist focus on one exclusive form of the sacred reality, whereas syncretists have no qualms in working with various forms of that reality, even if the official versions condemn or deny ideas about this. Of course, syncretists may take this religious plurality as one holistic cosmos, in which they have learned to move skilfully. But holistic view or not, the least one can say is that syncretists reject an exclusive view of the sacred reality. They thus resist the power structure that accompanies such a singular view, whether it is fundamentalist or not. The positivist belief system presupposes a reality 'out there,' as given, just as, in the fundamentalist belief system, the one sacred reality is presupposed, with only one 'grand' story to be told about it. Incidentally, in the positivist view, one is not allowed to intervene in that reality while researching it. In the case of both fundamentalist believers and positivist scholars, laws and rules drive the reality they focus on. The constructivist paradigm opts for *realities*, in the plural, and is even hesitant whether these realities are really 'out there'. Many stories in a variety of versions can be told about these realities.

There is a difference, though: syncretists have a stauncher belief in their realities than constructivists in theirs. They believe in the realities that other religions suggest, at least as long as they work in solving problems. Syncretists play with different realities in forming their religious identities. An improvising flexible and practical use is made of whatever regularity or causality presents itself.

Finally, just as fundamentalists and syncretists have different backgrounds as far as power processes and mechanisms are concerned, scholars may be said to play different power games in the way they practice science. Fundamentalists and positivists seek to impose a rather monopolistic, centripetal, law-based and strict view of the world. Both are, in their own ways, modernist. Syncretists and constructivists seem to resist this view. They adopt a mode of reflection that is tuned to the human capacity to think an unlimited number of realities with a centrifugally expanding number of identities that are open to improvisation when the conditions demand this. They are much more postmodernist.

Conclusion

In this chapter, I have shown how believers and scholars of diverse orientations opt for a different use of the repertoires that are available in their worlds, whether religious or academic. It was suggested that, within a framework that focuses on the relation between meaning-making and power, fundamentalists and syncretists occupy contrasting positions, among each other, in dealing with outsiders, as well as in approaching the sacred. In addition, unexpected similarities were identified between fundamentalists and positivists on the one hand, and between syncretists and constructivists on the other. An exclusive and centripetal use of one single repertoire was contrasted with an inclusive and centrifugal use of a series of repertoires. Scholars and believers thus have more in common than the usual separation of religion and science appears to suggest.

Bibliography

Baird, Robert D. (1971): *Category Formation and the History of Religion*, Mouton: The Hague.

Canclini, Néstor García (1995): *Hybrid Cultures: Strategies for Entering and Leaving Modernity*, Minneapolis: University of Minnesota Press.

Droogers, André (1998): Syncretism: The Problem of Definition, the Definition of the Problem, in: Gort, Jerald et al. (eds.): *Dialogue and Syncretism: An Interdisciplinary Approach*, Amsterdam: Rodopi and Eerdmans, 7-24.

Droogers, André (2001): Syncretism, in: *International Encyclopedia of the Social and Behavioral Sciences*, London: Elsevier, 15386-15388.

Droogers, André (2003): The Power Dimensions of the Christian Community: An Anthropological Model, *Religion: A Journal of Religion and Religions*, 33, 3, 263-80.

Droogers, André (2005): Syncretism and Fundamentalism: A Comparison, *Social Compass*, 52, 4, 463-471

Gort, Jerald et al. (eds.) (1989): *Dialogue and Syncretism: An Interdisciplinary Approach*, Amsterdam: Rodopi and Eerdmans.

Greenfield, Sidney M.; Droogers, André (eds.) (2001): *Reinventing Religions, Syncretism and Transformation in Africa and the Americas*, Lanham: Rowman and Littlefield.

Guba, Egon G. (1990): *The Paradigm Dialog*, Newbury Park: Sage.

Hannerz, Ulf (1992): *Cultural Complexity: Studies in the Social Organization of Meaning*, New York: Columbia University Press.

Lawrence, Bruce B. (1998): From Fundamentalism to Fundamentalisms: A Religious Ideology in Multiple Forms, in: Heelas, Paul (ed.): *Religion, Modernity and Postmodernity*, Oxford: Blackwell, 88-101.

Marty, Martin E.; Appleby, R. Scott (eds.) (1991): *Fundamentalisms Observed*', Chicago: The University of Chicago Press.

Stewart, Charles; Shaw, Rosalind (eds.) (1994): *Syncretism/Anti-Syncretism: The Politics of Religious Synthesis*, London: Routledge.

Yinger, J. Milton (1970): *The Scientific Study of Religion*, New York: Macmillan.

Appropriation, Alienation and Syncretization: Lessons from the Field

Hans Peter Hahn

Die Autorität des Neuen ist die des geschichtlich Unausweichlichen. Insofern impliziert es objektive Kritik am Individuum, seinem Vehikel: ästhetisch schürzt im Neuen sich der Knoten von Individuum und Gesellschaft.

(Adorno 1955: 38)

We live in a world that submits itself to the logic of infinitely accelerating the consumption of goods and their production. One of the tacit assumptions of this logic is our readiness to alienate our workforce permanently in order to acquire these objects.[1] It is with these thoughts in mind that Dominique Perrot (1979a) introduces a collective volume discussing the significance of objects people call their most appreciated goods. Perrot's point is that anthropological and sociological views of these highly esteemed objects may help to explain the fatal attraction of the material world. Perrot goes on to say that it is not only work and production but the objects themselves that play a crucial role in the diverse processes of alienation in the modern world.

In this chapter, I will basically follow Perrot's thoughts in discussing the role of cherished goods, but I chose my examples from a society which may be correctly described as belonging to the 'Less Affluent World'.[2] The patterns of material possessions in the African society I studied are undergoing rapid change, which makes it possible to gain new insights into the processes of appropriation and alienation.

---

[1] This is idea has been expressed already by Simmel ([1907] 1989: 620) and others.

[2] I borrow this term from Ger and Belk (1996: 273), who define it as 'societies not fully integrated into mass consumption'. As a matter of fact, in my case study, material possessions do not exceed an average of 120 objects per person.

This chapter also deals with the acquisition and handling of global goods in a rural society in West Africa.[3] Obviously, the global goods in question may be regarded as syncretistic objects, and it is no coincidence that most scholars dealing with globalization regard consumption and the ever-increasing importance of global goods as one of the main appearances of globalization. This chapter will narrow its focus to the consequences of the ubiquitous role of these global goods. As I will show, wherever these consumer goods are appropriated and subsequently become part of the local culture, another change in the significance of everyday things occurs, which is juxtaposed to the process of appropriation.[4]

For this process, I use the term 'cultural alienation' in the sense of Georg Simmel and others. The term 'alienation' has sometimes been called an 'old battlefield' in debates inspired by the Marxian thought of alienated work and modes of production (Israel 1971),[5] even before Israel Plessner (1960: 15f.) showed that Marx had borrowed the term 'alienation' from Hegel, who, however, used it in a much larger sense. For Hegel, *Entfremdung* and *Entäußerung* ('alienation' and 'objectification', but used as synonyms by Hegel) are only consequences of man's dealing with the material world. After the objects have been made they become autonomous, and there is an

---

[3] This is the title of a research project carried out from 2000-2006 by the author, Gerd Spittler and Marcus Verne with support from the DFG through a collaborative research programme at the University of Bayreuth entitled 'Local Action in Africa in the Context of Global Influences'. I would like to express my gratitude to my colleagues for discussing earlier versions of this paper and the Deutsche Forschungsgemeinschaft for its financial support.

[4] The process of appropriation is part of the theoretical framework of our research project. Remarks on our working definition and its general implications are available in Hahn 2004a.

[5] In the context of a book review of Daniel Miller's *Material Culture and Mass Consumption*, Gell (1988) criticizes Miller (1987) for relating alienation and objectification to Hegel. Gell asks for (ibid.: 47) a second cultural point of reference that he calls 'symbolic culture in the mode of imagination'. In defence of Miller, I would stress that the larger sense of Hegel's *Entfremdung* and *Entäußerung* include these subjective and imaginative aspects.

estrangement between man and things that leads to the freedom of the former from the material conditions. In his discussion of alienation, Plessner stresses that Hegel's view must be related to the epoch's dominant romanticism.[6]

The way Perrot and, much earlier, Simmel use the term goes beyond this meaning when they name the consumption and the allure of certain goods as principal reasons for alienation. As underlined by James Carrier (1994), cultural alienation is not related to work or production, but to distribution and consumption. Moreover, the precise meaning of the term 'cultural alienation' should be understood as being close to 'cultural estrangement', a term suggested in the *Encyclopedia Britannica* (N.N. 2001) as one of the meanings of alienation. Based once again on Simmel, the *Encyclopedia* describes this meaning of alienation as 'removal from established values in society'.

Perhaps because the connection between appropriation and cultural alienation is only indirect, in many publications on the topic these two processes have not been related sufficiently to each other. In the context of this common neglect, it seems to me that Adorno is an exception. He has felt very well the relatedness between appropriation (which he calls the authority of the new) and alienation (i.e. the historically inevitable). Thus, in the quotation above Adorno makes the point that the authority of the new imposes itself over the historical process, but also that both processes become reality on the level of the individual, bringing in the new and – at the same time – alienating himself from the old.

My chapter is organized in three parts. The first part explains the process of appropriation with reference to everyday objects. I will use the bicycle as an example and report from my own case study of

[6] In a similar way, Popitz ([1953] 1967: 123) explains Hegel's use of alienation as a kind of distanciation that happens on different levels: on the levels of the individual, of the society as a whole and of class differences.

a small village called Kollo in the south of Burkina Faso.[7] The term 'appropriation' is used in many different contexts and belongs to a variety of terms which have had a great career in the anthropology of globalization. The creative aspects of the process of appropriation are always being stressed: appropriation produces new meanings of things, it creates specific ways of handling them, and finally it creates new cultural spaces which allow objects that are at first strange or unspecific to become part of the local culture or identity. The second part of this chapter will be dedicated to certain criticisms of these idealistic perspectives on appropriation. The term 'cultural alienation' will be explained with reference to certain observations concerning dealing with locally made objects and their shifting contexts. One of the consequences of these shifting contexts is the uncertainity concerning the evaluation of local goods. Thus, alienation seems to constitute a very seldom reflected and rarely articulated countertendency to appropriation. Subjectively felt, alienation is not so much an orientation to new things, i.e. consumer goods, but rather a question of the perspective on one's own culture. The third part of the chapter deals with the relationship between the two terms 'appropriation' and 'alienation'. Both processes may parallel each other, but they take a different course. They even differ on the level of consciousness. While appropriation is a matter of agency and a topic of negotiation, cultural alienation often occurs unnoticed. I will argue that their relationship is a dialectic one in so far as appropriation initiates alienation, while alienation can be regarded as a countertendency to appropriation and may call the latter into question.

The anthropological observation of syncretisation is not meant to be restricted to the study of more or less syncretistic objects. Here I follow Charles Stewart (1999), who suggests that it is more impor-

---

[7] I carried out research from 1993 to 2001 in Kollo, a village in the Province du Nahouri in central south of Burkina Faso. A preliminary version of the findings has been published in Hahn 2004b.

tant to ask who is allowing syncretisation to take place, who is facilitating it and perhaps wh is hindering it. As we have seen in the quotation from Adorno, the individual is at the crossroads between appropriation and alienation: how successful the new is is a matter of how individuals act. In the context of Stewart's remarks, we may translate this into some precise research questions: Who are the individuals actively involved in the processes of syncretisation, appropriation and alienation? What are the contexts in which appropriation and alienation are being articulated? The intention of this contribution is to acquire a deeper understanding of the role of consumer goods in the rural milieu in West Africa and thus to be able to explain how these two processes, appropriation and alienation, may interfere with each other.

Appropriation

In the village of Kollo, consisting of about 2,000 people mainly living from agriculture, approximately half the properties in the households we examined may be categorized as global goods.[8] Some global goods have already been introduced to the area some decades ago, while others have only recently become objects of everyday use. Global goods in their entirety allocate an important part of the households' financial resources. Most of these items have been industrially manufactured and make their way into the local society as commodities. In this sense, a fundamental contrast is constituted with locally produced goods to which no important financial resources are dedicated.

---

[8] As Markus Verne (2005) has shown, the category of 'global good' is a very problematic one. There is no clear-cut boundary between local and global goods, and the framework of appropriation in particular tends to blur these categories. Nevertheless, for the purposes of our research project we used a working definition, based on the geographical origin of the material object itself. Thus, objects coming from outside of Africa are global goods.

What is the context for the appropriation of global goods? I will illustrate this issue by referring to the bicycle because it stands for a typical global and industrially manufactured good. In West Africa bicycles usually come from China, where British bicycle models are still being produced under license today. Local traders offer them in markets in Ghana and Burkina Faso. From the perspective of potential customers in the West African savannah, purchase one involves making an extraordinary investment, unlike the context of acquisition in Western societies. Usually the purchase requires several years' worth of savings. A frequent and alternative strategy of acquisition is connected to labour migration, which is very common in this region. Either the migrants themselves purchase a bicycle at the time of their permanent return, or else they buy one and give it away to their relatives during a stay at home.

The purchase is the beginning of a multi-facetted process of appropriation. Another important element is the local naming of the bicycle. While in Germany a bike may be called a 'Drahtesel' in a not quite respectful way, and in English equally contemptuously a 'boneshaker', in kasIm, the local language in the region of my case study, it is called an 'iron horse'. Obviously, the local name associates the object with the institution of horse keeping, which is very important to the status of the local chiefs. Donkeys are comparatively common, and many families have one at their disposal, to be used as beast of burden as well as to pull carts or ploughs. Keeping horses, on the other hand, is the privilege of a small number of 'noble' families and the chief himself. Though horses are hardly used in everyday life, the high status of the horse seems to have played a role in giving this name to the bicycle.

As a matter of fact, bicycles too have high status. The high costs of purchase from a local point of view are one indication of this. Another sign is the decoration and alteration of new bikes. Certain things, like a seat cover or new handles, are best understood as obligatory accessories, even though they may be more focused on aesthetic standards. They are bought right at the time the bicycle is purchased.

Other alterations constitute merely pragmatic adaptations to the local use of bicycles, for example, racks produced by local blacksmiths, which soon replace the original ones. But even more important is the removal of certain parts which are not really necessary, such as the chain box, mudguards, dynamo and front brakes, which are regarded as presenting a hindrance to the frequent and inevitable repairs (for example, of leaking tyres) or – like the front brakes – as an avoidable danger for the cyclist. These changes show the great importance of bicycles as a means of transport. Frequently transporting heavy loads, like large sacks of cereals, they play an important role for farmers in this region. At the same time, the modifications reflect the bad quality of the road surfaces, which is no surprise at the sight of the frequently used ways and paths. The frequency of repairs, ranging from patching tyres to changing the ball bearings and the not uncommon welding of rims and frames – apart from the problem of bad road conditions – also indicates how intensively bicycles are used.

The contrast between the form of the bicycle as a global good and its form as used in West Africa is great, as can readily be seen at first sight. Typically bikes in Kollo which have been used for a number of years consist merely of the frame, the rack and the minimum of indispensable parts. The frames may show traces of welding, usually the original paint is gone, and the tyres have often been sewed or wrapped in cloth in order to extend their use.

Appropriation in this context is to be understood on two levels. On the one hand, bicycles are highly appreciated as shown by the names they are given and their intensive use. The global good 'British-Chinese bicycle' is a model, and its acquisition a goal for many people in the village. On the other hand, bikes are considered imperfect when new and are accordingly materially redesigned in order to improve their functioning. In Kollo I have talked to owners of bicycles about the differences between new and localized bikes. The farmers confirmed that new bikes were somehow ‘nice’ in their own way, and that each part and their arrangement as a whole did make sense. This is articulated by seeing the engineer of the bike as a European. The farmers acknowledge that ‘Europeans aren’t stupid’. – After that, some criticism follows: he is nonetheless not able to understand the daily difficulties in Kollo. Perhaps a ‘bike of the Whites’ may brake better and, during the rains, one doesn’t get dirty thanks to the mudguards. But concerning reliability and the possibility of maintenance, everybody will affirm the advantages of the alterations to the bike which are made in Kollo: the rack, easily carrying 80 kg, the chain being easy to put back in its place when necessary, and wheels which are effortlessly removed and which allow thorns etc. to be discovered easily because of the missing mudguards.

The appropriation of the bicycle has become a local routine and takes place again and again with every new bike that is bought. The routinized appropriation may be identified by what I describe here as ‘culturally framed object biographies’. The experiences of handling the object during many decades have been incorporated, and became a cultural standard in the local society. For this reason I speak not only of the appropriation of several bicycles, but of the iron horse as a category of material objects. The appropriated bike is about a mixture, a syncretistic object containing global as well as local aspects. The peoples’ initiation and the propagation of this particular process of syncretisation shows that the bicycle owners are proud of their possession and recognize the quality of the global (the origin of the bicycle) and the local (their modifications).[9] It is to be presumed that a successful appropriation always ends in a way in which the mixture is thought of as better, more useful and also more meaning-

[9] In this respect, the local form of the bicycle is close to what Barber and Waterman (1995) describe for particular styles of Yoruba music, which contain references to the local as well as to the global.

ful, compared to the unaltered global good. This is the point at which appropriation and syncretism merge and create a common evaluation of the cultural role of the new objects.[10]

In his studies of appropriated goods in Trinidad, Daniel Miller (1992a) states: 'Only imported goods constitute authentic culture'. According to Miller, Trinidadians retrieve their own identities especially through the local interpretation of American soap operas. Nothing produced on Trinidad could be as authentic as these TV programmes (Miller 1992b). Among others, the copying of clothes as seen in the movies and the dialogue of the actors belongs to the acting in respect of this medium. The syncretism thus articulated may, according to Miller, present a more important contribution to the identity of consumers in Trinidad than any other, perhaps locally produced TV programme. In respect to my African case study, one is left with some scepticism as to whether bicycle owners would rate the role of their specific bicycle design that high. Surely, this kind of appropriated bicycle is something new, unique and superior to any other kind of bicycle. But still, it is necessary to ask where the limits of this perspective on appropriation lie, and how they are negotiated.

Alienation

The owners of bicycles mentioned so far have a special, prestigious position in the local society. At the same time, very often they are migrants or ex-migrants. This means that they have been away from home for months or even years. Nonetheless a few bicycle owners are not migrants themselves, but have a brother or a son who is, by whom they were given the bicycle on the occasion of the latter's visit

---

[10] As Moser (1994) stresses, appropriation has much to do with recycling. Recycling means reinventing objects and usages from things that have been already considered as waste. Recycling appropriation and syncretization thus opens up new spaces for culturally defined meanings and usages, particularly for the poor and powerless, who do not have the opportunity to participate in the consumption patterns of Western society.

to the village. Thus the bicycles – like a limited number of other things (jeans, wristwatches etc.) – are items which are much more common in the households of migrants than in other households. In the context of those households that count these things among their possessions, one can speak of a particular 'way of life'. This lifestyle belongs to the migrants and their families, something in which they differ from other households.

This way of life is not just a way of life among others in Kollo, but it stands for rare opportunities to articulate social differentiation and group formation. Visiting or returning migrants always bring with them considerable amounts of global consumer goods, some to keep for themselves, others to give to friends or relatives. Many of these things, such as clothes, are understood instantaneously as a sign of migration and are used conspicuously by the migrants.[11] The events when such behaviour is to be observed include, for example, visits to the local markets, where meeting friends and the exchange of news are especially important. Someone returning from migration or the arrival of a brother is important information on these occasions. New clothes, sunglasses or bicycles conspicuously displayed serve as a kind of proof emphasising such reports.

Other consumer goods are of more everyday use. Enamel bowls, tin buckets, stainless steel dishes and plastic mats count among them. All these things are to be seen in the context of appropriation and belong to the things which are regularly used in the household, the kitchen, at meal-times and in welcoming guests. They show the great importance of the goods that have brought back, even beyond the

---

[11] For more details on the art of giving of the returning migrant, see Hahn 2004c. Benfoughal (2002) documented a similar context among the Tuareg in southern Algeria, where labour migration is the starting point for the local appropriation of global goods brought back by returning relatives. Benfoughal further differentiates between the goods themselves and the ideas and concepts of their usage, the latter being of even greater importance.

context of conspicuous consumption observable in the market.[12] Of lesser importance to my argument, but indispensable for a vivid image of the role of the migrants is the fact that the number of the useful items mentioned is exceeded by the number of goods which are useless or rapidly lose their usefulness. The households of migrants are bursting with things like plastic bathtubs, broken tape-recorders, nylon bags and unused foam mattresses.

It is part of the logic of appropriation that neither the new leisure goods nor the novelties of everyday use immediately displace local goods. Women I interviewed said they used all types of goods, plastic bowls next to calabashes, ceramic water pots next to buckets, and so on. The interest in new things is thus based on the idea that one can possess these things too, without having to give anything up. It is this coexistence of local and global goods, resulting in the rapid expansion of material possessions, which I was particularly interested in.[13]

Comparing peoples' ways of dealing with local objects and the new things, there are considerable differences. So far I have discussed mainly the contexts of the new: their acquisition is in most cases connected to migration, and their handling is at least partly moulded by conspicuous consumption. I have stressed the difficulties involved in affording these things, which are much more expensive than the local goods. But what about local goods themselves?

The acquisition of local goods is much less difficult, since all the necessary raw materials are found in the region, and only very few financial means are necessary. In almost all compounds in the village there are artisans who can manufacture these things themselves. Men

---

[12] This term refers to Thorstein Veblen's (1899) classical work. More recent studies have shown very well the limits of this approach, particularly when reintegration into a social structure and hedonism collide (Walsh 2003).

[13] According to literature from European anthropology, the increase in material possessions is only one kind of the dynamics of material possessions (Bringéus 1986).

produce calabashes, women collect fibres for brushes and mats, and they also know how to make them. The availability of the materials and the many people who can be considered potential producers are aspects of their effortless availability. Normally all these things can be obtained within the family or through the help of one's neighbours. Thus, for example, straw mats are usually made and given away by old women who have been asked to do so by neighbours without receiving a great deal of material compensation for their effort. The same applies to men who are known to be skilled calabash carvers, who are often invited to split the calabashes for their neighbours, and to clean and prepare them for use. These practices of neighbourly help are based on quite definite rules in the local society. Whoever needs any item from the group of locally made things will not experience any problem in receiving help in manufacturing the object. This is a clear contrast to things brought back by migrants, because nobody can know when an absent member of the household will come back, nor what kind of objects he will bring.

But the differences may be interpreted a step further, when we ask about the perspective of the mat weaver on local and global goods. I know some women who have in their households dozens of ready woven but not yet used mats, as well as bundles of raw materials waiting to be transformed into straw mats. Although these women have hardly any plastic mats, there is no reason to exclude them from the attitude reported earlier towards the increase in material possessions: 'We want all things!' A feeling of ambivalence becomes apparent in these remarks by this woman. She cannot simply give up manufacturing mats because people will continue to ask her forthem, but her desire for plastic mats will never be fulfilled in this way. The local goods are there, they are still there, but, speaking metaphorically, they have moved aside, and are no longer any good for fulfilling people's desires.

With the new things, the social order is called into question. Money and, in the sphere of the subsistence economy, the crops in the fields are usually under the control of the elders or the household head.[14] Contrary to this rule, the migrants decide themselves whether to keep the objects they have brought or whether and to whom they give some of them. But it is not only a question of distribution and participation: even more important is the fact that these objects stand for a new world for which the returning migrants are the collectively recognized experts. With this articulation of superiority, which also suggests that those left behind do not even know the right way of handling these new things, the migrants create a distance.[15] Surely this may be interpreted by others as a provocative gesture.

The sphere of local objects, for which neighbourhood and mutual help are sufficient, is separated from the sphere of global goods by limitations of access and knowledge. This separation is sometimes formulated as criticism of the new things: what happens if the plastic mat becomes tattered after a year and the son or the brother doesn't return from labour migration and doesn't bring a replacement? It is better to carry on having some straw mats in store in order to be able to resort to them. This context makes local goods appear in a new light. They are no longer everyday things but have been relegated to being mere substitutes in case the desired new things suddenly become inaccessible. It would be wrong to claim that these things have turned into strange things. In order to stress the shifting of contexts, it would be more appropriate to suggest that these objects are now somehow no longer as close to the everyday routine as they

---

[14] A similar process has been documented from a migrant context in Senegal by Michael Lambert (1999).

[15] The unrestrained admiration for plastics and the other typical materials of mass-produced consumer goods is the object of El Maleh's (1997) provocative account of migrants' perspectives on the country of his origin.

were before. Local goods are not valueless or about to be discarded, but their context has become different.[16]

Another example points out even more clearly the shift of contexts. As harvest time comes closer in Kollo, the farmers usually have an idea whether it is going to be a good harvest and whether it should be kept in temporary granaries close to the fields or in the large mud granaries in the compound. One of the proverbial courses of action is the request of a man who, in anticipation of a good harvest, asks his wives to make a large number of baskets. But as I observed several times, the women comply with the request only reluctantly because, after weaving the baskets, the hard work of transporting them when heavy then awaits them. Instead, they expect the man to rent a bicycle or a donkey to transport the crops. However, this is not easy since at harvest time all households need their means of transport for themselves. Incidentally, there are such baskets in most households. During my interviews on objects and meanings, the women did not hesitate to quote the proverb and associate the baskets metaphorically with a good harvest. But the obligation to transport the harvest in locally made baskets is nowadays rarely and only grudgingly performed. The local things are still there, but they are no longer the same.[17]

Yet another change of contexts must be mentioned. In comparison the migrants (and their families) possess fewer things than the inhabitants of other households in which, for instance, older people

---

[16] In their study of the material culture of a village in Hungary, Edith Fél and Tamas Hofer (1974) distinguish between the things in the 'first line' and other things, kept in reserve, for the case of an eventual use. This distinction is close to what I mean here: local goods move from the first line to the second, without, however, being disapproved as a result.

[17] In northern Côte d'Ivoire, Mona Etienne (1980) reports the same change concerning the locally woven cloth: clothing made from it stillexists, but its use is now restricted. In everyday contexts, other kinds of clothing are preferred. Etienne (ibid.: 230) calls this 'alienation and the reversal of relationship'. As women's participation is no longer necessary, their interest in this aspect of material culture is no longer important either.

live. Surveys of households showed that the number of material possessions and the rate of acquisition of global goods are closely connected to age and livelihood strategies. Young people, including migrants, have few things but a larger proportion of global goods; older people and those who depend on their cultivating and their animals have more things in total, but a smaller proportion of global goods. Naturally older men and women often live in such households; they are unable to participate in labour migration because of their age.

The correlation of age and increasing material possessions is universal, as cultural psychology confirms (Dittmar 1991). It would not be worth mentioning at this point if it did not have consequences for how personal property is valued. As an example, I refer to the situation of the two individuals with the largest personal property in my case study. Both of them are widows, one living alone, the other with a child. Although their personal properties are the largest in quantity, they belong to the people with the lowest incomes in the village.[18] While one of them tries to generate a small income by selling firewood in the market in the little town nearby, the other has to rely on food donations form her neighbours. How do these women perceive their own property? At any rate they do not see it as 'wealth'. They know that all these things do not help them cope as widows with the shortcomings of their everydaylives. It is not that they would like to get rid of the things or that they would like to exchange them for a smaller number of global goods. Many objects in their households, though mal-functioning or simply unused, are highly valued and kept for the sake of memories. The silent but painstaking storing of objects is the widows' way of 'dealing with things'.[19]

---

[18] Complete documentation and a statistical analysis of the households can be found in Hahn 2002.

[19] Perrot (1979b) makes the point that speaking about objects always involves interpreting their significance. In order to understand the role of material possession,

The ambivalence between respect for local objects and frustration at the impossibility of acquiring global goods explains the significance of cultural alienation in the context of my case study. Alienation here means not simply dissociation, detachment or getting rid of something. Alienation leaves a space for an irrevocable entanglement with the object of alienation. Even though the value may be contested and usage decreasing, the objects will remain in a relationship with the person on the level of meaning and handling.[20] In this respect, I see alienation as part of a syncretistic process because it relates to a new perspective which evolves due to the presence of the new, i.e. global goods. Alienation is certainly about distance, about the feeling that local things are inappropriate or even unpractical. Ger and Belk (1996: 283) refer to a very similar process when they describe 'the loss of confidence and pride in local goods and material culture' in the context of the appearance of new goods.

A third example may explain even better the fact that although alienation certainly implies ambivalence, it goes beyond this in creating a new structure for the assignment of meanings to the object in question. One day in Kollo, I met a young man in the neighbourhood who had been back for several weeks from a long stay in Ghana. He was making a *nayIra tampOgO*, a shepherd's bag, out of grass fibres. Normally he would have been too old for such a thing, for these bags are normally used by 10-15 year-old boys, who, as young cowherds, keep their provisions in them when they are out and about with the cattle all day. In response to my question, he ex-

---

Perrot urges us to observe the silent moments involved in dealing with things. This is particularly important in the context of alienation, as this process is seldom made the focus of attention.

[20] Barber and Watermann (1995: 258ff.) describe how, in the creation of a new musical style containing many elements related to the global, something like a consciousness of Yoruba identity emerges at the same time. In the moment of integration into the global world order, local elements are identified as 'Yoruba style'. See also Morgan for the creation of 'being Aborigine' as a new context for urban Aborigines in Australia.

plained that, after his long stay in migration, this activity reminded him of former times, when he had not yet known the douth, the cities in Ghana. Needless to say, he will have no use for the bag, which for him represents just the memory and the articulation of an emotional bond.[21] Both these are aspects found in the concept of cultural alienation.

The presence of the cowherds' bag or the old things in the widows' homes and their valuation on a level that has almost nothing to do with practical usages must be regarded as part of the process of alienation. I know some Kasena living in Ouagadougou, the capital of Burkina Faso, who, upon returning to Kollo on holiday, sometimes take back with them one or several objects of everyday use, even if they have no use for them. This particular kind of reappropriation is at the same time an expression of alienation, because these things express the ambivalence of an indissoluble bond and an insurmountable distance.[22]

Appropriation and Alienation: A Dialectic Process

In the context of the appearance of the new, i.e. of the global goods, appropriation and alienation are relevant processes. As the migrants and their families boost the consumer goods brought back from migration, people develop a feeling of the limited use of locally made things. In a certain sense, alienation is a dialectical counter-

---

[21] In an account on the history of material culture studies in European anthropology, Gottfried Korff (2000: 31) questions whether the emotional perspective on things has not been neglected from the social scientists' point of view. What if the local concepts of 'subjective meanings of goods', of the 'holiness of things' and of 'the soul of the objects' had been taken seriously? Is the scientific reduction of man's possessions into the logic of signs and symbols the right way to deal with the material world? Cf. Ritzer 1998.

[22] Cultural alienation never happens in the context of objects with particularly high symbolic meanings. The regalia of lineages, the equipment of fortune-tellers and the altars of the ancestors are not used in everyday life, therefore they are not part of the ambivalent coexistence which causes dissociation.

process to appropriation. In many cases, the popular praise of appropriation as a creative and vital cultural process neglects the fact that the one would not be possible without the other. Whenever we observe appropriation, we should be very sensitive to any alienation that might be involved too. Or, from the perspective ofthose whose personal property is being subjected to a fundamental change, the experience of a special kind of distance from local things is a precondition for appropriating global goods. Alienation here means the ambivalence that arises from the shifting contexts of the local goods.

This is the first result of my observations. It also sheds fresh light on Daniel Miller's case studies, mentioned above. Miller has certainly correctly identified the ways in which syncretistic objects attain more importance than all the others for one's identity. Transferred to my African example, this could go equally well for the bicycle. However, a question mark might be added to Miller's interpretations. Without knowing the contexts in Trinidad, on the basis of my own case study, I suggest that part of this process is the alienation of certain local things that occurs simultaneously with the gaining of new meanings.

In conclusion, another aspect merits being revealed. Appropriation does not necessarily lead to a loss of social coherence in the local society. I have mentioned that consumer goods brought back by migrants are frequently presented as gifts to members of the family. Thus, giving such objects away is central for the social integration of the objects themselves, as well as for the returning migrant. To a limited extent, the giving away follows the patterns of mutual help in the manufacture of local things. Thus we can suggest that the fact of giving them away and the option to integrate them is more important than what kind or origin they have.[23]

---

[23] Gertrude Stotz (2001), who discusses how cars are treated by Aborigines in Australia, therefore suggests we speak of the 'socialization of global goods' instead of using the term 'appropriation'.

Bibliography

Adorno, Theodor W. (1955): *Ästhetische Theorie*, Frankfurt a.M.: Suhrkamp.

Barber, Karin; Waterman, C.A. (1995): Traversing the Global and the Local: Fuji Music and Praise Poetry in the Production of Contemporary Yoruba Popular Culture, in: Miller, D. (ed.): *Worlds Apart: Modernity through the Prism of the Local*, London: Routledge, 240-62.

Benfoughal, Tatiana (2002): Ces objets qui viennent d'ailleurs, in: Claudot-Hawad, H. (ed.): *Voyager d'un point de vue nomade*, Paris: Editions Paris-Méditerranée, 113-35.

Bringéus, Nils-Arvid (1983): Bedürfniswandel und Sachkultur, in: Köstlin, K. (ed.): *Umgang mit Sachen: zur Kulturgeschichte des Dinggebrauchs* (23. Deutscher Volkskunde-Kongress), Regensburg: Lehrstuhl für Volkskunde, 135-48.

Carrier, James G. (1994): Alienating Objects: The Emergence of Alienation in Retail, *Man*, 29, 2: 359-80.

Dittmar, Helga (1991): Meanings of Material Possessions as Reflections of Identity: Gender and Socio-material Position in Society, *Journal of Social Behavior and Personality*, 6: 165-86.

El Maleh, Edmond (1997): Itinéraire: critique de la critique, *Horizons Maghrébins*, (33/34): 10-15.

Etienne, Mona (1980): Women and Men, Cloth and Colonization. The Transformation of Production-Distribution Relations among the Baule (Ivory Coast), in: Etienne, M. and Leacock, E. (eds.): *Women and Colonization: Anthropological Perspectives*, New York: J.F. Bergin, 214-37.

Fél, Edit; Hofer, Tamás (1974): *Geräte der Atanyer Bauern*, Budapest: Akadémiai Kiado.

Gell, Alfred (1988): Anthropology, Material culture and Consumerism, *Journal of the Anthropological Society of Oxford*, 19: 43-7.

Ger, Güliz; Belk, Russel W. (1996): I'd like to buy the World a Coke: Consumptionscapes of the 'Less Affluent World',*Journal of Consumer Policy*, 19: 271-304.

Hahn, Hans P. (2002): *Die Dinge des Alltags und materielle Kultur in Kollo (Kasena, Burkina Faso)* (unpublished Habilitation thesis), University of Bayreuth.

Hahn, Hans P. (2004a): Global Goods and the Process of Appropriation, in: Probst, P. and Spittler, G. (eds.): *Between Resistance and Expansion: Explorations of Local Vitality in Africa* (Beiträge zur Afrikaforschung, 18) Münster: Lit, 211-30.

Hahn, Hans P. (2004b): Die Aneignung des Fahrrads, in: Beck, K.; Förster, T.; Hahn, H. P. (eds.): *Blick nach vorn: Festgabe für Gerd Spittler zum 65. Geburtstag*, Köln: Köppe, 264-80.

Hahn, Hans P. (2004c): Zirkuläre Arbeitsmigration in Westafrika und die Kultur der Migration, *Afrika Spectrum*, 39, 3: 381-404.

Israel, Joachim (1971): *Alienation, from Marx to Modern Sociology. A Macrosociological Analysis*, Boston: Allyn & Bacon.

Korff, Gottfried (2000): Ein paar Worte zur Dingbedeutsamkeit, *Kieler Blätter zur Volkskunde*, 32: 21-33.

Lambert, Michael C. (1999): Have Jola Women Found a Way to Resist Patriarchy with Commodities? (Senegal, West Africa), *Political and Legal Anthropology Review*, 22: 85-93.

Miller, Daniel (1987): *Material Culture and Mass Consumption*, Oxford: Blackwell.

Miller, Daniel (1992a): Imported Goods as Authentic Culture, in: Eisendle, R. (ed.): *Produktkulturen: Dynamik und Bedeutungswandel des Konsums*, Frankfurt a.M.: Campus, 271-88.

Miller, Daniel (1992b): The Young and the Restless in Trinidad: A Case of the Local and the Global in Mass Consumption, in: Silverstone, R. (ed.): *Consuming Technologies: Media and Information in Domestic Spaces*, London: Routledge, 163-82.

Morgan, George (2003): Autochthonous Australian Syncretism, *Current Sociology*, 51 (3-4): 433-51.

Moser, Walter (1996): Le recyclage culturel, in: Dionne, C.M.S. und W. Moser (Hg.): *Recyclages: Économies de l'appropriation culturelle*, Montréal: Éditions Balzac, 23-53.

N.N. (1974): Alienation, in: Benton, W. (ed.): *Encyclopaedia Britannica*, 15th edn., Chicago: Encyclopaedia Britannica.

Perrot, Dominique (1979a): Réflexion pour une lecture de la domination à partir des objets, in: Perrot, D. (ed.): *Objets chers et funestes: dimensions matérielles de l'impérialisme et de l'aliénation culturels* (= Cahiers de l'Institut universitaire d'études du développement, 10), Paris: Presses Universitaires de France, 13-31.

Perrot, Dominique (1979b): Car le mot déjà est regard, l'objet action: quelques principes méthodologiques en vue de l'étude des objets, in: Perrot, D. (ed.): *Objets chers et funestes: dimensions matérielles de l'impérialisme et de l'aliénation culturels*, (Cahiers de l'Institut universitaire d'études du développement, 10), Paris: Presses Universitaires de France, 41-91.

Plessner, Helmuth (1960): *Das Problem der Öffentlichkeit und die Idee der Entfremdung: Rede anlässlich der Übernahme des Rektorats der Universität am 7. Mai 1960*, Göttingen: Vandenhoeck & Ruprecht.

Popitz, Heinrich (1953): *Der entfremdete Mensch: Zeitkritik und Geschichtsphilosophie des jungen Marx*, Basel: Verlag für Recht und Gesellschaft.

Ritzer, George (1998): Introduction [to the English translation], in: Baudrillard, J. (ed.): *The Consumer Society*, London: Sage, 1-24.

Simmel, Georg (1989): *Philosophie des Geldes*, Frankfurt a.M.: Suhrkamp. (original: 1900, reprint of the 2nd edition Leipzig 1907).

Stewart, Charles (1999): Syncretism and its Synonyms: Reflections on Cultural Mixture, *Diacritics: A Review of Contemporary Criticism*, 29, 3: 40-62.

Stotz, Gertrude (2001): The Colonizing Vehicle, in: Miller, D. (ed.): *Car Cultures*, Oxford: Berg, 223-244.

Verne, Markus (2005): Auf der Suche nach dem 'globalen Gut', in: Loimeier, R.; Neubert, D. and Weißköppel, C. (eds.): *Globalisierung im lokalen Kontext: Perspektiven und Konzepte von Handeln in Afrika*, Münster: Lit, 85-124.

Walsh, Andrew (2003): 'Hot Money' and Daring Consumption in a Northern Malagasy Sapphire-Mining Town, *American Ethnologist*, 30: 290-305.

Conceptual Blending in Language, Cognition, and Culture. Towards a Methodology for the Linguistic Study of Syncretic Concepts

Hans-Jörg Schmid, Dymitr Ibriszimow, Karina Kopatsch and Peter Gottschligg

1. Introduction: Blended Concepts in a Post-Colonial African Context

Many post-colonial nations in Africa are marked by a highly complex linguistic situation, with a variety of Standard English co-existing as a lingua franca of (secondary and) tertiary education, or even as an official language, alongside a number of native African languages. Among the educated urban population in countries like Nigeria or Kenya there is a high proportion of multilingual speakers who are fluent in English and one or more indigenous languages. Switching to and fro between languages as they move through their daily lives, these speakers have to juggle ideas and concepts from totally different historical and cultural contexts. For example, as will be shown with data compiled in Northern Nigeria, the English word cap does not seem to be associated with the same concept as the Hausa word *hula* in the minds of bilingual speakers, although the two words are given as referential equivalents in bilingual dictionaries (e.g. Abraham 1962, Bargery 1993, Newman and Newman 1977). What our findings indicate is that in Nigerian English the word *cap* seems to evoke some sort of conceptual blend between the concept associated with the native English word *cap* ('baseball cap') and the concept associated with Hausa *hula* ('sown ornamental cap worn by men').

The minds of African multilingual speakers thus seem to provide a fertile ground for the emergence of culturally *blended concepts*.

The subjects of this paper, however, are not only blended concepts with inputs from different sources, but what we call *syncretic concepts*. These are defined as the results of conceptual blending[1] in a linguistic and cultural contact situation whose cognitive structures are different from the two (or more) input concepts to such an extent that they can be seen as emergent, qualitatively new concepts in their own right, emancipated from their sources.

2. Method

In this study we focus on blended and syncretic concepts in the variety of English spoken by educated native speakers of Hausa in Northern Nigeria, sometimes referred to as *Hausa English* (Bamgbose 1997). These are compared with corresponding Hausa concepts, on the one hand, and American English concepts, on the other. The rationale behind this twofold comparison is that as an English-as-a-Second-Language variety, Nigerian English is subject to competing influences from native varieties of English and the local Hausa culture.[2] Since we are also interested in the potential influence of modernization and globalization on blended concepts, it is the American variety of English, the major representative and source of 'Global English', that was chosen as a reference point,

---

[1] Readers familiar with the cognitive-linguistic theory of "conceptual blending" (for a recent account see Fauconnier & Turner 2002) will realize that the basic setup of blended concepts is vaguely inspired by the latter approach. However, as blending theory deals with the online construction of meaning, while our concern is the nature of more or less fully entrenched concepts, not constructed on the fly but stored in long-term memory, the similarity remains somewhat superficial. On the other hand, what blending theory may be well able to handle are the early stages, when L2 speakers of English become familiar with a new English form and concept from Western culture, both of them blended with the speakers' own cultural backgrounds.

[2] We are of course aware of the fact that the notion of 'Hausa culture' is a hopeless idealization. We use the term as a shorthand reference to the culture that was elicited in our tests, i.e. the knowledge to a large extent shared by the Hausa-speaking informants.

rather than British English, the historical mother variety of Nigerian English.

We will report on findings from research carried out in Maiduguri/Borno State, Nigeria and St. Barbara/California, USA. 45 Hausa-speaking students from the University of Maiduguri and 47 students at the University of California at St. Barbara participated. The same Nigerian informants were presented with Hausa words and English words at independent sessions separated by several days. Since some of them did not turn up for the English session or felt unable to respond to certain English words, there are only 39 responses to the English stimuli.

The method applied was the so-called "attribute-listing task" used by the psychologist Eleonor Rosch in the 1970s to investigate the conceptual structures of cognitive categories (cf. Rosch 1975, Rosch and Mervis 1975). In this test, informants are confronted with everyday words like *camel, cap* or *bicycle* and asked to list attributes that are shared by all the entities which can be referred to by the words. Typical answers for the stimulus *bicycle*, for example, include attributes like 'has pedals', 'has two wheels', 'is used as a vehicle' and so on. In the analysis of the lists provided by the individual subjects, attributes are cumulated and ranked according to the number of informants who wrote them down. Attributes named by a large proportion of informants like 'has pedals' are considered to be more important aspects of the conceptual structure of a word than idiosyncratic ones (like 'my uncle has one' for *bicycle*), and are taken to be significant for the formation of a 'prototype' of the corresponding cognitive category.[3]

As will be shown, the conceptual structures of individual blended concepts are subject to a large number of factors, including the language of the words encoding them, the nature of the entities they represent, the culture in which they are embedded, and the concep-

[3] For a summary of the so-called 'prototype theory' of categorization and its methodology see Ungerer and Schmid (2006: Chs. 1 and 2).

tual domain to which they belong. The fact that blended concepts are determined by a complex network of interrelated parameters raises a number of serious methodological issues that will be discussed in this paper:

- Is it possible to distinguish 'real' syncretic concepts, i.e. emergent and new ones, from less spectacular cultural adaptations and contextualizations?
- Is it possible to determine the specific source of syncretization for individual concepts?
- Where are the methodological limits of the study of syncretic concepts?

Our aim is thus twofold: we want to show that there are degrees of conceptual 'blendedness' and we want to reflect on the potential and limitations of methods of investigating conceptual blending and syncretic concepts. Before we tackle these more theoretical issues, we will look into a selection of our findings from the attribute-listing tasks.

3. An Illustrative Selection of the Findings: *airplane*, *wheelchair* and *cap*

In this section we will discuss a number of salient aspects of the attribute-lists collected for three concepts lexicalized as E. *airplane*/H. *jirgin sama*, E. *wheelchair*/H. *keken guragu* and E. *cap*/H. *hula*. These case studies will help to illustrate the range of factors influencing the degrees of conceptually blended concepts to be found in Nigerian English. The lists providing the attributes named by the three groups of informants and the number of informants who named them are attached in the appendix to this paper.[4]

---

[4] For the readers' convenience, the majority of whom is probably not conversant with Hausa, the Hausa attributes are presented only in an English translation in this paper. It should be kept in mind that the English translations are quite imperfect in mirroring the concepts behind the Hausa attributes.

3.1 *Airplane*

Table 1 in the appendix gives the findings for the Hausa lexeme *jirgin sama* and the Nigerian English and American English lexeme *airplane.* As the table shows, there is a large number of attributes that are named by the informants of all three groups, among them 'fly/flying', 'engine', 'passengers' and others. Perhaps the most striking feature of the Hausa list is that no equivalent to the English attribute 'pilot' is given. On the other hand, the attribute 'sky', which seems to be motivated by the literal meaning of the Hausa lexeme (*jirgin sama* 'sky vehicle') and is named by 40% of the Hausa informants in response to the Hausa word, is not included in the reactions to the English lexeme airplane (from the same informants!).

By and large, the Nigerian English concept seems to be closely related to the American English concept, but information about the usual procedure on board is missing ('bad food', 'movie' etc., and also 'stewardess', 'flight attendant').

3.2 *Wheelchair*

The results for *wheelchair* (see Appendix, Table 2) pattern in an altogether different way. The attributes given by the informants indicate that the Nigerian English concept is more similar to the Hausa one than to the American English one. What the attribute lists seem to reflect is the noticeable difference between the objects in Nigerian and Western culture: while in the West, wheelchairs have engines or rings attached to the wheels that allow riders to move forward, Nigerian wheelchairs are equipped with a chain and pedal-like handles which riders use for self-propelled motion.

In contrast to *airplane*, we also notice an influence of the Hausa word *keken guragu* (literally 'bicycle for cripples') in the attributes given for the English word *wheelchair.* For the attributes given in response to the Nigerian English lexeme include literal translations of the Hausa lexeme.

3.3 *Cap*

The attributes for Nigerian English *cap* (see Appendix, Table 3) again reveal indisputable similarities with the Hausa concept. Coinciding attributes include 'round(ed)', 'hand made', 'worn by men', 'sown', 'made of wool/cotton'. What is not included in the Nigerian English list but plays an important role in the responses for Hausa *hula* is the ornamental function. This is an attribute related to the everyday interaction with the referents, reflecting attitudinal and emotional associations with them. It is a significant finding also for other words like *shoe* or *window* that these interactional and attitudinal attributes are not named by the same informants in response to the English word, but only given in response to the Hausa word.

Comparing the list of attributes given by the American informants with the one produced by the Nigerians in response to the English stimulus, we see that the American English concept is markedly different from the Nigerian English concept. What the Americans seem to have in mind is undoubtedly the picture of a baseball cap, while the Nigerian English speakers visualize the local *hula*-type of headgear. In contrast to *wheelchair*, there is no noticeable impact of the Hausa form on the Nigerian English concept.

Taken together these selected findings give a glimpse of the multifaceted and multivariate situation with regard to the nature of blended concepts. In order to interpret the whole set of findings it is essential to develop a theory of blended concepts and a set of parameters that allow us to determine the degree of blending involved in individual concepts. The starting point in this endeavour is an extended version of Ogden and Richard's (1923) well-known semiotic triangle serving as an idealized version of 'pure concepts'.

4. Theoretical Aspects: Blended Concepts

4.1 Pure concepts

Extending the semiotic triangle introduced by Ogden and Richards (1923), we assume that concepts must be considered on the four dimensions represented in Figure 1:

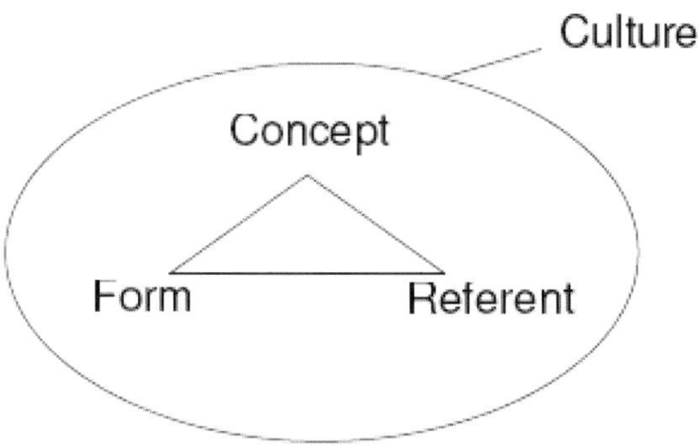

Figure 1:

Representation of „pure concept"(adapted from Ogden and Richards 1923)

The *concept*, in a narrow sense, in people's minds creates an association between a linguistic *form* and an extra-linguistic *referent* or set of referents in the world. In Ogden and Richard's terms, the *word* "symbolizes" the *thought* which "refers to" the thing. Though there is a line at the bottom of the triangle it should be clear that there is no direct link from form to referent, but only an association mediated by the concept. In addition to the components of the original semiotic triangle Figure 1 represents the idea that concepts are inevitably embedded in cultures. In order to distinguish concepts from words, on the one hand, which are traditionally marked by italics, and referents, on the other hand, we will mark them by small capitals. Thus the word *cap* encodes the concept CAP which stands for real caps in the extra-linguistic world.

The defining characteristic of *pure concepts* is that all three components of the triangle – form, concept and referent – 'belong' to one language and one culture, in the sense that they are historically and psychologically rooted and entrenched in them. It must be emphasized, however, that the notion of *pure concept* is an idealized theoretical construct, potential manifestations of which will always be open to historical, linguistic, psychological, ethnological and anthropological controversy. The main function of the notion of pure concept is to serve as a backdrop for the following explanation of the basic setup of blended concepts.

4.2 Blended concepts: The basic setup

Risking a smack of triviality, one can say that blended concepts are the results of the mixture of two pure concepts from two cultures, typically in one of these cultures. This basic setup is represented in Figure 2.

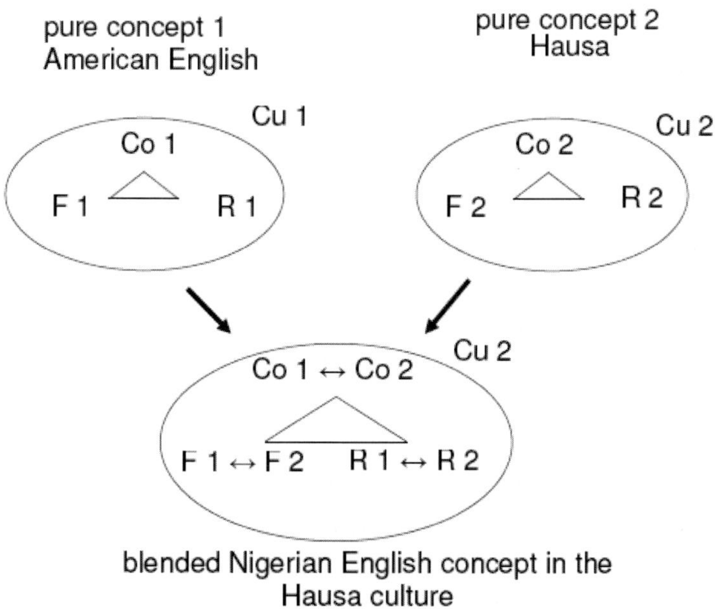

Figure 2: Basic setup of blended concepts (Co = concept, F = form, R = referent, Cu = culture; ↔ = variable degree of influence)

The double-pointed arrows in the blended concept indicate that the three components of the concept can be influenced to different degrees by each of the two pure concepts. Applied to the present data this means that Nigerian English concepts can be like American English concepts, on the one hand, like Hausa concepts, on the other hand, but they can also incorporate input from either of these sources to a greater or lesser degree. The internal complexity of blended concepts is further compounded by the fact that the three components of the blended concepts do not have to be related to the same source. For example, the Nigerian English word *wheelchair* takes its form from English. As we have seen, however, the concept associated with the word by Nigerian speakers is more similar to the corresponding Hausa concept KEKEN GURAGU, and the typical Nigerian referent is also distinctly different from the typical Western specimen of a wheelchair. These considerations show that there is an enormous range of variants of blended concepts depending on which aspects of the concepts are affected by blending and on the sources of the input into the components of the blended concept. As already hinted at, there are a large number of potential factors determining the particular composition of a blended concept. In the next section we will isolate the most important factors in order to create an analytical tool for the study of blended concepts.

5. Parameters Determining the Degree of Conceptual Blending

The parameters determining the degree of conceptual blending will be presented in three groups each of which relates to one component of the semiotic triangle: referent-related parameters, concept-related parameters and form-related parameters.

5.1 Referent-related parameters

a) Degree of difference between the classes of referents in Hausa and Western culture

This parameter captures the similarity of the typical referents of a word in the Hausa culture as compared to Western/American referents. For example, while American baseball caps are considerably different from Nigerian referents of Hausa *hula*, there is no noticeable difference for the referents of the word *airplane* in the two cultures.

b) Degree of appropriation of referents in Hausa culture

This parameter applies especially to items introduced into Nigeria from the West. The question is to what extent the referents have become part of everyday Hausa culture. What is the frequency and intensity of people's interaction with the referents? Airplanes, for example, exhibit a low degree of appropriation by Nigerians because only a small minority of them has the opportunity to fly. This of course explains the rather detached view of airplanes from the outside reflected in the attributes lists collected from the Nigerian informants. Cars and busses, on the other hand, have become an integral part of Hausa culture since many people use them and interact with them in a variety of ways (e.g. as drivers, passengers, mechanics, dealers, owners, pedestrians etc.).

c) Degree of cultural adaptation of referents to Hausa culture

This parameter tends to correlate with the previous one, because adaptation tends to be the result of intense appropriation: Nigerian trucks are more adapted to the Nigerian context than Nigerian airplanes. As a result, it would be difficult to tell apart a Nigerian jet from an American one, but easy to recognize a Nigerian truck. The degree of adaptation is also related to parameter a), because objects that have been highly adapted to Hausa culture are more different from corresponding American objects than objects taken without any cultural adaptation.

5.2 Concept-related parameters

While the set of parameters explained in the previous section concern the appearance and characteristics of things, the ones to be discussed now are located in people's minds.

d) For Nigerian English: Degree of conceptual adaptation of English concepts to corresponding Hausa concepts, as compared to concepts in American English

This parameter is the conceptual counterpart of parameter c). It captures the degree of *contextualization*, *Africanization* (cf. Wolf 2003) or *nativization* (Bamgbose 1997: 11) of concepts encoded by English words to the local culture. As has been shown, the Nigerian English concept WHEELCHAIR, for example, is more similar to the corresponding Hausa concept than to the American English one. The English concept thus seems to be adapted to the local culture.

e) For Nigerian English: Degree of conceptual emancipation of Nigerian English concepts from American English concepts

This parameter captures the extent to which a concept in Nigerian English differs from the concept in American English encoded by the same word. Although there is often a correlation to parameter d) – concepts highly adapted to Hausa culture tend to be more emancipated from English culture – the two cannot be subsumed on one dimension, because it is possible for Nigerian English concepts to be both emancipated from American English and not adapted to Hausa culture. Blended concepts of this type are particularly good candidates for the status of syncretic concepts, because they are qualitatively different from their conceptual and cultural input. The concept WINDOW emerges as an example of this type from our study; the conceptualization of the English word by our Nigerian informants differs significantly from both their conceptualization of the corresponding Hausa concept TAGA and that of the American English informants.

f) For Hausa: Degree of conceptual adaptation of Hausa concepts to English concepts

This is the counterpart to parameter e) from the Hausa perspective. The question is whether a particular Hausa concept has undergone a conceptual adaptation to an English concept. Processes of this type may be the result of a cultural *alienation* caused by the English language and the Western culture and world-view transported by it all over the globe. This is a particularly intriguing question in view of the heated debate on how the presence and use of English affects post-colonial societies; strong catchwords in this controversy are *linguistic imperialism*, *linguistic genocide*, English as a *killer language* (see Mühlhäusler 1996, Skutnabb-Kangas 2000). Unfortunately it is impossible to focus on this issue here because of a methodological problem: there is no external reference-system for Hausa comparable to American English as a 'global' reference-system to which Nigerian English can be related. Hausa speakers entirely unaffected by English, which would be candidates for supplying such a reference-system, can only be found in remote rural areas, where attribute-listing tasks cannot be applied due to the illiteracy of most informants.

5.3 Form-related parameters

g) Effects of forms on concepts

This parameter captures what is traditionally known as linguistic *interference*. The concept WHEELCHAIR provides an interesting example: as already discussed, the Nigerian informants named attributes like 'handicap bicycle', 'bicycle' and 'has a chain', which are hardly comprehensible from a Western perspective. The most likely source of these attributes lies in the Hausa word for wheelchairs, *keken guragu* and 'bicycle for cripples/handicapped people'.

The attributes given by the informants for English *wheelchair* indicate that the form of the Hausa word leaves its mark on the corresponding concept in Nigerian English.

h) Origin of the form: English or Hausa?

All Nigerian English words investigated are originally English. Words borrowed from Hausa such as *tuwo* ('staple food'), *gari* ('fried cassava flour') or *gyara* ('"makeweight" given by seller', cf. Wolf and Igboanusi 2003: 74ff.) were not taken into consideration, because they have no American English equivalents. Many Hausa words, especially in domains dominated by modernization such as vehicles or computing, are loanwords from English (e.g. Hausa *jif* 'jeep' and *tasi* 'taxi').

i) Existence of a form in English and Hausa

Not all of the Nigerian English words investigated have equivalents in Hausa. For example, there is no need for Hausa words corresponding to English *cheese* or *pizza*, for the simple reason that the referents can hardly be found in Nigeria and consequently speakers have little opportunity to refer to them.

Having established parameters that can guide the assessment of individual concepts, we will now present some further case studies demonstrating the highly complex interplay between the parameters and then move on to the methodological issues mentioned above.

6. Case Studies

The following seven case studies of Nigerian English words are arranged in three groups according to parameter (a), 'difference of referents', and analyzed according to the concept-related and form-related parameters listed in 4.2 and 4.3. First two examples will be presented where Nigerian and Western referents are more or less identical, then three cases with similar referents and then two words with distinctly dissimilar referents. Throughout the focus lies on the conceptual structure of the concepts, since they were the target of the attribute-listing experiments described above.

6.1 Same referents

6.1.1 *Camel*

Referent-related parameters: We assume that camels are perceived, at least by the general public, as being more or less identical in their outer appearance in Nigeria and the USA.

Concept-related parameters: The assessment of the concept-related parameters is based on the findings from the attribute-listing experiments presented in Table 4 in the appendix. The attribute-lists from the three groups of informants yield a closer similarity between Nigerian English and Hausa than between the former and American English. The American informants are preoccupied with stereotypical knowledge about camels such as 'humps', 'desert' and 'spits', some of which are also given by some of the Nigerian informants. The lists for Nigerian English and Hausa, on the other hand, include important shared attributes with similar scores: 'tall', 'long neck', 'long legs', 'carries goods' and 'meat'. These attributes reflect a richer cognitive model of camels derived from a more intense interaction with these animals.

The findings for the concept CAMEL thus suggest that we are dealing with a case of contextualization here. An English word for referents of local origin and relevance has been conceptually adapted to the local context and shows clear signs of similarity with the concept underlying the referentially equivalent Hausa word *raƙumi*.

6.1.2 *Airplane*

Referent-related parameters: Airplanes are of Western origin and, as already mentioned above, especially long-distance jets exhibit a low degree of appropriation and adaptation. There is no perceivable difference to Western referents.

Concept-related parameters: As already explained in Section 2.1, the Nigerian English concept AIRPLANE shares attributes with both

Hausa and American English (cf. Table 1 in the appendix): 'flying', 'transport', 'passengers' and others are obvious examples. What distinguishes the Nigerian English concept from the American one is that the American informants display more inside knowledge about the props and events during the flight. They clearly activate some sort of plane-flying script including aspects like 'stewardess', 'flight attendants', 'movies', 'bad food' and 'peanuts'. Not surprisingly, the Nigerian informants, on the other hand, take an outside view and focus on the parts of airplanes ('engine', 'tyres', 'wings' and 'propeller') in response to both the English and the Hausa stimulus. The attribute 'pilot' is given for the English stimulus, but not for the Hausa word.

Form-related parameters: Interestingly, an effect of the literal meaning of the Hausa word *jirgin sama* ('sky vehicle') is only noticeable in the Hausa list ('travels in the sky'), but not in the Nigerian English one. Thus there is no indication of linguistic interference of the Hausa form on the Nigerian English concept. On the other hand, the list for the Nigerian English stimulus includes references to 'air'. The first element of the compound, *air*, seems to be responsible for this.

The evidence suggests that the concept AIRPLANE has mustered more resistance against adaptation to the local culture than the concept CAMEL. This is probably due to the low degree of appropriation, which is reflected in the removed view of planes emerging from the attribute lists. An effect of the linguistic form is only noticeable in the attribute 'air' given for the Nigerian English word. The fact that there is no interference from Hausa is particularly noteworthy, as such interference has been found for the concept WHEELCHAIR to be discussed below (see 5.3.2).

6.2. Similar referents: banana, shoe, window

6.2.1 *Banana*

Referent-related parameters: Although they are a natural product, bananas come along in different colours and sizes and with different tastes in Nigeria and the USA. The referents are thus similar, but less identical than e.g. camels or airplanes.

Concept-related parameters: Viewed in their entirety, the three lists in Table 5 in the appendix are surprisingly dissimilar. As before, there are of course attributes included in all three lists, but there is little convergence with regard to their frequency scores. The Nigerian English list shows clear signs of cultural adaptation in several attributes referring to the growing of bananas: 'leaves', 'roots', 'tree', 'plant' and 'stem'. The same attributes can be found in the Hausa list, but except for 'tree', they are absent from the American one. This does not mean, however, that the Nigerian English concept is identical to the Hausa one, because the attitudinal attributes 'delicacy/desired' and 'pleasant/nice' given for the Hausa concept AYABA are missing in the Nigerian English list.

What these findings indicate is that the Nigerian English concept banana seems to be sufficiently different from the American English concept to be regarded as highly adapted and thus emancipated. All the aspects related to banana plants (rather than the fruits themselves) only play a role for the Nigerian informants, but not for the American ones. The fact that the attitudinal attributes given for the Hausa concept are missing is open to several interpretations: it could be a sign of an ongoing, uncompleted adaptation process or of the emergence of a syncretic concept, blending conceptual material from the two sources in a qualitatively new way.

6.2.2 *Shoe*

Referent-related parameters: Like bananas, shoes are essentially similar but not identical in the two cultures.

Concept-related parameters: Attributes shared by the Nigerian English and the American English concept are 'foot wear' and 'protect feet' (see Table 6). Apart from these two attributes, there is little overlap between the two English lists. The Nigerian English list shares with the Hausa list the attributes referring to 'legs' or 'feet' respectively, to the materials 'leather, skin, hide' and 'rubber' and to 'protection'. It is worth mentioning that the Nigerian English list does not contain references to 'thorn' as potential dangers for the feet; the ornamental function of shoes is also not given by the Nigerian informants in response to the English stimulus.

As was the case for BANANA, there is considerable evidence for an adaptation and contextualization of the English concept SHOE. And again, the Nigerian English concept lacks attributes given for the Hausa word *takalmi*, which are so to speak 'closer' to people's everyday lives and experiences, namely the reference to 'ornaments' and to 'thorns'. The Nigerian English attribute list seems to reflect an emotionally more detached view of the same referents than the Hausa list.

6.2.3 *Window*

Referent-related parameters: At least as far as their perceptual properties are concerned, Nigerian windows differ considerably from typical windows in the West in that they tend to be covered.

Concept-related parameters: The perceptual difference is clearly reflected in the attribute lists in Table 7. While American informants focus on attributes related to light and brightness ('light', 'clear', 'see through/look out', '(good) view', 'sunshine'), Nigerian informants stress the ventilation function of windows both in the Nigerian English and the Hausa lists, but also mention the fact that windows tend to be covered. Interestingly, the attribute 'brightening room / brightness' is named only for the Hausa word *taga*. Other associations unique to the Hausa responses are 'lock', 'nail(s)' and 'key'. These are again reflections of the interaction with local specimens of the category which do not seem to be triggered by the English word.

6.3 Dissimilar referents: cap and wheelchair

6.3.1 *Cap*

Referent-related parameters: The objects referred to by the word *cap* in Nigerian English and American English differ markedly. In the Nigerian context, a cap is a colourful round ornamental item of headgear, usually hand-sown or woven and worn exclusively by men. For Americans, the typical cap is of course a baseball cap.

Concept-related parameters: Looking at Table 3, there can be no doubt that the Nigerian informants call up the image of a Nigerian type of cap when they respond to the attribute listing task, no matter whether the stimulus is English *cap* or Hausa *hula*. This shows in the attributes 'round', 'hand made', 'worn (mostly) by men', 'sown', 'made of wool/cotton' and '(many) colours'. However, as before, the adaptation of the English concept to the local culture seems to stop when it comes to attitudinal and interactional attributes: there are no correspondences of the Hausa attributes 'ornamental', 'thread', 'yard' and 'woven'. The attributes given by the American informants, on the other hand, do not only make it clear that they have baseball caps in mind, but they also reflect the polysemy of the lexeme *cap* in attributes like 'bottle', 'lid' and 'closes something'.

6.3.2 Wheelchair

Referent-related parameters: Unlike Western wheelchairs, Nigerian ones typically feature handles that allow the people using them to propel themselves forward by means of a chain transmission, if they are capable of doing that. In the West, wheelchairs are pushed by other people or propelled by electric motors.

Concept-related parameters: The strong association between wheelchairs and handicapped, physically disabled or 'crippled' persons emerges from all three attribute lists in Table 2. An essential part-whole attribute included in all three lists is the reference to 'wheels', but the answers with regard to the number of wheels vary from two to four. What is of particular interest here are attributes which seem to be influenced by the linguistic forms of the compounds *wheelchair* and *keken guragu* (lit. 'bicycle for cripples'). On the one hand, it is remarkable that the attribute 'chair' occurs only in the Nigerian English list, but not in the Hausa one. On the other hand, the Nigerians also refer to wheelchairs as resembling bicycles. While this could of course simply be due to the perceptual and functional similarity between Nigerian wheelchairs and bicycles, it is striking that the Nigerian English list includes verbatim translations of the Hausa word as 'handicap bicycle' or 'bicycle for crippled'. The combination of these two findings calls for an explanation in terms of linguistic interference: it seems that both the English form *chair* in *wheelchair* and the Hausa form *keke* ('bicycle') in *keken guragu* leave their marks on the conceptualizations emerging from the attributes given in response to the Nigerian English word. This is in contrast to the concept AIRPLANE where we found no traces of linguistic interference of the Hausa word on the English concept.

7. Discussion

Taken together, even the small number of cases yields some interesting results, but gives also an insight into the complexity of the investigation of culturally blended concepts. The following tendencies can be observed.

The conceptual setup in Nigerian English of the two concepts with more or less identical referents, CAMEL and AIRPLANE, seems to be related to the cultural relevance of the referents in Hausa culture. Being of greater relevance to the local culture, camels are conceptualized very much alike in Hausa and Nigerian English but clearly differently from the latter two in American English. Due to the lack of appropriation, the Nigerian English conceptualization of airplanes sides more with the American view than with the local Hausa one. The origin of the referents, African for camels and Western for airplanes, seems to play a role here as well.

A finding common to the three concepts with more or less similar referents, BANANA, SHOE and WINDOW, is that there is a marked degree of conceptual adaptation to the African cultural context. Clearly the words *banana, shoe* and *window* do not 'mean' the same to Nigerian and American speakers of English, even though they apparently speak the same language. However, it is not the case that Nigerian speakers simply transfer their Hausa concept to Nigerian English. Important attitudinal associations as well as attributes extracted from everyday interaction with the objects do not emerge in the Nigerian English list, although they are given for the corresponding Hausa terms. The Nigerian English concepts seem to be emotionally more detached and less 'rich' than the Hausa concepts. This may be a reflection of the status of English: for all the speakers who acted as informants, it is a language acquired by institutional education rather than inside the family and a language whose use is reserved for occasions on the formal end of the scale. The question whether the detachment is a reflection of the fact that English has remained a foreign language representing a foreign culture must remain open.

While both Nigerian caps and wheelchairs are markedly different from American caps and wheelchairs, the underlying Nigerian English concepts do not yield similar patterns on the conceptual level. CAP behaves in a way comparable to SHOE or WINDOW, showing distinct evidence of cultural adaptation with missing attitudinal and interactional attributes. The concept WHEELCHAIR, on the other hand, seems to be a true blend of the two cultures, which is influenced by the linguistic form of the words in English and Hausa. The Nigerian attribute list for *wheelchair* reveals both associations with chairs, which are not triggered by the Hausa word, and with bicycles, which are not activated in the minds of American speakers. That Nigerian English WHEELCHAIR shows signs of linguistic interference, while the other compound AIRPLANE does not, may be due to the lower degree of appropriation of airplanes.

None of the Hausa concepts shows signs of an influence from the Nigerian English concepts. Even for AIRPLANE, a technological item associated with modernization and globalization and thus a particularly good candidate for phenomena of this type, an alienating effect of English could not be discerned.

8. Conclusion

The investigation of blended concepts has proved to be a methodological challenge. Three crucial sources of the complexity of the problem can be extracted from this discussion: first, the variable degrees of influence from the two cultures and languages (more or less Hausa influence vs. more or less English influence); second, the lacking correlation between referent-related and concept-related parameters; and third, the unpredictable influence of linguistic forms on concepts, which seems to be subject to referent-related parameters.

With these issues in mind, we can return to the methodological questions raised at the outset of this paper:

a) Is it possible to distinguish 'real', i.e. new and original, syncretic concepts from less spectacular cultural adaptations and contextualizations? We believe that this question must be answered in the negative. While we have found evidence for concepts whose structures display distinct signs of conceptual blending with an input from two cultures, it seems impossible to decide whether something new has emerged. Inevitably there are traces of the input of the source concepts and cultures. What seems to be the case, on the other hand, is that the input does merge in a qualitatively new way in the blended concepts, and it is in this sense that one might say that syncretic concepts have been found after all. The best candidates are the concepts with a distinct mixture of conceptual components from the two sources, which tends to be caused by an extra-linguistic difference between the referents. As far as the possible influence of globalization is concerned, our findings suggest the conclusion that the degree of adaptation of global concepts depends on the degree of appropriation in the local culture. For example, the increasingly global food concept pizza, which we have also investigated but not discussed in details here, does not seem to be entrenched in the minds of Nigerian speakers: only very few informants are able to provide attributes, and those who are stick to very general properties like 'round', 'flat' or 'food'.

b) Is it possible to determine the specific source of blending for individual concepts? Again we are rather sceptical and believe that the evidence is limited. While it is tempting to assume cultural causes for conceptual effects, the link is apparently not that straightforward. As we have seen, purely linguistic factors like the interference of lexical forms are at work as well. Unless there is fairly clear evidence in the attributes given by the informants – as was the case for wheelchair – it is difficult to distinguish between conceptual blending triggered by linguistic interference and conceptual blending caused by cultural adaptation.

c) Where are the methodological limits of the study of syncretic concepts? As we have seen, the complexity of the task at hand arises from the interplay between linguistic forms, extra-linguistic referents, mental concepts and tacit cultural knowledge. As linguists, we have more or less sufficient information on linguistic forms and their history. By means of attribute-listing tasks, we have tried to collect intersubjectively valid information about concepts. For information about material culture we must rely on our own unsystematic observations, information given by members of the culture and on results of anthropological investigations. The latter, however, tend to be influenced by the perception and linguistic proficiency of the field worker, and we have seen how much the Nigerian English concepts of everyday items can differ from the corresponding Western ones. The material collected on the conceptualizations of everyday goods may thus in fact be helpful for anthropological research.

What we hold to be crucial from a methodological point of view is that blended concepts can only be investigated with a comparative approach. It is not reasonable to speculate on the blended or syncretic nature of a concept unless one is able to collect systematic and reliable information on the potential linguistic, conceptual and cultural input systems. Blended concepts should never be blended concepts as such, but must inevitably be blended concepts in relation to input systems. In fact, other approaches to the study of syncretism, e.g. in the fields of art, religion or material culture, must be put under the same constraint. It would be rather naïve to assume that the situation is less complex here, because researchers in these areas do not have to bother with linguistic forms and concepts. After all, knowledge about culture is inevitably conceptual knowledge. In addition, the methods in these academic fields largely rely on the use of language as a medium of communication and we have seen that even for the most basic and common everyday words a correspondence between Nigerian English concepts and American English or Global English concepts can by no means be taken for granted. We hope, therefore, that the material we have collected on the conceptualizations of everyday goods may in fact be helpful for anthropological, ethnological and sociological investigations as well.

Finally, we want to emphasize that it seems impossible to give well-founded judgments on individual blended concepts. The degree of blending discernible in one concept will always have to be determined in comparison with other blended concepts with linguistic, conceptual or cultural similarities.

Table 1: Attribute lists for Hausa *jirgin sama* and Nigerian and American English *airplane*

Hausa	**n = 45**		**Nigerian English**	**n = 39**		**American English**	**n = 47**	
jirgin sama	**freq.**	**weight**	***airplane***	**freq.**	**weight**	***airplane***	**freq.**	**weight**
transport (commercial) / used for transport	19	0,42	engine	16	0,37	wing/wings	35	0,74
(travels) in the (open) sky	18	0,40	flying	15	0,35	pilot/pilots	28	0,60
carrying people / passenger / travellers	15	0,33	pilot	12	0,28	fly/flying	23	0,49
engine	12	0,27	transport(ation) (means of ~)	11	0,26	passengers	17	0,36
flying (off)	12	0,27	has (small) tyres/wheels	9	0,21	(jet) engine/engines	16	0,34
has tyres	12	0,27	(two) wings	8	0,19	stewardess	14	0,30
(carrying / travelling with) goods	11	0,24	carries many people / passengers / goods	7	0,16	travel/travelling	10	0,21
has (long) wings	11	0,24	moves/lies in air	7	0,16	fuel/jet fuel	10	0,21
vehicle	10	0,22	vehicle	7	0,16	seats	9	0,19
propeller	7	0,16	airport	6	0,14	sky	8	0,17
runs very fast /travelling fast	5	0,11	propeller	6	0,14	airport/airports	8	0,17
passengers' seats / seats	5	0,11	passengers (conveyance of ~)	5	0,12	transport(ation)	8	0,17
			seats	5	0,12	fast	7	0,15
						movie/movies	6	0,13
						flight attendants	6	0,13
						first class (vs. coach)	6	0,13
						crash	6	0,13
						cockpit	6	0,13
						luggage	6	0,13
						bad food	5	0,11
						peanuts	5	0,11
						air	5	0,11
						wheels	5	0,11
						windows	5	0,11

Table 2: Attribute lists for Hausa *keken guragu* and Nigerian and American English *wheelchair*

Hausa	**n = 45**		**Nigerian English**	**n = 39**		**American English**	**n = 47**	
keken guragu	**freq.**	**weight**	***wheelchair***	**freq.**	**weight**	***wheelchair***	**freq.**	**weight**
vehicle for a cripple(s)	26	0,58	tyres/rollers/wheels (two/three/four)	33	0,84	wheels	35	0,74
tyres / two tyres	19	0,42	chair (type of ~)	16	0,39	handicapped	18	0,38
chain	14	0,31	used by /disabled handi-capped/ crippled people	16	0,39	chair	15	0,32
(type of) vehicle / riding	13	0,29	seat (one ~)	10	0,24	physically disabled person	13	0,28
(has) three tyres / wheels	13	0,29	handle(s)	6	0,15	injury/injured	10	0,21
seat / saddle	12	0,27	handicap bicycle/ rider/bicycle for crippled/ resembles bicycle	5	0,12	old/elderly people	9	0,19
pushing / is being pushed	10	0,22	made of steel/iron/metal	5	0,12	hospital	8	0,17
(is used for) transport (of cripples)	9	0,20	mostly used in hospital /hospital utensil	4	0,10	electr(on)ic	8	0,17
driving/driven per/by hand	9	0,20				sick/ill	7	0,15
metal	7	0,16				metal	7	0,15
brakes / hand brakes	6	0,13				seat	7	0,15
sitting / place to sit / sth. to sit	6	0,13				ramps	6	0,13
pedal / hand pedal / pedal for driving	5	0,11				cripple(d)	6	0,13
						transportation	6	0,13
						push	6	0,13

Table 3: Attribute lists for Hausa *hula* and Nigerian and American English *cap*

Hausa	**n = 42**		**Nigerian English**	**n = 39**		**American English**	**n = 47**	
hula	**freq.**	**weight**	***cap***	**freq.**	**weight**	***cap***	**freq.**	**weight**
head-cover / is put on the head	29	0,69	(used on) head	15	0,38	baseball	45	0,68
(only) men (use it) / male	22	0,52	round(ed)	9	0,23	hat	37	0,56
ornamental / put on for ornamentation	16	0,38	(many) colours	8	0,21	head	20	0,30
to sow / sowing / sown (by hand)	14	0,33	hand made	7	0,18	bottle	12	0,18
(there is) thread in it	11	0,26	cover	7	0,18	protects from sun	11	0,17
type of cap	11	0,26	worn (mostly) by men	6	0,15	covers (hair)	11	0,17
clothes	10	0,24	medium size	6	0,15	wear	9	0,14
weaving / woven	6	0,14	soft/hard	5	0,13	lid	9	0,14
sth. to wear	6	0,14	sown	5	0,13	(cap) gun	9	0,14
yard of textile material	6	0,14	cloth	4	0,10	sports	9	0,14
(different) colour(s)	5	0,12	made of wool/cotton	4	0,10	brim	9	0,14
(part of) garment	4	0,10				team	7	0,11
cap (syn. of *hula*)	4	0,10				button on top	9	0,14
						hair	7	0,11
						bill	7	0,11
						boys/guys	8	0,12
						logo	5	0,08
						sun(shine)	4	0,06
						screw on	6	0,09
						closes something/closing device	7	0,11

Table 4: Attribute lists for Hausa *raƙumi* and Nigerian and American English *camel*

Hausa	n = 45		Nigerian English	n = 39		American English	n = 47	
raƙumi	**freq.**	**weight**	***camel***	**freq.**	**weight**	***camel***	**freq.**	**weight**
animal	31	0,69	animal	32	0,82	hump(s)	40	0,85
(used for) carrying loads (for payment)	23	0,51	legs (four), long	22	0,56	desert	36	0,77
tall	23	0,51	(used in)desert	20	0,51	spit	24	0,51
has long neck	18	0,40	tall	17	0,44	animal	16	0,34
(used for) transport	15	0,33	transport(er/ation) (means of ~)	14	0,36	water (storage)	15	0,32
vehicle / riding	12	0,27	long neck	13	0,33	means of transportation	14	0,30
to wander/travel in Sahara /in desert environment	8	0,18	carry loads/goods	7	0,18	4 legs	11	0,23
has long legs	8	0,18	hunchback	7	0,18	Egypt(ian)	10	0,21
hump / hump on the back	8	0,18	vehicle	6	0,15	brown	10	0,21
desert / living in the desert	7	0,16	eyes	5	0,13	cigarettes (ad)	9	0,19
(four / two) legs	7	0,16	carry people	4	0,10	Arabian	9	0,19
short tail / small tail / tail	6	0,13	meat	4	0,10	no need for water	7	0,15
meat	6	0,13	travelling	4	0,10	(accustomed to) heat/hot	7	0,15
(is used to) travel	6	0,13				sand	7	0,15
lead-rope of camel	5	0,11				(Middle) East	7	0,15
eats thorn / thorn	5	0,11				tall	7	0,15
big, huge	5	0,11				travel(ing)	6	0,13
						(big) hooves	6	0,13
						ride	6	0,13
						fur/furry	6	0,13
						slow	5	0,11
						yellow	5	0,11

Table 5: Attribute lists for Hausa *ayaba* and Nigerian and American English *banana*

Hausa	**n = 42**		**Nigerian English**	**n = 39**		**American English**	**n = 47**	
ayaba	**freq.**	**weight**	***banana***	**freq.**	**weight**	***banana***	**freq.**	**weight**
food / food stuff / eating / is eaten	28	0,67	fruit	20	0,54	yellow	55	0,85
(is) sweet / sweet stuff	17	0,40	sweet	14	0,38	fruit	35	0,54
delicacy / desired	12	0,29	edible (when ripe)	13	0,35	(waxy) peel/peelable	31	0,48
shell, bark	11	0,26	leaves	13	0,35	long	24	0,37
garden	10	0,24	roots	10	0,27	monkey	23	0,35
leaf / has leaves	9	0,21	tree (derived from ~)	8	0,22	tree	15	0,23
garden stuff / garden fruit	8	0,19	plant	7	0,19	curved/crescent shaped/irregular shape	15	0,23
fruits / tree fruits / fruit	6	0,14	soft	7	0,19	sweet	13	0,20
soft	6	0,14	food	6	0,16	slip/slippery	12	0,18
planting / (is) planted	6	0,14	green/yellow	6	0,16	healthy/good for you	12	0,18
(obtained from) a tree	6	0,14	peeled/cover that has to be removed	6	0,16	green (when not ripe)	10	0,15
pleasant, nice	6	0,14	flowers (before producing plant)	5	0,14	tropical	10	0,15
green / green back (bark)	6	0,14	carved /curved shape/semicircle	4	0,11	cereal	9	0,14
white inside / white / inside (white)	5	0,12	stem	4	0,11	mushy	9	0,14
peeling / is peeled before eating	4	0,10	vitamins	4	0,11	potassium	8	0,12
root / has roots	4	0,10				soft	7	0,11
						tasty/delicious/yummy	7	0,11
						Chiquita	7	0,11

Table 6: Attribute lists for Hausa *takalmi* and Nigerian and American English *shoes*

Hausa	**n = 42**		**Nigerian English**	**n = 38**		**American English**	**n= 47**	
takalmi	**freq.**	**weight**	***shoes***	**freq.**	**weight**	***shoes***	**freq.**	**weight**
(made of) skin / leather shoe	27	0,64	(made of) leather / hide / skin	23	060	(wear on) feet	38	0,58
(made of) rubber / rubber shoes	22	0,52	feet/ foot wear / used on feet	18	0,47	(with/without) socks	22	0,34
legs / is worn on the leg	19	0,45	cover(ed) shoes/top	13	0,34	boots	22	0,34
protection (against thorn, heat, sun or stumbling)	18	0,43	rubber	13	0,34	protection (protect feet)	20	0,31
ornament	14	0,33	protect feet (from injury) / protection	9	0,24	running	20	0,31
putting on / is put on	10	0,24	foot cover	6	0,16	sandals	19	0,29
heel	6	0,14	pair	6	0,16	laces	18	0,28
rope	5	0,12	part of dress(ing) / dress	6	0,16	(high) heels	17	0,26
clothes	5	0,12	size(s) (different ~)/big and small	6	0,16	comfort(able)	14	0,22
walking	4	0,10	colour(s) (different ~)	5	0,13	sneakers	12	0,18
			slippers	5	0,13	walk	11	0,17
			female	4	0,11	flip-flops	10	0,15
			male	4	0,11	tennis	10	0,15
			sandals	4	0,11	leather	9	0,14
						sole	8	0,12
						colour(ed)	8	0,12
						brands	7	0,11

Table 7: Attribute lists for Hausa *taga* and Nigerian and American English *window*

Hausa	**n = 42**		**Nigerian English**	**n = 39**		**American English**	**n = 47**	
taga	**freq.**	**weight**	***window***	**freq.**	**weight**	***window***	**freq.**	**weight**
(place for) air (entrance)	19	0,45	air going in and out, ventilation	28	0,70	glass	50	0,77
wood	13	0,31	part of building	9	0,23	open	26	0,40
room / inside/part of the room	11	0,26	(part of) room	9	0,23	light	23	0,35
glass	10	0,24	glass	8	0,20	panes	22	0,34
house / inside the house	9	0,21	wood	8	0,20	outside	17	0,26
brightening room / brightness	9	0,21	cover(ed)/not open	7	0,18	clear	15	0,23
iron	8	0,19	opening (not very wide/to the outside) (~ in building/room)	7	0,18	sight/see-through/look out	15	0,23
lock (inner)	8	0,19	metal/iron	5	0,13	view(s) (good ~)	16	0,25
nail(s)	7	0,17	part of house	4	0,10	house	13	0,20
building / part of the building	6	0,14	square (opening)/rectangle	4	0,10	close(d)	13	0,20
curtain	6	0,14				sun(shine)/sunny	11	0,17
sth. to close / closed with the window cover / to close	5	0,12				curtains	9	0,14
to open	5	0,12				(necessary in) building	9	0,14
key	5	0,12				car(s)	8	0,12
						square/rectangular	7	0,11
						clean	8	0,12
						breaking/breakable	7	0,11

Bibliography

Abraham, R. C. (1962): *Dictionary of the Hausa Language*, London: Hodder & Stoughton.

Bamgbose, Ayo (1997): English in the Nigerian environment, in: Bamgbose, Ayo; Banjo, Ayo; Thomas, Andrew (eds.): *New Englishes. A West African perspective*, Ibadan: Mosuro, 9-26.

Bargery, G. P. (1993): *A Hausa-English Dictionary and English-Hausa Vocabulary*, with Supplement and new introduction by N. Skinner, Zaria: Ahmadu Bello University Press.

Fauconnier, Gilles; Turner, Mark (2002): *The way we think. Conceptual blending and the mind's hidden complexities*, New York: Basic Books.

Mühlhäusler, Peter (1996): *Linguistic ecology. Language change and linguistic imperialism in the Pacific region*, London: Routledge.

Newman, Paul; Newman, Roxana Ma (1977): *Modern Hausa-English Dictionary*, Ibadan: University Press.

Ogden, C.K.; Richards, I.A (1923; 1949): *The meaning of meaning. A study of the influence of language upon thought and of the science of symbolism*, 10th ed., London: Routledge.

Rosch, Eleonor (1975): Cognitive representations of semantic categories, in: *Journal of experimental psychology*, general 104, 193-233.

Rosch, Eleonor; Mervis, Caroline B. (1975): Family resemblances: studies in the internal structure of categories, *Cognitive psychology* 7, 573-605.

Skutnabb-Kangas, Tove (2000): *Linguistic genocide in education or worldwide diversity and human rights?*, London: Erlbaum.

Ungerer, Friedrich; Schmid, Hans-Jörg (2006): *An introduction to cognitive linguistics*, 2nd ed., London: Longman.

Wolf, Hans-Peter (2003): The contextualization of common core terms in West African English: Evidence from computer corpora, in: Lucko, Peter; Peter, Lothar; Wolf, Hans-Georg (eds.): *Studies in African varieties of English*, Frankfurt: Peter Lang, 3-20.

Wolf, Hans-Peter; Igboanusi, Herbert (2003): A preliminary comparison of some lexical items in Nigerian English and Cameroon English, in: Lucko, Peter; Peter, Lothar; Wolf, Hans-Georg (eds.): *Studies in African varieties of English*, Frankfurt: Peter Lang, 69-81.

Creolization and Simplification: A Linguistic Perspective

Jonathan Owens

Concepts

In an enterprise so large and diverse as the SFB-FK 560 in terms of the themes it treats and the disciplines which treat them, it is useful at times to step back and compare important concepts from the different projects. In doing so one will confirm, or perhaps discover, that different projects are doing the same thing, as it were, but that the similarities have been masked because of the different terminologies used. Equally, it may emerge that ostensibly similar concepts mask what in fact are fundamental differences, which reflect further differences in the underlying reality the research is dealing with.

In this brief chapter I concentrate on the second aspect of the problem: highlighting the notion of simplification in contemporary research on creolization. Creolization is most developed as a branch of linguistic research, though it has been invoked in a cultural sense as well (Hannerz 1987), and the term has been adduced in research in our B domain on syncretization, which has been the main focus of the colloquium on which the proceedings are based. In this chapter I summarize the main points of the current debate, and in the concluding section generalize to a comparison between simplification and creolization on the one hand, and the notion of syncretization on the other.

1. Simplification in Creolization

Creoles are a class of languages which for many years were ignored by linguistics but became very popular from around 1970, and have since become established as a niche domain within linguistics. Their enduring interest resides in the fact that in many cases they are languages which arise and acquire a community of native speakers within a very short period of time, as short as one or two generations. For students of historical linguistics and language change, they therefore enjoy a privileged position for the potential insights they offer into linguistic processes.

The question has been much debated whether and in what sense creoles in fact form a linguistic class unto themselves. There are a number of aspects to this debate. For instance, do creoles belong in a genetic sense to their so-called lexifier parent: is Jamaican English or Sranan a changed form of English, is Haitian Creole a changed form of French. Some answer yes, some no. The 'yes' answer can be defended by citing regular sound correspondences between the lexifier and the creole. Sound correspondences are a classic method in historical linguistics for demonstrating genetic relationships. In the following (1), for instance, it is clear that one can 'explain' the presence of Saramaccan /k/ (Surinam) in the following words as an inheritance from English:

1. English k = Saramaccan (Surinam) k (Ham 1999)	
back	*báka*
count	*kónda*
because	*bikáa*
work	*woóko*
clothes	*koósu*

Those who answer 'no' to the above question fall into a number of different camps. Some maintain that the creoles in fact have a parentage with their substratal language, in the case of the Caribbean creoles, for instance, with a West African language (Haitian Creole with Fongbe; Lefebvre 1999). Others argue that they have no genetic affiliation, but here again there are various interpretations. Some argue that the 'changes' which creoles undergo are so radical and occur in such a short period of time that they are not a changed form of any language but are linguistically a-genetic (Thomason and

Kaufman 1988). Others sidestep the question of genetic affiliation and see in the development of a creole structure the workings of universal linguistic processes (Bickerton 1984). Recently, in a series of articles (1998, 2001, 2002, 2004), McWhorter has seized upon simplification as a means of identifying creoles as a class of languages. It is this perspective which I would like to discuss in greater detail.

The idea that creole languages have undergone a stage of simplification is nearly as old as the study of the languages themselves. Its interpretation, of course, has been differentiated. In a classic, early formulation, Hymes (1971) concentrates on the so-called pidgin-creole life-cycle. Languages are simplified in a process of pidginization; a resulting pidgin stabilizes and becomes more complex. In this perspective, the question of the simplification of creoles is finessed: creoles are characterized by their complexity relative to their pidgin ancestor. It is the pidgin which has simplified.

Turning to McWhorter's recent claims, he argues his case from a broad typological perspective. His criteria are refreshingly clear, linguistically defined and hence discussable. Creole languages are compared to various 'normal' languages, which McWhorter assumes to be those which have developed over a long, unbroken chain of transmission. Creoles lack a series of characteristics which other languages have, all of which are subsumed under the idea of simplification. Simplification is treated in two ways by McWhorter. First, it is identified by specific linguistic forms (1998: 792-9). For instance, creoles are languages which:

Lack suprasegmental morphology
Have reduced inflectional morphology
Have regular rather than irregular derivational morphology

While these morphological aspects of simplification are well known in creole studies, McWhorter contends that creole grammar as a whole is simpler. From a syntactic perspective, for instance, creoles:

Lack ergative structures
Lack inherent reflexivity markers
Lack a grammaticalized distinction between alienable and inalienable possession (see (2) below)

Elsewhere, simplification itself is given general attributes (2004: 80-3), being characterized in phonology by a lack of marked phonological features. The Khoisan languages, for instance, with their large inventory of click sounds, are more complex than Polynesian languages, which lack clicks and indeed often lack marked sounds generally. Syntax is simple to the extent that it lacks the processing of many rules or lacks overt marking of syntactic distinctions such as transitive vs. middle vs. passive voice. In general, inflectional morphology is a criterion of complexity. Finally, non-compositional derivation is a mark of complexity (comparable to 'regular derivational morphology', above). The meanings of 'understand', or 'verstehen' for instance, are not reducible to their components parts, 'under' and 'stand' in the first instance, 'ver' and 'stehen' in the second.

Given these characteristics, McWhorter argues that creoles form a class against all 'older' languages, the reason being that creoles, having become simplified along the given parameters, have not had time to develop the complexity which otherwise characterizes languages. McWhorter thus adjoins structural parameters to known chronological facts – no known creole language is older than five hundred years, and many are younger – and from this derives a class of languages, the creoles. The idea is straightforward and, perhaps, verifiable against linguistic data.

Of course, McWhorter realizes that not all older languages have all the attributes of the non-creole class: he simply argues that all creoles have them. His parameters sufficiently and exhaustively define the class of creoles.

McWhorter (2002) develops the concept of over-specification to encapsulate the difference between creoles and non-creoles. He identifies a set of twenty basic distinctions in language in general which are needed for communication, a distinction between singular and plural nouns, between nouns, adjectives and verbs, a way of marking near and far demonstratives, and so on. Older languages will have not only these basic distinctions, but many others as well, which McWhorter considers superfluous to communicative needs. Creoles, on the other hand, will manifest these distinctions, and not many more. They are too young to have developed them. They lack the 'ornamentation', as McWhorter terms it, of older languages.

McWhorter illustrates his thesis with various creoles, though he concentrates on various Caribbean and South American ones, Djuka, Saramaccan and Haitian in particular. In different studies these varieties are shown to be simpler when measured both against their lexical donor language and their African substrate language (Fongbe).

McWhorter's thesis is interesting especially for its claims about language evolution. He appears to argue that languages go through stages, that they are born in a simple form and become more complex over time. While this idea is not new, the suggestion that this claim is verifiable among today's living languages is new. Creoles in this sense are not a-genetic, as Thomason and Kaufman (1988) would have it, but are, as it were, typo-genetic. They represent a coherent class, not in the traditional genetic sense of being derived via certain changes from an ancestor, but in the sense that the circumstances of their birth lead them to discard attributes normally found in languages, this process of simplification resulting in the common class. This is, in a sense, a variant of Bickerton's perspective that creoles evince common structures due to their common circumstance of origin.

There have been four types of responses or alternatives to McWhorter's work among creolists.

The first is to redefine the question of creole genesis in formal, universal grammatical terms. Morphological simplification is taken as a given, and the resulting creole grammatical structures are, as much as possible, analysed as 'falling out' or deriving from the architecture of language universals. The problem with this approach, as McWhorter (2004) points out, is that there are a great many creole structures which do not fall out automatically from universal parameters, given morphological simplification. Too much of creole grammar is left unexplained, or must be specified in an ad hoc manner. The argumentation involved here is rather arcane, and I will not discuss it here.

A second response represents a new twist in the creole linguistic literature, namely to cast the claim of simplification in terms of political correctness. DeGraff (2003) attacks the claim of creole simplification on the in my view aprioristic grounds that it singles out creoles as an exceptional class of languages; for DeGraff, by definition, all languages are normal and, presumably, can only be differentiated using recognized parameters of differentiation, such as the comparative method or the previously mentioned universal grammar. The problem with DeGraff's intervention here is, besides its guilt by association style – i.e. those who countenance creole simplification are also those who endorse the validity of an American Secretary of States' statement in the early nineteenth century that Haitian creole is 'Niggers speaking French' – that it appears to disallow any historical inferences based on the structural parameter of simplification. This, however, flies in the face of what, outside creolist circles, is the non-controversial observation that structural simplification can be a fundamental part of language change and genesis. McWhorter, it should be noted, goes to some length to disavow any link between claims about creole language simplification and inferences about the cultural or cognitive capabilities of those who speak creole languages. Here again I believe that McWhorter's perspective remains a valid one, and so I move on to the other two criticisms.

A third perspective takes a differentiated view of the issue. This appears to be the majority view, as exemplified recently in Siegel (2004). Siegel points out familiar problems in McWhorter's approach. In his view it is difficult, for example, to characterize entire languages as simple or otherwise: at best, only components or modules of them can be. Moreover, the entire question of creole simplification turns on a logical characterization of the problem. It is generally accepted that, in their incipient stages, the original speakers of the creole were not fluent in the lexical donor language (English, French etc.). This being the case, they cannot be said to have simplified these languages, since they did not speak them in the first place. It is only the outside observer who reconstructs a potential parentage with a predecessor language or languages.

Such points aside, Siegel does side with the linguists, as it were, allowing that creole genesis is a crucial question and that the simplification of creoles is a fact characterizing their being and is therefore in need of explanation. It is clear from his literature review that this is also broadly the position of most creolists who have dealt with the question. He draws structural parallels between creole genesis and general attributes of second language learning, for instance, the claim that in many creole societies, constant influxes of new second language learners would have exerted a steady pressure towards simplification, as is attested in second language learning.

Siegel does not commit himself on the general appropriateness of McWhorter's characterization of creoles as new languages which have not had the time to complexify linguistically, but at least aspects of Siegel's second language learning explanation for simplification are compatible with it.

A fourth position I describe echoes issues raised elsewhere, but compels a focus on the central question of simplification. It is a simple, parochial, descriptive problem which derives from one of a number of African creoles which are systematically excluded from creole studies. I say 'systematically', arguing that creole linguistics, like sociolinguistics and I believe many of the social sciences generally, rarely stray from languages and societies familiar to the West, and therefore it frames its theoretical discussion ultimately on an impoverished comparative database.

The language is Nubi, a creole language spoken in Uganda and Kenya and closely related to the so-called Juba Arabic pidgin/creole spoken in particular by southern Sudanese. It arose from Arabic in the second half of the nineteenth century. Like other creoles, comparing it to its lexical source language, the Arabic of the Sudanic region, reveals a drastic degree of morphological simplification, as well as a high degree of restructuring. Both points can be seen in a comparison of the following two sentences translating ‘they are being beaten’, one from Khartoum Arabic, the other from Nubi.

(1) Khartoum Arabic	Nubi
(hinna) b-yi-n-d∞arub-an	bi-gi-durubú ‘they were being beaten’
(they.F) b-3-PASS-hit-F.PL	FUT-CONT-hit. PASS

The following table summarizes the grammatical categories realized in the verb forms.

Khartoum Arabic	Nubi
Lexical content	lexical content
Tense-aspect (verb stem)	tense-aspect (*bi-*, *gi-*)
Person (*yi*)	voice (final stress signaling passive)
Gender (*-an*)	
Number (*-an*)	
Mood (*b-*, = roughly 'indicative')	
Voice (*-n-*) (passive)	

The Nubi verb realizes three grammatical categories, the lexical content of the verb, the tense-aspect markers *bi-gi*, and a passive voice, marked by the word final stress. Khartoum Arabic, on the other hand, marks many more categories: lexical content, person (*y-*), gender (*-an*), number (*-an*), mood (*b-*) and voice (*-n-*).

A closer descriptive look at Nubi, however, reveals that in many respects the simplification perspective is too simple. An overall quantification of a 'simplicity' index for Nubi relative to Sudanic Arabic or such substratal languages as Bari or Madi – as seen above, controversial in and of itself – is well outside the scope of this paper. One may be struck, however, at how many obvious and in some cases surprising respects Nubi provides simple, substantive contradictions to truths that have become embedded in the contemporary canon of creole linguistic structures. To take an obvious example, McWhorter writes,

> '… there is no creole known to this author which distinguishes alienable from inalienable possession overtly'
>
> (McWhorter 2002: 12)

However, it is well known that Nubi does make such a distinction (Wellens 2003: 83).

(2) Alienable, with marker *ta* 'of'	Inalienable
gurun ta ragi	gurun bagar
horn of man	horn cow

'The man's horn' (that he owns) cow horn

Even more significant are features such as the following:
Suprasegmental grammatical markers: Nubi has four contrastive verb shapes distinguished only by suprasegmental means: *ásrubu* 'drink', *asrúbu* 'drinking', *ásrúbu* 'to drink', *asrubú* 'drunk'

Crucially in this respect, neither Sudanic Arabic nor potential substratal languages like Bari, Mamvu or Moru/Madi have comparable suprasegmental marking. As seen above, McWhorter argued early (1998) that lack of grammatical suprasegmentality was a hallmark of creoles, yet in Nubi it is a feature gone wild, as it were (see Owens 2001 for detailed discussion). Furthermore, it was pointed out some time ago (Owens 1997: 150) that Nubi has developed an 'in situ' passive marking system that remains otherwise unattested among the 5,000 or so languages of the world.

The point of these observations is to caution that creoles not only innovate, they can innovate in ways, to echo Sapir, that vary without limit. Of course, on an ex post facto basis, plausible explanations for the Nubi innovations can be proposed. However, they represent clear complications, which in McWhorter's terms are ornamental as far as the fabric of language goes.

2. Simplification, Creolization; Creolization, Syncretization

When backed up against a wall and forced to name attributes of linguistic creolization, it has been suggested here that simplification would stand out as among the most prominent named by most creolists. Except perhaps for a handful of syntactic formalists, most would recognize it as a feature which characterizes all creole languages when compared to possible source languages. Certainly it is an open question as to how broad the phenomenon is among discretely identifiable grammatical components, and the fact that in some well-attested creoles, at least, such as Nubi, simplification is also accompanied by unpredictable innovation indicates that simplification does not exclude a temporally simultaneous complication and ornamentation.

If simplification is an inherent aspect of creolization, a linguistic definition of the phenomenon is difficult to carry over into other cultural domains. Except for McWhorter, most creolists adopt a cautious component-by-component interpretation of simplification: identifying discrete cultural domains against which a simplification criterion can even be applied is impossible. While anthropologists such as Hannerz have spoken of the creolization of cultures, the association has to be understood as a metaphorical one.[34]

Still, similarities between concepts that are well established or becoming well established in the social sciences and linguistic creolization can hardly be passed over. The enduring controversy in creole studies, for instance, over the relative influence of superstrate (i.e. the lexical donor language) or substrate languages in determining the structure of the emerging creole in principle echoes the notion of cultural syncretization. In both it is assumed that elements of an emerging or emerged system can be identified as belonging to one parent system or another. Furthermore, just as syncretized systems can desyncretize when one of the constituent components becomes dominant, so too can creoles decreolize through contact with the superstrate language.

Even if parallels between syncretization and creolization may be discerned, it is necessary to remember that their interpretation remains elusive.

First, it may be pointed out that other phenomena than linguistic creolization should be invoked in parallels with syncretization. For

[34] Hannerz was looking for a concept to characterize a fluid cultural mixture, 'different cultural streams engaging one another' (1987: 555), found in particular in post-colonial African urban areas, as well as its extension to European metropolises, and he found it in the idea of creolization. Interpreting the different senses of creolization thus entails a broad consideration of the relationship between language and culture.

instance, students of historical linguistics recognize another 'extreme' instance of language change, namely that attested in the relatively few cases of mixed languages. For instance, Michif, which is still spoken in the Upper Great Plains regions of Canada and the US, has a verb system based on Athabaskan (Cree) and a nominal system based partly on French and partly on Cree (Bakker 1996). Media Lengua, spoken in Ecuador, has a lexicon from Spanish and a grammatical system from Quechua, while what I term Central Asian Mixed Arabic, spoken in Uzbekistan, has basically an Arabic morphological system and lexicon, but fundamental syntactic rules from Uzbek or Tadjik (Persian). These situations are probably more amenable to a simple analogical comparison with syncretism than is creolization.

Secondly, explanations of creole genesis evaluate the role of language mixture in very different terms. Well known contributions such as Bickerton's Bioprogram give language mixture very little importance. Chaudenson (1979), McWhorter and others correlate the relative influence of substratal vs. superstratal languages with demographic and socio-historical factors. Degree of mixture is considered to derive automatically from non-linguistic factors. Whereas mixture is a sine qua non of syncretization, it plays a secondary, and for some scholars a negligible role in creolization.

Thirdly, along the same lines, as already noted, the simplification implied by creolization has no cultural correlate. Indeed, as far as languages go, simplification correlates in no obvious way with vitality, power, geographical spread, survivability or any other extralinguistic characterization of language. At the one extreme, Tok Pisin is an English-based creole which has become the major lingua franca of New Guinea. At the other extreme, Arabic is morphologically a rather complicated language, which in my view has undergone relatively little simplification and is spread over a very large area. Communicative instruments are perhaps the ultimate adaptive devices, allowing culture and meanings to be transmitted in a myriad of forms.

Given these key differences, it may be doubted that there is much to be gained by even dwelling on an extended comparison between syncretization and creolization. Parallels can be certainly be found, but when one tries to pull them together in a systematic fashion, neither coherence nor a vital common denominator emerges.

My response to this is as follows. Rather than try to play down differences between a social scientific concept such as syncretization and linguistic ones such as creolization, one should rather determine whether the differences do not in fact reflect differences in underlying realities. It will have been noted in the relatively brief exemplification of the linguistic controversies surrounding the idea of simplification that the criterial units are small and measurable. At the smallest end, phones (sounds) and affixes (morphology), for instance, are measured in milliseconds. Even the largest syntactic structures, e.g. ergativity structure, are based on the sentence, which, to give a comparative measure, represents a unit which can be spoken in less than a second. Syncretic religious practices, rituals of various sorts, on the other hand, can be very long. At first glance, finding a common denominator, for instance in cognitive terms, between the linguistic units invoked in the discussion of creole genesis and the concepts underlying syncretic practices is not so much hopeless as misguided.

The overall conclusion that I draw is not that cultural phenomena are too vast to be reasonably integrated into a common research perspective, but rather that their extreme differentiation needs to be recognized as a starting point for establishing reasonable, common goals.

I should note that this is not so much an insular approach as a realistic one, which all disciplines taking part in this SFB can consider. In the final analysis, a sceptical approach is often the one which yields the most interesting results. To take an example from the field of linguistics, as noted above the linguistic discussion around creole genesis hinges around units which are relatively easy to define, such as phones, morphemes and the like. A look at the much broader horizons treated by a domain such as cultural syncretization probably has its linguistic correlates as well, though perhaps it does not. Much depends here on what the elements of language are, where the boundaries between language and the world lie, and whether indeed they exist at all. This could be a topic for future research.

Bibliography

Bakker, Peter (1996): *A Language of our Own*, Oxford: Oxford University Press.

Bickerton, Derek (1984): The Language Bioprogram Hypothesis, *Behavioral and Brain Sciences*, 7: 173-221.

Chaudenson, Robert (1979): *Les créoles français*, Paris: Nathan.

DeGraff, M. (2003): Against Creole Exceptionalism, *Language*, 79: 391-410.

Ham, William (1999): Tone Sandhi in Saramaccan: A Case of Substrate Transfer, *Journal of Pidgin and Creole Languages* (JPCL), 14: 45-91.

Hannerz, Ulf (1987): The World in Creolisation, *Africa* 57: 546-59.

Hymes, Dell (1971): Introduction, in: Hymes, D. (ed.): *Pidginization and Creolization of Languages*, Cambridge: Cambridge University Press, 65-90.

Lefebvre, C. (1999): *Creole Genesis and the Acquisition of Grammar: The Case of Haitian Creole*, Cambridge: Cambridge University Press.

McWhorter, John (1998): Identifying the Creole Prototype: Vindicating a Typological Class, *Language*, 74: 788-818.

McWhorter, John (2001): The World's Simplest Grammars are Creole Grammars, *Linguistic Typology*, 5: 125-66.

McWhorter, John (2002): The Rest of the Story: Restoring Pidginization to Creole Genesis Theory, *Journal of Pidgin and Creole Languages* 17: 1-48.

McWhorter, John (2004): Saramaccan and Haitian as Young Grammars: the Pitfalls of Syntactocentricism in Creole Genesis Research, *Journal of Pidgin and Creole Languages* 19: 77-138.

Owens, Jonathan (1997): Arabic-based Pidgins and Creoles, in: Thomason, Sarah (ed.): *Contact Languages: A Wider Perspective*, Amsterdam: Benjamins, 125-72.

Owens, Jonathan (2001): Arabic Creoles: The Orphan of all Orphans, *Anthropological Linguistics*, 43: 348-78.

Siegel, Jeff (2004): Morphological Simplicity in Pidgins and Creoles, *Journal of Pidgin and Creole Languages*, 19: 139-62.

Thomason, Sarah; Kaufman, Terence (1988): *Language Contact, Creolization and Genetic Linguistics*, Berkeley: University of California Press.

Wellens, Ineke (2003): *An Arabic Creole in Africa: The Nubi language of Uganda*, PhD thesis, Nijmegen University.

Negotiating the New

The *Baraza* in Zanzibar: Local Sitting and Transnational Thinking in a Cosmopolitan Setting

Roman Loimeier

Introduction

Space and space-related terms such as 'sphere' (public sphere) or 'scape' (landscape, seascape, ethnoscape, etc.) have become very trendy words in recent years. The concept of 'scapes' as formulated by Arjun Appadurai was quickly expanded to many different contexts. When discussing 'space', however, we should also take into account the concept of the 'public sphere' as developed by Jürgen Habermas (1962/1989/1990), who defines 'public sphere' as a '*Form von bürgerlicher Öffentlichkeit*' (a form of civilian public) which allows for the free circulation of information and ideas, outside the control of the state (Habermas 1990: 86ff.). This concept was taken up by Robert Launay and Benjamin Soares in their discussion of an 'Islamic sphere' in French West Africa in the colonial period and defined as 'a space conceptually separate (though obviously not entirely autonomous) from particular affiliations...but also from the colonial (and later the post-colonial) state', a space that was consequently hotly contested, in particular with respect to the definition of public ritual, the fixing of dates and religious holidays, the public modes of prayer, etc., or 'Islam' as such (Launay and Soares 1999: 468ff., 483), and became, thus, space for the negotiation of influence and power, in the struggle for *Deutungshegemonie*, that is, the power to define religious, social or political issues in an hegemonic way or more literally the 'hegemony of meaning'. However, the idea of thinking societies in spaces has diverted attention from another, equally important perspective, namely that of thinking societies in times, and to then link (social) time with (social) space, although one small group of neo-Marxist authors such as David Harvey has already been thinking exactly along these lines. In addition, Anthony Giddens has contributed considerably to the discussion of times and spaces by introducing the concept of time-space distanciation (Giddens 1997: 28ff). In the following, I would like to focus on this idea of linking space and time by presenting a case study from Zanzibar, where I was led to 'discover' the *baraza* as a major site for the negotiation of all kinds of things in both local and truly translocal terms.

The Space, Place and Time Dimensions of the *Baraza*

The term *baraza* (pl. *baraza/mabaraza*)[1] itself has many different meanings, though has so far it not really been discussed in the academic literature. To the best of knowledge, only Marc J. Swartz (1991) and Mohamed Ahmad Saleh (2004) have provided first academic definitions of the *baraza* by defining it as 'a place of public audience or reception, a veranda, a stone seat in the entrance hall, a bench against the wall outside a house or a raised platform with stone seats and sometimes roofed over in front of the house, for receiving visitors, holding an audience, transacting business, for gossiping, where men gather on a fairly regular basis, usually between *magharibi* and *isha* prayers. It is a male place of socialization par excellence with contrast to *ua*, the courtyard, where female members of the society get together (*uani*) for their talks and their domestic activities' (Swartz 1991: 317; Saleh 2004: 16).[2] Mw. Ramadhani

---

[1] Mohamed Ahmed Saleh has pointed out that the plural of *baraza*, namely *mabaraza*, is applied only when referring to the 'meetings of a council' and other forms of organization that are not necessarily linked with a specific place. When refering to the *baraza* as a place, people form the plural by saying, for instance, 'he is sitting in three *baraza*s', i.e. '*anakaa katika baraza tatu*'. In my text, I will follow this rule instead of applying the grammatical plural *mabaraza* (Mohamed Ahmed Saleh, personal communication, 2.4. 2005).

[2] Swartz's definition of the *baraza* was developed in the context of his research on the Bena in Tanzania, where the term means, as in many other 'mainland' societies,

Kututwa has added to this definition by remarking that in rural (*shamba*) areas there are also *baraza* in the form of (public) sheds in either the village or along the roadside, often wooden, but sometimes mud or concrete constructions (*kibanda*, *makuti*) with benches (*magogo*) and mats (*mkeka*, *gamvi*, *busati*) to sit on (Mw. Ramadhani, personal communication 2.8.2004). The oldest Kiswahili dictionary of Krapf (1882) defines the *baraza* as 'a stone seat or bench table, either outside of the house or in the hall, where the master sits in public and receives his friends; hence the public audience held by the Sultan and the council then held; meeting of a council' (quoted in Haugerud and Njogu 1991: 8). The Arabic root of the term, namely, *b-r-z* (to jut out, to protrude and to stand out) reflects the architectural meaning of the term as a 'platform' which 'protrudes' from a building. The term '*majlis*' (council, meeting) would thus be a better translation of the term into Arabic, at least with respect to its social meaning. Also, *majlis* refers to a corresponding social 'institution' of communal sitting and communicating in, for instance, southern Arabian cultural contexts.[3]

The term *baraza* essentially points thus to three different dimensions of interpretation, namely the organizational, spatial and temporal, i.e. time-linked notions of the *baraza*. All of these notions should be seen as reflecting a spectrum of possibilities:

a) In organizational terms, a *baraza* may represent different degrees of formality/informality, institutionalization and abstractness. A

---

a 'session to settle disputes' (Swartz 1991: 317). This reflects the fact that the term *baraza* has acquired, in different societies and at different times, different meanings. I am grateful to Pat Caplan for directing my attention to Marc Swartz's work.

[3] Corresponding institutions may be found in many societies, such as the *majlis* in Arabia, the 'shadow tree' in the West African savannahs, the *bangwe* in Rwanda and Burundi, the *piazza* in Italy, the German *Stammtisch*, the Bavarian 'beer garden' or the *café de commerce* in France. As the topic of 'sitting local' has not been a major focus of my research, I am unfortunately not aware of any academic literature on these places of socialization, although there should be a great number of texts on it. I sincerely apologize for this gap in my knowledge and would be grateful for any kind of *irshâd* (guidance).

baraza might be a simple (informal) 'meeting' of people, but also a 'council', or, in historical times, the 'audience' of the Sultan of Zanzibar, which was described as a *barza* (Ruete 1998: 125), or, finally, a huge range of clubs, unions or associations such as the '*Baraza la kiswahili la Taifa*' (National KiSwahili Council), the '*Baraza la Musiki za Taifa*' (National Council of Music), the '*Baraza la Sanaa la Taifa*' (National Board of Industry), the '*Baraza Kuu la Waislamu wa Tanzania*' (Supreme Council of Tanzanian Muslims), or the '*Baraza Kuu la Jumuiya na Taasisi za Kiislamu*' (Supreme Council of Islamic Organizations and Institutions in Tanzania), organizations whose membership is defined in more or less formal terms;

b) In spatial terms, the *baraza* represents a spectrum of places where people meet, such as the veranda in front of a house (see above), or, especially in *shamba* areas, a place near the local mosque. Inside a house, a *baraza* is a parlour for receiving visitors such as, again, the 'audience chamber' of the Sultan of Zanzibar; this 'inside' *baraza* also corresponds to the *majlis* mentioned above. In Zanzibar, the Sultan had several *baraza*, the most important being the '*baraza al-`îd*', which met each morning after the '*`îd al-fitr*' (i.e. at the end of Ramadhân) at 10 am, and then continued as a state reception until dinner in the evening (ZNA AB 10 and 83). In addition to these meanings of the term, any kind of place where people would meet in different functions could acquire the notion of a *baraza*, agency thus being the defining issue. Globalization (*utandawazi*) has finally added another dimension to the spatial notion of the *baraza*, namely the cyber-*baraza*, which should be seen, according to Farouk Topan, as consisting of e-mail networks and chatrooms, i.e. the electronic forum of the global Zanzibari diaspora, as well as of those globalized Zanzibaris who are united in one virtual *baraza*, the 'Zanzinet' (Topan forthcoming: 10);[4]

c) In temporal or time-linked terms, a *baraza* is connected with the specific times of the day when its members meet, such as the *baraza za wazee*, the 'old men's *baraza*', at Jaws' corner, which is frequented daily between *`asr* and *maghrib* prayers. In fact, a single *baraza* (in the spatial sense of the term) could be occupied in the course of a 'day'[5] by a number of different groups. In addition, as mentioned above, each *baraza* is linked with the stories of that specific place and its people, and, thus with local history. It would be possible, in fact, to write a social history of Zanzibar by recording the histories of the different *baraza*.[6]

In more abstract terms, the *baraza* could be characterized as 'inscribed places', spaces which have been defined in meaningful terms by the people of a specific place, who have thus transformed undefined space into defined place (Low and Lawrence-Zuniga 2003: 13). A *baraza* may therefore be regarded as a 'space' (*Raum*) which has come to life as a 'place' (Augé 1992/: 79ff.). Consequently, a *baraza* has stopped being 'something in between', i.e. pure (undefined) 'space', and has become 'something', namely a distinct '*Platz*', a place, which is known for the stories associated with it, for its specific history, as well as for the people who meet there. These notions of 'place' (*Platz*) and 'space' (*Raum*) have not only been discussed prominently by Low and Lawrence-Zuñiga (2003) and by Augé (ibid.), but also by Smith (1987) and Harvey (2004), who

---

[4] It would be interesting to see whether other forms of 'virtual' *baraza* exist as well, for instance, a *baraza* of the 'spirits' (*wapepo*).

[5] A 'day' in Zanzibar is divided into *siku* (daytime) from 6 am, 7 am being the 'first' hour of the day, or, in Kiswahili 'time', *saa moja asubuhi* (one o'clock in the morning), until 6 pm (*saa kumi na mbili*, i.e. twelve o'clock); and *usiku* (night-time), starting from 6 pm, 7 pm being the first hour of the night, until 6 am (*saa kumi na mbili usiku*).

[6] Georg Deutsch has started to do this with his history of Soko Mohogo treet (publication forthcoming).

support, in their respective work, Low and Lawrence-Zuñiga's definitions of space and place. Smith, following a Chinese geographer, Yi-Fu Tuan, defines the space-place continuum as follows: 'Space is more abstract than place. What begins as undifferentiated space becomes place as we get to know it better and endow it with value ... If we think of space as that which allows movement, then place is pause; each pause in movement makes it possible for location to be transformed into place.... When space feels thoroughly familiar to us, it has become place. Thus, abstract space, lacking significance other than strangeness, becomes concrete place when it is filled with meaning' (Smith 1987: 28).

David Harvey, while stressing that 'place, in whatever guise, is like space and time, a social construct', also maintains that 'place', much more than 'space', is connected with 'permanences' (Harvey 1996: 293), thus linking space/place and time. Such permanencies (i.e. all kinds of human agency) come to occupy 'a piece of space in an exclusive way (for a specific period of time) and thus define a place – their place – (for this period of time)' (Harvey 1996: 293). The concept of 'place' is thus intrinsically linked with concepts of time, namely the concepts of time of those who transform, through their 'permanences', space into place when they meet at specific times at specific places. While space may exist in an independent way, place is always situated in a time-continuum, namely the time-continuum of those who frequent specific places. As soon as these temporal permanencies cease, place ceases to be place and returns again to undefined and 'non-used' 'space'. Places are consequently 'spaces' where time has become 'condensed' through the 'permanences' of specific persons or groups. In places such as a *baraza*, time becomes, as a consequence, 'visible' (Harvey 1996: 294). Places are therefore ultimately 'constructed and experienced as material ecological artefacts and intricate networks of social relations. They are the focus of the imaginary, of beliefs, longings, and desires. They are an intensive focus of discursive activity, filled with symbolic and representational meanings, and they are a distinctive product of institutionalized social and political-economic power' (Harvey 1996: 316).[7]

In this context, finally, it should be added that *baraza* are not the only form of grassroots organization or organization of places and spaces known in Zanzibar. There are, for instance, the numerous 'clubs' and associations, in particular of the young, often football fans who meet in their own 'spots' (*kijiwe*), marked in Zanzibar by little flags, often just a shed as protection against the sun. In addition, there are the so-called *maskani* associations, the meeting places, usually simple sheds with benches, for the supporters of a specific political party which started to form in the early 1990s in Zanzibar in the context of the emergence of a multiparty system (Crozon 1998: 41ff.). The Zanzibari ruling party even equipped some of its *maskani* with a TV set in order to attract people (Mohamed Ahmed Saleh, personal communication, 2.4.2005). In contrast to the *baraza*, however, the *maskani* are associatedwith specific aims and have a more formal character than a *baraza* (for a detailed discussion of the political background to the development of the *maskani*, see Bakari 2001: 189ff.). Finally, there are the *kikao*, the 'places to sit', where specific agendas are discussed, *kikao* thus representing rather formal meetings (Mw. Idris, personal communication, 27.7.2004). It should also be mentioned in this context that in recent decades *baraza* have spread to the mainland under the influence of Nyerere's policies, since he supported the *baraza* as an instrument to propagate his ideas of social reform in mainland Tanzania (Mw. Idris, personal communication, 19.6.2004).

---

[7] As such, the *baraza* even seems to fit into Heidegger's definition of 'place' 'as the locale of the truth of being': '*der Ort, an dem sich 'Sein' vollzieht und darstellt*' (M. Heidegger, 1971, *Poetry, Language, Thought*, as quoted in Harvey 1996: 299).

The Phenomenology of the *Baraza*

Baraza therefore seem to represent a rather broad spectrum of different forms of organization, as well as different notions of place and space, which are again defined in different temporal terms. *Baraza* may consequently appear as to represent a rather vague notion of the organization of '*Öffentlichkeit*', i.e. the 'public sphere' as well as 'public times', in Zanzibar. Yet *baraza* are not entirely amorphous, but rather follow a distinct set of rules and are linked with a distinct code of behaviour which we could call '*baraza* etiquette'. These rules and codes of behaviour also apply to the form of the *baraza* I would like to highlight in my paper, namely the Zanzibar Stone Town street *baraza* on Unguja Island.[8]

Walking through Zanzibar Stone Town,[9] one encounters *baraza* be virtually everywhere. Major concentrations of *baraza* are to be found in the Darajani (market) area, but also in Mkunazini: from Vuga Street down to Mskiti Jibrin (Jibrin mosque) at least nine or ten *baraza* are located at different times of the day, and Jaws' corner, in

---

[8] Together with the island of Pemba and some smaller islands such as Tumbatu, Unguja Island forms the Zanzibar archipelago. Unguja can again be divided into three major socio-geographical zones: Zanzibar Stone Town proper, i.e. the historical and political centre of Zanzibar (ca. 20,000 inhabitants as of today); Ng'ambo, i.e. the urban areas of Zanzibar Town on the 'other side' (*ng'ambo*) of the 'creek' (which almost cut Stone Town off from the rest of the island until it was filled in in the colonial period), today, a major urban agglomeration (ca. 390,000 inhabitants) consisting of numerous quarters such as the different 'Miembes' (Miembeladu, Miembeshauri, etc.), Kikwajuni, Kisiwandui, Saateni, Kilimani, Jang'ombe, Mwanakeregwe, Gulioni and others; and the rural areas (*shamba*) on the island with a population of about 200,000. The island of Pemba has about 350-400,000 inhabitants, but, apart from some smaller towns, no urban agglomeration comparable to Zanzibar.

[9] Stone Town is defined here as the old and most densely settled area of Zanzibar Town west of Creek Road between the Mnazi Mmoja hospital in the south and Fungoni in the north, comprising the quarters of (from north to south) Malindi, Kiponda, Kokoni, Darajani, Hurumzi, Forodhani, Hamamni, Mkunazini, Soko Mohogo, Baghani, Vuga, Kibogoni and Shangani, an area of approximately one square kilometre (3 km north-south, 200-1,000 metres east-west) and a maze of narrow alleys of more than 20 kilometers in length.

the very centre of Stone Town, alone accounts for at least six *baraza*. Other concentrations are to be found in the different parts of Baghani, Vuga, Kokoni, Malindi, Kiponda and Hurumzi. Hamamni, Kajifijeni and Shangani, by contrast, seem to have only a few *baraza*, while Forodhani is a place for picnicking and tourist activities, and thus not really a place for *baraza* but for family evenings.

Nonetheless, even though *baraza* have existed in Zanzibar, in particular in *shamba* areas, for a long time, they are a comparatively recent feature of many parts of Stone Town, only starting to develop essentially after the revolution of 1964. This rather surprising development is connected with the fact that until 1964 Stone Town had been an area for the rich and aristocratic, who would never sit 'in the street' as they had their in-door '*majlis*'. Sitting 'in the street' in a *baraza* was thus, until 1964, a feature of the 'poor' in Stone Town or of the 'Africans' living in Ng'ambo or *shamba* areas. Before 1964, therefore, *baraza* were mainly confined to Stone Town, the markets (i.e. Darajani, Mkunazini and Kokoni), the mosques (such as Mskiti Ruta) and public places, or the poorer and 'popular' quarters of Stone Town, such as Malindi. Like today, therefore, *baraza* were, and still are, spatial expressions of the social context in which they are situated (conversation E. Meffert, 7.8.2004). The development of *baraza* has to be seen, consequently, as a feature of social change (and development), which, for some parts of Stone Town – such as Shangani, where *baraza* scarcely existed before 1964 – could be characterized as a development from '*majlis* to *baraza*', i.e. from meetings inside the house to meetings outside it). In a broader sense, a change in social context will also influence the social character of the *baraza* of a specific locality.[10]

When walking through Stone Town, one readily en counters *baraza* 'in session'. In fact, it might be said that virtually every house

[10] In this context, it should be added that *baraza* in *shamba* areas and Ng'ambo did not necessarily have a 'social function', but were often built only to protect houses against heavy rainfall (E. Meffert, personal communication, 7.8.2004).

in Zanzibar (Stone Town, Ng'ambo and *shamba* areas) has its own *baraza*. Most of these, however, are *baraza* for the house and the people of the house only, not 'public' ones. Only a few *baraza* have become truly 'communal' or 'public', although even their number may number, in Stone Town alone, more than 300 or 400 (see map), even though the number of 'famous' public *baraza* is smaller, probably between 50 and 60. It is therefore necessary to differentiate again between 'private' *baraza* and 'public' as well as 'communal' *baraza*, although the boundaries between them are fluid. Most 'private' *baraza* are only attended by those people, men and women,[11] who actually live in a specific house, or passers-by greeting somebody from the house who happens to be sitting in 'his' *baraza*. 'Communal' *baraza*, by contrast, would not necessarily be associated with a specific house any more, but be situated at 'strategic' places such as small openings in an alleyway or at an intersection of several alleyways, and consequently attract more people from diverse backgrounds, yet still the neighbourhood, who would come at specific times of the day, night or week to sit in 'their' *baraza*. 'Public' *baraza* are thus all those *baraza* who attract people from a still wider geographical background. For these public *baraza*, residency is no longer a defining factor. Also, public *baraza* are situated at 'strategic' places, such as one of the small places in Stone Town, as, for instance, Jaws' Corner in Soko Mohogo or the place in front of and around the Spice Inn in Kokoni. In terms of numbers of members, communal and/or public *baraza* normally bring together groups of more than two (but often less than ten) individuals, such as the *baraza* of the *wazee* of Jaws' Corner, which regularly has from two to six or seven members.[12] Finally, there are a small number of

[11] Sitting in *baraza* is, so far, gendered. I have not seen any mixed *baraza*, although women may sit, but at different times of the day, on the same 'spot' as men (see also below).

[12] *Baraza* in Zanzibar Stone Town thus seem to be smaller than corresponding *baraza* in Mombasa (see below).

(male) 'in-door' *baraza*, as in the Masomo bookshop, where local politicians meet, or the Tembo Hotel, which brings together members and friends of the Muzamil family.[13] However, these contemporary in-door *baraza* are characterized by the fact that access is not open to everybody that *baraza* discussions often refer to sensitive issues such as politics or business, and that one has to be invited to become a member of such a *baraza*, even for a short period of time.[14]

Some of the public or communal *baraza* have acquired particular fame, such as, in historical times, the *baraza* of the Sultan mentioned above; the *baraza* of the *qâdîs* of Zanzibar, which in the 1890s met each day (except Fridays) from 4-5 pm. in front of the clock tower (N. Oberauer, personal communication, 28.9.2004); the different *baraza* at Mskiti Ruta;[15] the *baraza ya* Khamis Machungwa in Majanini; the Passing Show Hotel *mbao* players' *baraza* of Nassor Bubek in Malindi; the *baraza* of Bwana Mkelle (the 'poets' *baraza*); the *baraza* of Sayyid Ba Wazir, close to Mskiti Barza; the *Baraza ya* Hollis Road (in Malindi); the 'Ice Krim Klabu' in Darajani; the Mizingani *Baraza* '*kwa* Mr Lasi'; or even famous Ng'ambo *baraza* such as the '*baraza ya* six four' (in Michenzani), the '*baraza ya msikiti* Nambani' and the '*baraza ya msikti* Mchangani' (Mw. Idris, personal communication, 19.7.2004); or, finally, *baraza* which became famous in the early years of the revolution such as 'Bright Brother', 'Peace Lover' and 'Jaws' Corner' (established 1974) (Burgess 2002: 293). At least some of these historical *baraza* continue to exist today, and have been complemented since the early 1980s by other popular *baraza* such as the *baraza* of the fans of Manchester United in Kokoni, the businessmen's *baraza* close to the

---

[13] Abdalazîz Lodhi, personal communication, 2.4.2005.

[14] In my chapter, I concentrate on communal and public *baraza* and exclude the multitude of purely 'private' *baraza*, even though these represent up to 90% of all *baraza*.

[15] Also shown in the documentary film *Jeder Wind hat seine Reise*, Bavarian TV and ARTE, produced by Along Mekong Productions, Heidelberg, 2002.

Cash&Carry supermarket in Darajani, the intellectuals' *baraza* close to the *manispaa* (the Municipality), the fishermen's *baraza* in Funguni, the Hamali (porters and rickshaw-pullers) *baraza* in Mkunazini and Darajani, as well as the taxi drivers′ *baraza* in lower Vuga street, Shangani, Forodhani and Darajani, etc., and numerous others, all around Stone Town. These *baraza* have become known for different occupational, communal and religious orientations, and quite a number for their distinct political affiliations, like some of those in Jaws' Corner, which have become famous for their sympathies for the Civic United Front (CUF), Zanzibar's main opposition party.

Today communal *baraza* are characterized by the fact that they are all situated in rather 'public' and 'strategic' places which serve many purposes, such as the market area (Darajani) or well frequented alleyways with many shops (Mkunazini, Kokoni, Gizenga).[16] Many *baraza* are also located in the vicinity of a mosque (such as Ruta, Istiqâma, Malindi), or finally at important places such as Jaws' Corner, where one can also find a coffeemaker,[17] *mbao* and domino-players, a TV set, a sugarcane-juice maker or the 'noticeboard' of the area for 'public announcements'.[18] Consequently, these places attract specific *baraza* such as a particular group of 'morning coffee drinkers', who come to 'their' baraza even from faraway places to get their morning coffee (or night coffee, as in Gizenga) from a specific

---

[16] These *baraza* are frequented, consequently, only during business hours.

[17] There are, in fact, quite a number of coffee-makers in Stone Town, such as in Jaws' Corner, in Gizenga Street (corner Cathedral Street, but only in the evening), at the Cash&Carry Supermarket in Darajani, in Narrow Street and Malindi, at the Passing Show Hotel in Malindi, at Mskiti Ruta, those close to the former Empire and Majestic Cinemas, at Muzamil's store in Darajani as well as in Mlandege market. In former times, these coffee-makers were mostly itinerant and moved from place to place selling their coffee. In recent times, they have become more attached to specific places and tried to attract customers to their places (Adam Shafi Adam, personal communication, 2.4.2005).

[18] Such as 'what is on in tonight's TV', 'who is going to give what kind of lecture in Barwani mosque', 'how did Manchester United play against Liverpool', etc.

coffee-maker. In addition, major places and their *baraza* also attract film-viewers (in the evening) or groups of card, domino or *mbao* players (usually in the afternoon). In recent times, however, the character of the evening *baraza* has been changing, as an increasing number of families have acquired private TV sets and can thus receive the numerous TV programmes offered by different providers by satellite dish. As a consequence video shops are closing down, and only those who cannot afford to buy a TV set still meet in the evenings in front of a communal set. These public video evenings are still financed by the *baraza* of the film-viewers, who usually pool the money to rent a film.[19]

Jaws' Corner, for instance, is today the home of numerous *baraza*, and during most parts of the day it is possible to meet simultaneously at least five or six *baraza*, as different *baraza* meet at different times of the day on the same spot. However, the most permanent *baraza* are the old men (*wazee*) of the area: scholars, teachers, retired bureaucrats and some traders from the northern Baghani quarter (i.e. Lebanon Brothers' Corner); the businessmen of upper eastern Soko Mohogo, mostly local traders of 'Arab' origin; the businessmen of upper western Soko Mohogo, mostly local traders of 'Indian' origin; the young dropouts and ne'er-do-wells of the area; the pious, affiliated with Soko Mohogo (Barwani) mosque and its imâm; and the residents of the neighbouring houses in the northern outlet of Soko Mohogo towards Darajani. Finally, there are always some passers-by who come to Jaws' Corner to drink coffee, chat and play cards or *mbao*, in addition to all those who pass through this area on their way to work and business, and who eventually stop for a moment to chat and exchange greetings.[20]

With respect to the social character of the Zanzibar Stone Town *baraza*, it should be noted that membership may appear to be rather

[19] Muhammad Alî, personal communication, 31.7.2004.

[20] As Georg Deutsch has been working on Soko Mohogo and Jaws' Corner in particular, I refer the reader to his work for more detailed information.

informal: there is in fact no formal membership, no membership fees or membership cards as in more formal associations, parties or unions. Yet membership is defined all the same: therefore everybody may theoretically join any *baraza*. As each *baraza* has a specific character, however, some may be more 'open' than others.[21] Thus, some *baraza* may be perceived as rather hermetic, its members probably stopping their conversation, possibly on sensitive issues such as politics, whenever an unknown person tries to join: one would have to be invited, essentially, to become a permanent member of such a *baraza*.[22] Recruitment is thus a process of conscious inclusion, to be initiated by the members of the respective *baraza*. Living in a specific neighbourhood, regularly passing by a certain *baraza* and respectfully greeting the people there, sticking to the rules of *heshima* (respect) and *adabu* (proper and good manners), the established rules of public as well as '*baraza* etiquette', having a friend or friends in the *baraza*, or having similar occupational, religious or political interests and orientations may help to speed up the process of being invited to join a specific *baraza* eventually; but they do not constitute an automatic transition from non-membership to membership, from exclusion to inclusion.

Most *baraza* are open, however, and welcome any 'non-member' to join, either on a permanent or a temporary basis, even for short periods of time, although some degree of continuity of residence in a specific area may help to speed up one's integration. The varying

[21] Some *baraza* may develop specific strategies to keep outsiders away. Thus, the 'intellectuals' *baraza*', close to the *Manispaa* (Municipality), excluded a night-guard from a neighbouring building who was suspected to be a government informer. The members of the *baraza* knew that this night-guard was afraid of death and diseases and consequently started to chat about these topics each time he came to sit down with them, until he eventually gave up (Abdul Sheriff, personal communication, 22.7.2004). Another *baraza* (of Comorians) in Kisimamajongoo would even disperse when unknown people approached, in order to reconvene later (Bi Meffert, personal communication, 4.8.2004).

[22] Personal communications from Hassan Mwakimako, 20.4.2004, and Mw. Idris, 20.5.2004.

open ness or closed-ness of *baraza* shows that it is very difficult to translate the concept into one of Max Weber's 'ideal types': Most of what is said about the *baraza* may be true in most cases, but not necessarily for all. Due to the semi-public, semi-formal, semi-open character of *baraza*, they defy any effort to classify them: *baraza* may, in fact, be described using the particle 'semi' in many respects.

The 'semi-character' of the *baraza* is also reflected in the character of *baraza* conversations, the *mazungumzo ya baraza* (or *kupiga soga*, i.e. chatting), which are semi-public, i.e. not 'official', though not really private either. In addition, *mazungumzo ya baraza* are different from formalized forms of public discourse, such as the *mihadhara*, the public lecture (for a further discussion of the *mihadhara* as another form of organization of the public sphere, see below). With respect to the *baraza* etiquette in Mombasa, Swartz mentions that *baraza* members avoid gossip: 'Each man is greeted on arrival by everyone already there with a handshake and a greeting consisting minimally of 'salaam aleikhum' (*sic*) and generally of a considerably more elaborate sort. This is true even when the gathering is very large. Thirty or forty men were the most I ever observed at a baraza, with five to eight being more usual, but whatever its size, greetings occupy a good deal of the group's time. The tone of the barazas I attended, whatever their particular content might be, was decorous, dignified, and restrained. The participants were invariably good humoured and agreeable in their relations with one another...' (Swartz 1991: 251). *Mazungumzo ya baraza* are therefore not necessarily 'chatty', though men in Zanzibar do not necessarily decline a 'good chat' as they seem to do in Mombasa. Usually, *baraza* conversations focus on specific topics of conversation, which the members of the *baraza* then discuss in a more or less structured way, though again topics may vary wildly, from politics and marriages to new fashions or the effects of aphrodisiacs.[23] An important

---

[23] Abdul Sheriff, personal communication, 19.6.2004.

feature of *baraza* conversation, however, is that discussions have to follow the established rules of *baraza* etiquette, which privileges its elder (*wazee*) over its younger members. This does not mean that the young are excluded from *baraza* conversations. Often, the question of age does not even arise, as the members of a *baraza* are of roughly the same age.

Baraza may therefore acquire a multitude of forms (*aina*) which have in common the fact that members of the *baraza* are usually a group of people following specific rules of conduct that are binding on them all. As such, *baraza* are natural networks of people who have known each other for some time and trust each other. As a consequence, *baraza* have acquired manifold functions: they provide security, and members of a *baraza* may vouch for each other and even lend each other money in case of need. Thus, Shaykh Masoud b. Alî ar-Riyâmî was famous 'to stand for any who entered his baraza' (Aley 1994, n.p.). Also, *baraza* go out and organize picnics in the *shamba* areas, especially in the month of Ramadhan, either for a day or even a weekend, and collect money for such purposes. Money may also be collected, of course, for the needy, for burials, for *maulidi* ceremonies, for parties and marriage ceremonies (*arusi*), and *baraza* members are usually also be the first to be invited to such festivities (Mw. Idris, personal communication, 19.7.2004). *Baraza* may thus be seen as a *lieu de sociabilité*, an important social institution, which ultimately also provides 'education', not only in the direct sense of *wazee* helping schoolchildren with their homework, but also in a broader sense, as places where the 'rules of social life' are practised as, for instance, with respect to the different ways of solving communal problems (Valcke 1999: 338).

As *baraza* are usually groups of people (mostly men) who chat and discuss all kind of seemingly banal things such as neighbourhood affairs or marriage arrangements, or comment on people passing by, a *baraza* may not even be perceived by outsiders as such an important *lieu de sociabilité* or a 'basic cell' of Zanzibar's social and political life, or, if perceived at all, may be seen simply as a group of men sitting 'idle', a standing 'handicap' to any kind of economic development. The manifold if hidden (or better: not very spectacular, visible) functions of the *baraza* in Zanzibar's social, political and economic life may explain, however, why they have so far not come under attack from, for instance, the *ansâr as-sunna*, the local activist Muslims,[24] or some 'development-minded' technocrats as an 'awful waste of time', a 'typical expression of the men's laziness'.

The *Baraza* as 'Gendered Space'[25]

So far, the impression may have been created that *baraza* are an almost purely male affair. However, there are numerous female in-door *baraza* or 'salons'. Which usually meet inside houses or in the courtyard of a house (*ua*).[26] And while women still tend to meet inside houses in most parts of Stone Town, this is again not true for Ng'ambo, where women form *baraza* outside their own houses in the evening, in particular after *maghrib* prayers. These female *baraza* could be seen as an extension of the houses' female sphere into the street. Female *baraza* have also started to expand into Stone Town recently, mostly through immigrants from Pemba, where female public *baraza* seem to be part of local social structures (Mw. Idris, personal communication, 20.5.2004). At the same time, female public *baraza* are not totally new or unknown in Stone Town either. Thus, there are at least three well-known female *baraza* in Shangani, Soko Mohogo and Vuga, and recently some more have formed in Vuga (at least one), Malindi (at least two) and Hurumzi (three) (personal observation, July/August 2004). So far, however, there are no mixed *baraza*, and most men in Stone Town still claim that *baraza* are male affairs. *Baraza* could thus still be seen as a visible

---

[24] Who are also called *watu wa bidaa*, the 'people of the innovations', as they tend to attack certain 'un-Islamic' innovations as *bida*.

[25] This term is derived from Low and Lawrence-Zuniga 2003: 13.

[26] See Saleh 2004: 16.

symbol of the male domination of Zanzibar Stone Town's public sphere.

With respect to female *baraza* in Mombasa, Swartz mentions that 'women´s gatherings are less formal and structured than men´s are. Unlike men´s gatherings, which almost always involve the same men meeting at the same place, at the same hour, and lasting some period of time, women come together whenever and wherever it is convenient and desirable. A woman may pop over to a neighbor´s house to borrow a cup of sugar, and while there the two may chat for a long or a short period depending on how busy the two of them are and how interesting their conversation becomes. Other women, if they are free and so inclined, may join the conversation and a casual group of four or five women might thus assemble. The same group of women could come together again within a short period of time, or no more than two of them might talk together again for weeks. Like the men's, the women´s gatherings are spontaneous, casual and irregular. Another difference between men's and women's gatherings is that in the latter, I am told, there is little or no reluctance to discuss particular people and events concerning them. Tales of who is doing what and with or whom are as common among the women´s groups as they are rare among the men´s. Also unlike the men´s groups, among the women interaction rather often includes heated statements, arguments, and personal remarks including compliments and insults. Women share their joys, sorrows, and angers with one another rather freely; men hardly do so at all' (Swartz 1991: 251).

In Zanzibar, *baraza* play a major role with respect to social control of the public sphere, as the members of a *baraza* usually remark on what is going on in a specific quarter. Also, the space around a *baraza* could be seen as a stage on which people perform to specific rules and are under constant supervision. This is particularly evident with respect to the movement of women. As a rule, women allowed to leave their houses in their *buibui*, the local form of the *hijâb*,[27] and to visit other women in other houses.[28] A major objection of Zanzibari men to women leaving the house since the late nineteenth century has been that they did so in the original form of the *buibui*,[29] which covered the women's faces completely and allowed them to leave houses incognito, the *buibui* giving them anonymity as well as inapproachability (see Fair 2001: 64ff.).

For men, this kind of complete coverage represented a lingering threat, as women could go where they wanted to go and allegedly could also do what they wanted to do, without being recognized. The 'modern' *buibui*, which leaves the women's faces free, has therefore not only strengthened male control over the movement of women, but has also made 'female' movement more transparent to the men sitting in their *baraza*. Consequently, it is not surprising that the move towards the '*niqâb*', i.e. the full veil which covers the face and seems to be mostly worn by the women of the *anâr as-sunna* groups, is again seen by some men as an implicit threat to male control of women's movements. In fact, women wearing a '*niqâb*' are often said to be prostitutes 'in reality' who move 'incognito' from house to house.

However, when I asked my *baraza* friends whether they would really did recognize these veiled ladies, they would consistently deny this 'stupid' assumption, and lectured me on how to tell women apart properly by their way of moving, talking and dressing, their henna patterns, sandals, and other little ways. Thus, the assumption that veiled women are part of a theoretically threatening, because anonymous, mass (as well as, of course, an oppressed one) appears to be a

---

[27] Today, the *buibui* does not cover the face any more.

[28] Even if it is possible, today, to see an increasing number of local women (in addition to those from the mainland) moving in public in *kangas*, costumes or western dress, in particular, blue jeans.

[29] Which was called the 'spider', as it was a construction of wires placed on the head which gave the *buibui* a tent-like appearance (see Fair 2003: 64ff.).

rather 'philological' (or, in German '*weltfremd*') idea and perhaps should only be applied to those social contexts in which women are indeed compelled to wear a style of *niqâb* which makes them 'unrecognizable', especially in metropolitan contexts. In a 'small' society such as Zanzibar, where that kind of (male) social control is inconceivable, women remain 'individuals' even when fully veiled, as they are largely free to follow their own desires with respect to fashion, even though outsiders would probably (if erroneously) claim that *buibui* or *niqâb* veiling are hardly amenable to 'fashionable designs'.[30]

Baraza discussions consequently revolve not only around issues of public morality and the question of women moving incognito in Zanzibar's streets, but also on the different forms of veiling up and down.[31] These fashions of the veil are perceived, in truly cosmopolitan pop-culture terms, after popular films: thus, in the 1950s and 1960s fully veiled women were called Vi-Zorro, while women in *niqâb* are nowadays addressed as 'Ninjas'.[32] The case of Zanzibar shows, however, that processes of veiling up and veiling down are not necessarily connected to specific ideological motivations. In late 2003 and early 2004, for instance, female teenagers 'suddenly' started to wear the *niqâb* in considerable numbers, yet, in a rather 'fashionable' way: i.e. the *niqâb* was beautifully adorned and worn in a rather conspicuous way, alongside equally fashionable sunglasses and sandals. This movement of female teenagers veiling up was not at all motivated in religious terms, however: rather, the female

---

[30] Of course, fashion exerts a powerful pressure on women as well. Thus, women who want to conform to the changing styles of local fashion, as influenced by different sources of inspiration, such as India, the Gulf States, Iran and the West, as well as competing African styles of fashion, have to spend considerable sums of money on dress and may therefore switch – for some time, at least – to the 'uniform' black *buibui* which allows women to economize.

[31] For the dynamics of 'veiling up and down', see Linda Herrera in *ISIM Newsletter*, 6 October 2000.

[32] Abdul Sheriff, personal communication, 15.8.2003.

teenagers in question argued that they 'were so smashingly beautiful, that men would die if they could see our faces'. At the same time, these rascally young ladies moved in rather conspicuous ways, i.e. in groups of three or four, through the narrow alleyways of Stone Town, chatting audibly and making caustic remarks about 'men', including those who were sitting (like me) in the *baraza* they were passing by (Marloes van der Bijl, personal communication, 15.7.2004; also personal observation). In this case, processes of veiling up in Zanzibar should be seen as an expression of a very local 'micro-fashion', not as the expression of a 'macro-fashion' of the wider Islamic ecumenism, which might be linked with ideological notions of 'proper Islamité'.

Baraza and Cosmopolitanity

Baraza are natural places for the exchange of information, not only as far as specific areas in Zanzibar Stone Town or Ng'ambo are concerned: as *baraza* usually meet outside houses, and as there is constant interaction between the different *baraza*, members of a *baraza* are perfectly informed about anything going on in town, and ideas pass quickly from one *baraza* to the next. Yet, networks of information are not confined to local news: at the time of the impending war against Iraq, in February 2003, for instance, everybody listened to the radio as well as the TV news, and discussed, in addition, a range of local and international papers. Members of at least some *baraza* therefore had a choice of at least six, seven or eight different sources of information, in particular CNN, the BBC World Service, the Swahili service of Deutsche Welle,[33] the local TV programme, the local radio programme and Radio Tanzania Dar es-

[33] The Swahili service of Deutsche Welle actually became very popular in the context of the Iraq war, as it was regarded as 'neutral' by contrast to the BBC or even CNN.

Salam, plus different newpapers such as *Dira, Maarifa, Nasaha, Zanzibar Leo* or *Mtanzania.*[34]

Most people were therefore probably better informed about things going globally than most Europeans or North Americans. As a consequence, the questions I was asked, when chatting with members of *baraza*, were often rather specific. In summer 2002, they often referred to the vast floods in the lower Elbe river valley in eastern Germany and how the German government was coming to terms with this catastrophe politically. In summer 2003, by contrast, I had to discuss extensively, in several *baraza*, a question raised by Salim Ahmad Salim in a public *mihadhara.*[35] In these discussions, my co-disputants not only displayed a thorough knowledge of African politics and history, but also surprising insights into European (as well as world) politics, in addition to a well-grounded knowledge of world economics, the development of trade unions in Europe and a series of other issues. Their sources were not only the locally accessible media, but also the life-experiences of a number of members of *baraza* who had been to Europe, North America, East Asia and Australia. One of my local interlocutors, Bwana Saleh Saloum, for example, had worked for a period of five years in the Quelle textile factory in Fürth, Bavaria, and had acquired a working

[34] In addition, there are other informal sources of information, gossip and rumor, such as the barber's shop, which were of considerable importance as a market place for information in pre-radio times (Mw. Idris, personal communication, 19.6.2004).

[35] The former OAU President had asked why some poor African countries such as Senegal were rather well off in political terms, while some rich countries such as Nigeria seemed to be suffering a permanent political crisis. My discussants not only pointed out to me that Salim's argument was not quite convincing, as there were also poor African countries suffering from political crisis, such as Somalia, while some rich countries such as Botswana appeared to be rather stable. In the end, questions of stability and instability in Africa would boil down to the question of whether outside forces were interested in destabilizing African countries or not. Multinational companies would profit, it was felt, from processes of disintegration, while on the other hand some European countries, such as France, had a historical record of stabilizing countries such as Senegal.

knowledge of the Franconian dialect, while another friend, Bwana Ahmedi, had seen most of the important harbours and port cities of the world while working as a seamen before retiring finally to Zanzibar, where he joined one of the Jaws' Corner *baraza*. The networks of information of individual members of a *baraza* may thus reach out over long distances, even to Franconia, through relatives, friends or acquaintances living abroad, in Oman, the Gulf States, Yemen, Britain, Singapore or Malaysia, networks that may be activated to mobilize financial, intellectual or political support. As such, *baraza* are not only the most local and most grassroots sorts of institutions possible, they are at the same time truly translocal and cosmopolitan, representing as such the 'polyphonous' character of Zanzibar´s location in East Africa's 'global now'.

I have used the term 'cosmopolitan' here in a rather conscious manner, as 'cosmopolitanity' (and 'being cosmopolitan') is often quoted, in Zanzibar, as being a major feature of the Zanzibarian national character (or at least self-imagination). In the Zanzibarian context, we could therefore define cosmopolitanity (Kiswahili *mchanganyiko*; literally 'mixture, amalgam'), as the 'natural acceptance of difference' (Abdul Sheriff, personal communication, 19.6.2004), i.e. as the perception of differences as part of everyday life and routines which do not have to be negotiated any more. In cosmopolitan contexts, differences are rather seen as an integral part of the cultural, religious or political imagination of a specific person, group, community or society. In this sense, cosmopolitanity has been a major, although not the only characteristic feature of Zanzibari life since the nineteenth century.

Zanzibar was indeed characterized in the nineteenth and twentieth centuries by its religious and ethnic diversity. Apart from the different Muslim (Sunni-Shâfi`î, Sunni-Hanafî, Shî`î-ithna `asharî, Ismâ`îlî – both Khoja and Bohora, and Ibadî) denominations, there were also influential Christian (Goan-Catholic, Anglican, Catholic, Lutheran), Hindu (several), Bahâ'î, Zoroastrian and even Buddhist groups. In ethnic terms, similarly, Zanzibar was not only home to an 'indigenous' population (Hadimu, Wapemba, Watumbatu), but also to a large spectrum of immigrant groups which had come to Zanzibar from many different places at different times: African mainlanders (Nyamwezi, Makonde and others), Comorians, Somaal, Bajuni, Hadhramis, Umanis, Baluchis, Persians, Gujaratis and Cutchis, as well as a small European community, all united by Kiswahili as the common language of communication.[36]

After the revolution of 1964, however, this religious and ethnic diversity was contested by the politics of the Karume government, which stressed Zanzibar's 'Africanité' and subsequently implemented politics of 'othering' which led to an exodus of many Indians, Arabs and even Comorians, who were not regarded any more as 'indigenous' Zanzibarians. The revolution led to an increasing narrowing of Zanzibar's range of ethnic and religious orientations and to a loss of cosmopolitanity. After 1964, Zanzibar experienced a process of ethnic and religious 'homogenization' which constituted a clear break with her cosmopolitan legacy of the past. Since the early 1980s, this process of ethnic and ideological closure has been stopped and reversed, though not in conscious political terms, as from time to time the ruling party still employs strategies of othering to marginalize the opposition. Yet, economic liberalization and the increasing integration of Zanzibar into Tanzanian mainstream policies have led to the return of exiled Zanzibaris, if only for holidays and the cultivation of old ties of friendship and kinship. This process has consequently led to a certain reassertion of Zanzibar's cosmopolitanity, which is valued at least by the people in the

[36] British colonial officers indeed had to acquire a working knowledge of Kiswahili in Zanzibar and had to pass an examination in it before being allowed to rise in the hierarchy of administrative positions. Some British officials were rather proud of their knowledge of Kiswahili, and one of them, William Hollingsworth (1896-1981), who had been working in the Department of Education from 1922 to 1944, even became a lecturer in Kiswahili at the School of Oriental and African Studies in London in the 1950s and 1960s and wrote a grammar of Kiswahili.

street and the *baraza*. I was personally confronted with this reassertion of Zanzibar's cosmopolitan character when, on 3 August2004, I met Khâlid Muhammad al-Sa`îd, a son of Sultan Abdallâh b. Khalîfa (r. 1961-63), who had come back to Zanzibar for the first time in his life after the revolution, as well as the leading member of his family, the formerly ruling Bû Sa`îdî dynasty, in order to look at some family pictures in the National Archives. After 1964, Khâlid Muhammad al-Sa`îd became a member of the Zanzibari diaspora, which could be regarded as the translocal expression of Zanzibar's cosmopolitanity in 'exile'. He grew up in Britain (Portsmouth), settled down in Oman, started a company in the Emirates, and had now come back to Zanzibar. Like many exiled Zanzibaris, he still spoke Kiswahili as his preferred language, as well as English and Arabic. With the return of exiled Zanzibaris from Britain, the United States, the Gulf, India, East Africa, Oman, Australia and even Hong Kong, Zanzibar's contemporary cosmopolitan cocktail is experiencing another round of re-mixing, which is defined, like earlier 'cocktails', by both (new) local and translocal choices, as well as by contemporary global power structures.

The Zanzibari example shows that cosmopolitanity is a process, not a 'state', and one which reflects, first of all, efforts to transcend purely national frameworks (in cultural, economic, political, religious etc. terms). Cosmopolitanity must also be understood as the result of an ongoing process of negotiation which constantly defines, re-defines and re-arranges its specific components. It is thus changing in character constantly, potentially increasing and decreasing, andthus reflecting the specific choices of a specific society in a specific period of time with respect to the specific composition of the cosmopolitan cocktail. However, the Zanzibari case also shows that there are historical periods in which cosmopolitanity is contested, as, for instance, in the colonial period or after the revolution in 1964, when different strategies of 'othering' were employed for political reasons in order to marginalize specific groups such as 'Arabs' or 'mainlanders'. However, these policies of 'othering' were criticized locally as being opposed to the 'innate cosmopolitan nature' of the Zanzibarians, who had allegedly accepted racial mixing as a rule. In order to prove their point, for instance, Zanzibaris would refer to independent Zanzibar's first postage stamp, which depicted a mosque, a church and a Hindu temple.

This working definition of cosmopolitanity is confirmed by the academic discussion of the term which has emerged from a background of long debates in cosmopolitan studies.[37] Turino (2000) thus defines the term 'cosmopolitan' as 'objects, ideas and cultural positions which are widely diffused throughout the world and yet are specific only to certain portions of the populations within given countries'. Cosmopolitanism can consequently be described as a 'specific type of cultural formation and constitution of habitus that is translocal in purview' (Turino 2000: 7). As cosmopolitanism involves specific practices, material technologies and conceptual frameworks, it also has to be realized in specific locations and in the lives of actual people and will be shaped by and be somewhat particular to each locale. Cosmopolitan formations are therefore always simultaneously both local and translocal. At the same time, cosmopolitanism is different from other types of transnational cultural formations such as diasporas or overseas immigrant communities because it lacks the specific factual or symbolic grounding around a single homeland or place of origin. Cosmopolitan cultural

---

[37] As influenced in particular by Clifford (1992), Brennan (1997) and Cheah and Robbins (1998). In their volume, Cheah and Robbins provide a long overview of debates on cosmopolitanity and cosmopolitics; see in particular Amanda Anderson's contribution, in which cosmopolitanism is defined as 'a flexible term, whose forms of detachment and multiple affiliation can be variously articulated and variously motivated. In general, cosmopolitanism endorses reflective distance from one's cultural affiliations, a broad understanding of other cultures and customs, and a belief in universal humanity' (Anderson 1998: 267). Additional major contributions to the debate on cosmopolitanity include those by Arjun Appadurai and Carol Breckinridge (1988) and Ulf Hannerz (1990).

formations draw on and comprise diffuse sources from an increasing number of local sites (Turino 2000: 7-8). As the Zanzibarian example shows, these cosmopolitan formations imply constant and differing re-mixes, which again reflect the influence of specific power structures in a specific setting at a specific period of time.In their manifold forms, the *baraza* in Zanzibar represent the constant changes in Zanzibari society and thus seem to fit the notion of cosmopolitanity rather well.

By Way of Conclusion: How I Became a Member of a *Baraza*...

Having passed by numerous *baraza* during my stay in Zanzibar in summer 2002,[38] and having chatted with some of their members for some time, I was rather surprised when I was invited one day by a member of the *baraza za wazee* in Jaws' Corner to join them. Having passed by at least twice every day for a couple of weeks, having respectfully greeted all the members present and having told them about the events of my day, my work in the National Archive, the interesting and curious things I had found there, the questions that had come up and my problems with Kiswahili, I never received the impression that I was anything more than a welcome break in the stifling boredom of their early evenings. However, as soon as I was invited to join the *baraza* of the *wazee* (and to shut up), I became aware that to be informed about anything going on in Zanzibar, or indeed the world, I only had to sit in 'my' *baraza* and listen.

At the same time, I was, of course, still welcome to pass on bits and pieces of information about Zanzibari history which I had read about in the archive and which turned out to be important for the *wazee* and their interpretation of local history. In addition, I constituted a further source of information to feed the curiosity of my fellow *baraza* members with respect to things going on in Europe,

[38] As well as before that, in early 2001, and later, in spring and summer 2003, and summer 2004.

and I was surprised to learn, just how well informed these truly cosmopolitan *wazee* were. I therefore realized that sitting, watching and listening made the *wazee* of my *baraza* the true sociologists of their quarter, and by extension, made them quite knowledgeable with respect to all kind of worldly and unworldly affairs. In the end, I probably learned more 'about' Zanzibari society by sitting and listening in a *baraza* than by sitting and reading in the Zanzibar National Archive.

Bibliography

Aley, Juma (1994): *Enduring Links*, Zanzibar: Union Printing Press.

Appadurai, Arjun (1996): *Modernity at Large: Cultural Dimensions of Globalization*, Minneapolis: University of Minnesota Press.

Augé, Marc (1992/2000): *Non-Places: Introduction to an Anthropology of Supermodernity*, London: Verso.

Bacuez, Pascal (2001): *De Zanzibar à Kilwa: relations conflictuelles en pays swahili*, Louvain: Peeters.

Bakari, Muhammad (2001): *The Democratization Process in Zanzibar: A Retarded Transition*, Hamburg: Institut für Afrikakunde.

Beck, Rose Marie (2003): Verbale und nonverbale Kleiderkommunikation am Indischen Ozean (Swahili, Ostafrika), in: *Feministische Studien*, 2 (special issue: Streitpunkte in islamischen Kontexten): 239-53.

Brennan, Timothy (1997): *At Home in the World: Cosmopolitanism Now*, Cambridge: Harvard University Press.

Burgess, Anthony (2002): Cinema, Bell Bottoms, and Miniskirts: Struggles over Youth and Citizenship in Revolutionary Zanzibar, *The International Journal of African Historical Studies*, 35: 2-3, 287-314.

Cheah, Pheng; Robbins Bruce (1998): *Cosmopolitics: Thinking and Feeling beyond the Nation*, Minneapolis: University of Minnesota Press.

Clifford, James (1992): Travelling Cultures, in: Grossberg, L.; Neson, C.; Treichler, P. (eds.): *Cultural Studies*, New York: Routledge.

Crozon, Arielle (1998): Les maskani et le parti: une alliance sans entente, in: Le Guennec, F.; Coppens; Parkin, D. (eds.): *Autorité et pouvoir chez les Swahili*, Paris: 41-60.

Deutsch, Jan Georg (2002): The Indian Ocean World and a Very Small Place in Zanzibar, in: Reinwald, Brigitte (ed.): *Space on the Move: Transformations of the Indian Ocean Seascape in the 19th and 20th century*, Berlin: Klaus Schwarz Verlag.

Fair, Laura (2001): *Pastimes and Politics: Culture, Community and Identity in Post-abolition Urban Zanzibar, 1890-1945*, Athens: Ohio University Press.

Giddens, Anthony (1997): *Konsequenzen der Moderne* (engl. 1990: *The Consequences of Modernity*), Frankfurt: Suhrkamp.

Habermas, Jürgen (1962 and 1990): *Strukturwandel in der Öffentlichkeit* (engl. 1989: *The Structural Transformation of the Public Sphere*), Frankfurt: Suhrkamp.

Harvey, David (1996 and 2004): *Justice, Nature and the Geography of Difference*, Oxford: Blackwell.

Haugerud, Angelique; Njogu, Kimani (1991): State Voices in the Countryside: Politics and the Kenyan Baraza, *African Studies* Working Papers No. 159, Boston: African Studies Center, Boston University.

Herrera, Linda (2000): Downveiling: Shifting Socio-religious Practices in Egypt, *ISIM Newsletter*, 6.

Kresse, Kai (2003): The Swahili Baraza: Socializing Intellectual Practice in Old Mombasa Town, University of Edinburgh: Paper presented at departmental seminar.

Lachenmann, Gudrun (2004): Weibliche Räume in muslimischen Gesellschaften Westafrikas, *Peripherie*, 95 (24, special issue: Gender und Islam): 322-40.

Launay, Robert; Soares, Benjamin (1999): The Formation of an Islamic Sphere in French Colonial West Africa, *Economy and Society*, 28: 467-89.

Loimeier, Roman (2007): Sit Local, Think Global: The Baraza in Zanzibar, in: A. Tayob (ed.): *Islam and Public Life in Africa*, London: Oxford University Press.

Low, Setha M.; Lawrence-Zuniga Denise (2003): *The Anthropology of Space and Place*, Oxford: Blackwell.

Ruete, Emily (1998): *Memoirs of an Arabian Princess from Zanzibar*, Zanzibar: Gallery Publications.

Saleh, Mohamed Ahmed (2004): Going with the Times (Kwenda na wakati). Conflicting Swahili Norms and Values Today, in: Caplan, Pat; Topan, Farouk (eds.): *Swahili Modernities*, London: Sage Publications.

Smith, Jonathan Z. (1987): *To Take Place: Toward Theory in Ritual*, Chicago: The University of Chicago Press.

Swartz, Marc J. (1995): *The Way the World Is: Cultural Processes and Social Relations among the Mombasa Swahili*, Berkeley: University of California Press.

Sheriff, Abdul (1995): *The History and Conservation of Zanzibar Stone Town*, London: James Currey and Ohio University Press.

Topan, Farouk (2007): From Coastal to Global: The Erosion of the Swahili Paradox, in: Loimeier, R.; Seesemann, R. (eds.): *Dini na Dunia: The Global Worlds of the Swahili*, Münster: Lit.

Turino, Thomas (2000): *Nationalists, Cosmopolitans and Popular Music in Zimbabwe*, Chicago: The University of Chicago Press.

Valcke, Sandrine (1999): Entrepreneurs: Business à Zanzibar, in: Baroin, Catherine; Constantin, François (eds.): *La Tanzanie contemporaine*, Paris: Karthala-Ifra: 335-48.

Material from the Zanzibar National Archives:

ZNA AB 10/83: Id al-Fitr Baraza.

ZNA AD 5/52: Baraza za Uchumi

ZNA AD 5/63: Baraza la Taifa la Lugha ya Kiswahili

ZNA AD 12/35: Minutes za Baraza-conference: Mkutano wa Baraza kuu Idara ya Futboli

My partners in conversation (in Zanzibar and beyond) were:

Adam Shafi Adam
Bi Fatma Alloo
Bi Marloes van der Bijl
Dr Duchi
José Kagabo

Mw. Ramadhani Kututwa
Prof. Abdalazîz Lodhi
Dr Erich and Bi Vaada Meffert
Mw. Muhammad Idris Muhammad
Dr Hassan Mwakimako
Mw. Muhammad Alî Sa`îd
Bw. Mohammed Ahmad Sâleh
Bw. Sâleh Saloum
Prof. Abdul Muhammad Hussein Sharif
Mw. Faridh Sulaima Sorago
Dr Issa Ziddy

Crossover and Fuzzy Edges in the Swahili *Taarab* Lyric: Some Theoretical Implications

Said A.M. Khamis

> Working right at the limits of several categories and approaches means that one is neither entirely inside nor outside. One has to push one's work as far as one can go: to the borderlines, where one never stops walking on the edge, incurring constantly the risk of falling off one side or the other side of the limit while undoing, redoing, modifying this limit.
>
> Trinh T. Minh-ha

A music complex like *taarab*, characterized by constant flux and interchange between cultures, hints at an art in which 'boundaries' inevitably raise the problematic of 'inside' and 'outside' and how to distinguish one from the other. Though *taarab* is more unstable now than it was twenty years ago, it is in the lyric that 'fuzziness' is strikingly perceptible. Whereas, over time, *taarab's* musical structure(s), singing styles and performance practices have yielded to the pressures of modernity, for a considerable time the lyric itself has resisted any significant change. Only when liberalization policies were introduced in Kenya and Tanzania in the 1990s has the lyric become visibly erratic, allowing other poetic styles to transgress its hitherto stable topography.

The aim of this essay is to examine the 'nature' of the new lyric, which is constantly re-mapping itself through a confluence with otherwise incompatible styles. The protean form of the new lyric, I argue, is replete with certain theoretical implications, as the change itself is not easily amenable, especially when one considers why it has taken place so 'pervasively' in recent years.

Features of Traditional *Taarab* Lyric

From the bulk of *taarab* lyrics circulating in East Africa from 1920, it is evident that, from the outset, the lyrics followed an earlier Swahili verse tradition that had adopted Arabic poetic conventions. The lyric, with its fixed patterns of syllabic measure(s), caesuras and rhyme scheme(s), usually consists of a triplet or quatrain with a rhyme at the end of each caesura, except for refrains which 'may' have variation in syllabic measure(s) and rhyme scheme(s).

(i) The Triplet:

—-6 metre—a —-6 metre—b
—-6 metre—a —-6 metre—b
—-6 metre—a —-6 metre—b

Buduri[1]

Buduri kanipendeza ikhwani nawahubiri
Buduri hunisangaza kila nikimbasiri
Buduri ni muijiza kwa haiba na fahari

The full moon beguiles me, I am telling you people
The full moon stuns me, whenever I look at her appearance
The full moon is a 'miracle', in her beauty and glory

(my translation)

[1] Waimbaji wa Juzi (1966:25).

(ii) The Quatrain:

—8 metre--f	—8 metre--g
—8 metre--f	—8 metre--g
—8 metre--f	—8 metre--g
—8 metre--h	—8 metre--k
	(chorus and refrain)

Pendo[2]

Risala mwenye adabu tumishi mwenye maana
Fika kwa wangu muhibu kanisalimie sana
Mwambie, 'Ataghadhabu! Watetao hupatana
Pendo za juzi na jana timiza, usizondoe!'

Take this message, my well-mannered and trustworthy servant

Go to my lover and give her my best regards

Tell her, 'Leave off your anger! Those who quarrel do come to terms

Fulfil our love of the past; do not remove it!'

(my translation)

As a rule, the traditional lyric addresses a variety of topics: social, political, cultural, religious, philosophical and psychological. However, the most ecstatically oriented lyric is about tender love, which may be particularly amorous, though often in subdued style. The individual verses share certain traits in that they are highly stylized and stereotypical, presenting the amorous theme through standardized expressions.

---

[2] Diwani ya Al-Ghassaniy Muyaka (1940:106).

The New Lyric and its Features

From the later half of the 1990s, some laxity appeared in the rules for composing the traditional lyric, opening up the traditional lyric at the margins by blending its features with those of other forms hitherto regarded as 'deviant'. This has resulted in a lyric called *mipasho*, – a syncretistic form that is structurally aberrant and semantically blunt, if not 'crude', in signification.

The 'erratic' nature of the new lyric is not, in fact, the main theme of this inquiry, for, in Kaminsky's words (1993: 60-1), '[a]ll literary taxonomies tend to lose clarity at the edges and relegate certain borderline phenomena to anomaly.' What is surprising about it is not that a particular terrain has been re-drawn, but the fact that different textual styles move into one another harmoniously. Yet the lyric appears variegated, subverting the usual binary oppositions pure/syncretistic, local/global, traditional/modern, or modern/post-modern. It is a terrain in which (inter)textuality is constantly at work, drawing its energies from alternative histories, chronologies, global media images, 'simulacra' and local urban (sub)culture(s) bubbling out with societal cacophonies, sociolects, cants and colloquialisms. Such a socio-cultural flux finds a correlation with what darts within the new lyric, due to the fact that several stylistic topographies are moving into one another. The 'shape' of the new lyric has the following features.

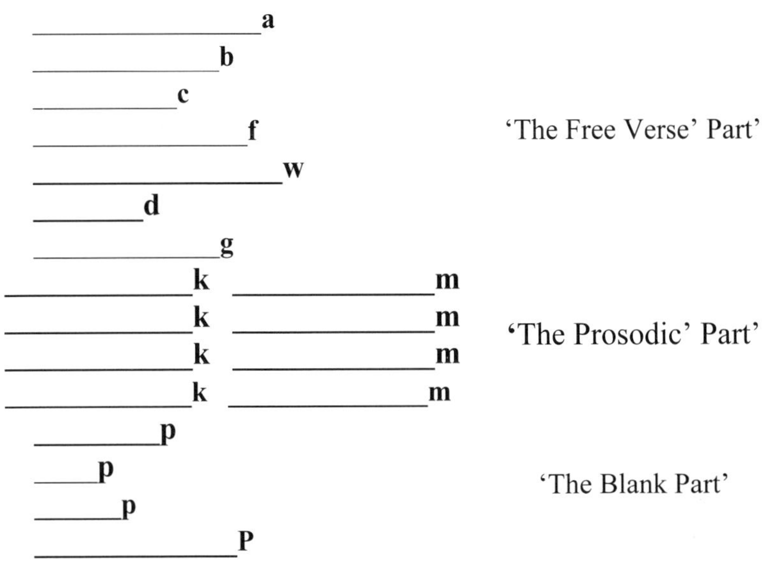

Fuzziness

Fuzziness is due not only to the fragmentary texture of the new lyric, but to a host of other factors. Unlike the traditional lyric, which is expressive, the new lyric is a narrative in which events and episodes are loosely combined and meaning(s) refracted and deferred, subverting stable meaning(s) embodied in the idea of *kujitosheleza*. This is the skill of co-joining linguistic constituents semantically, without which the whole poem is rendered *guni* (deviant). Even in a 'prosodic' fragment of the song *Mimi ni wa Karne ya Ishirini na Moja*, meaning 'I am of the Twenty First Century' by the East African Melody, fuzziness is observable in the analogy between the 'figure' woman and computer which appears incongruent. The association between the computer's high technology and the woman's qualities that render her saleable seems to be comparable at first glance but are actually blurred, discordant, if not strange. This is because the analogy between these objects cannot be based on common vehicle.

Whereas the computer is functionally useful and has high market-value, the woman's qualities are not regarded socially as useful and positive and her value is relegated. The only common attribute that is derivable from the two objects is that: one – the woman, appears to be 'randy' and another – the computer, is just a gadget whose utility is global. Therefore these objects must both be considered as commodity, though not of the same value as we are made to believe in the lyric.

Fuzziness is also engendered by the fact that the lyric is composed from the point of view of what Nicol (2002: 5) calls 'virtual space', in which the composer of the lyric, the singer and audience are all divorced from those aspects of life which are regarded as authentic, genuine and real. A 'structural irony' that revolves around knowledge in art is that there is no such a thing as a fixed meaning or meanings. Any meaning is pregnant with others and can be altered subtly into something quite different through a modulation of tone and context. In fact, as Nicol (5) observes: '[o]ur physical and linguistic space has been colonized by the discourses of the mass media, which constantly recycle images that have been completely detached from their original context and thus rendered meaningless'. Thus, it is not stable or fixed meaning(s)[3] that matter, but the impression and illusion that the singer creates in order to show that *anakwenda na wakati* ('s/he is moving with time'), thus making the language appear highly self-reflexive, as in this 'eulogy' or 'advertisement' of a woman:

Mimi kwenu natesa mutambuwe wezangu
Teknolojiya ya kisasa hiyo ndiyo fani yangu
I am to you a tormentor, you should know that
The modern technology is my specialization
(my translation)

[3] If we say, for example, *Nakupenda*! 'I love you', there is less contention, but if I say *Kinyang'unya si mkeka*, 'An old rag is not a mat', the statement is open to many interpretations.

Code-Mixing

Another feature that makes meaning(s) appear relatively 'blurred' in the lyric is 'code mixing'. The sense of blurring in this case is due to the opacity caused by newly imported terms. Though this is an important strategy in the *taarab* lyric, it has hitherto been based generally on Arabic as the 'foreign' entry. The new lyric often draws on English, though the influence of Arabic is not totally absent. Thus, a change in choice signifies a change in time, as the influence of English is becoming more 'global' and that of Arabic being eclipsed. Indeed, globalization is often associated with the 'power' of English.

In the new lyric, code-mixing manifests itself in two ways. First, foreign items are fully Swahilized, as in <*kwenye netwaki* (network)>, <*nafanya mantenens* (maintenance), *kwa hadiweya* (hardware)>, <*topteni* (top ten)> or <Makrosofti *staili* (microsoft style)> etc. Secondly, there appear to be direct imports from English, as in <darling *n'naye*>, <*kwenye* channel *kusogea*>, <New Millennium>, <conductor *kasema*>, <passenger *'meduwaa*>, <'C' Licence>, <one sweet *hi*yo>, <sorry *kwa huyo siye*> etc.

Co-occurrence of Old and New Images

The juxtaposition of local images formerly used in *ngoma* (local dance), like *bomu, lelemama, kibiriti-ngoma* and *mbwa-kachoka* (*beni*) (now re-appearing in the new lyric after being in disuse for decades[4]), as well as new ones from sociolect, slang, cant and colloquialism (emerging as a sub-cultural idiom), seems to cause semantic obscurity in the new lyric. Utterances like <kinyang'unya si mkeka> (an old rag is no match for a mat), <kibiriti ngoma> (explosive dance beat), <kanzu yako ya rubamba> (your rubamba-dance

---

[4] After the 1964 revolution in Zanzibar some of these *ngoma* disappeared, as the whole cultural landscape was deliberately changed to serve the revolutionary propaganda.

attire), <yangojee ya kilingeni> (wait for real things) and <kiber-enge> (trolley)> which had lost vitality in the past, are now being re-vitalized to fit a new situation. In this case, we can refer more to discursive meaning(s) than fixed and absolute ones, or even to meaning(s) that are rendered meaningless.

New local or (trans)local images found in expressions like <ngangari feki> (fake smartness), <unachemsha> (sweating for nothing), <buzi> (boozer), <mapaparazi> (paparazzi), <kizaizai> (scandalous person) and <taksi-bubu> (unauthorized taxi) emerge out of creative 'spume' as part of urban popular culture, with its cargo mentality, wishful thinking, rivalry, competition and struggle for the fittest, as expressed in the overloaded metaphor *nchi ya bongo*, a reference to Tanzania as being a country in which one has to use tricks to survive.

Repetition

Repetition (call repetition or antiphonality) is also a salient feature of the new lyric. Normally, traditional and new lyrics are both written first before being sung. However, due to the lavish occurrence of call and antiphonal repetitions, the new lyric seems to ascribe more to the flexibility and variation of orality than to the fixity and neatness of the scribal. That notwithstanding, 'length' due to repetition caused by the interface between orality and literacy on the same matrix makes the edges appear more blurred.

Repetition is rated variously in literature. In scribal literature it is normally viewed with caution or as a out-and-out flaw. In oral literature, its merit lies in variation, in which slow and quick tempo, rising and falling tone, intonation waves, pitch, stress, voice quality and the artistic manipulation of the voice provide vibrancy and vitality. In the singing of the new lyric the repetition is superfluous; hence its robust presence is justified by the accompaniment of music and the percussive effect that is intended to capture the audience.

Theorizing Space, Boundary and Mapping

Space as a metaphor, referring to generic categories in literature, is used to account for mobility and interaction by subliming the categories into tangible entities as kinds of maps. Thus, in using the metaphor(s) of 'mapping' the new lyric with all the particular assumptions and practices that cartography involves, a number of theoretical issues can be discussed.

To begin with, 'space' as used in literature is pregnant with ambiguities, as Crang and Thrift (1995: 1) correctly point out: '[T]he problem is not so much that space means very different things, what concepts do not, but that it is used with such abandon that its meanings run into each other before they have been properly interrogated...' This notwithstanding, space in literary theory is often considered as a kind of textual operator used to shift registers, a framed entity that strives to maintain a kind of stability by preserving its internal rules, which give a form a unique shape. Space is thus defined by '[d]eterminable borders and limits, marking its structure, unity and referentiality...' (Henderson 1995: 2).

Crang and Thrifts' suggestion is clearly a rigid, formalistic, intratextual way of looking at space. Texts do not always appear impermeable, especially when one looks at them through binary oppositions such as 'internal/external edge-line of a given text' and/or text's 'internal mechanism versus external/societal drive' as a trigger of change within a text. Thus, the criterion 'containment', which serves to limit the literary canon through its assumption of absolutism, does not offer much apart from its emphasis on inner structural rules as the semiotic grid through which the elements of language relate to each other. This structural view of space is static since it operates as a closed system: it provides a very specific and limited sense of what space might mean.

Tracing Mobility

In studying what may be considered to be a 'newly mapped terrain' of the Swahili *taarab* lyric, an appropriate theoretical parameter would merely be one that sees space as a process and as in process, thus serving to 'deconstruct' the spatial structure itself. There may be several such models. We will briefly concentrate on 'three' that are helpful to this study.

Continuum Model

By using a sense of continuity and fluidity associated with orality, a continuum model can establish where the new comes from, locate where it is, and interrogate its status after the crossover in which orality and literacy merge to form a new self-standing textual terrain. The relevance of this model is tied to the fact that in Africa things are in a state of flux, converging and yet diverging, compelling people to enter a continuum at several points and be caught in a series of interlocking continua. In fact, the continuum model thrives on what Ong (1982: 11) calls 'secondary orality', a kind of '(inter)culturalism' in which orality is sustained by high technology through the media. In the same vein, though differently worded, Mazrui (1986: 97) sees a 'triple heritage' in Africa consisting of a fusion of African indigenous culture with Arab/Islamic and Western/Christian influences: '[A]frica is a cultural bazaar. A wide variety of ideas and values, drawn from different civilizations, competes for the attention of potential African buyers. The marketing of cultures in Africa has been going on for centuries, but a particularly important impact has come from 'Semites' (especially Arabs and Jews) and the 'Caucasians' (especially Western Europeans)'.

Mazrui's 'cultural bazaar' is a boundless artistic mobility for diversity and choice, where decisions to act and react are made in accordance with certain drives, where artists may not just parody the global, but tame or twist it to suit local demands. This is a given 'order' in a cultural milieu, where the 'contact situation' is a strong determiner. It is an 'established status quo', which African artists, like African politicians and businessmen, cannot ignore if they are to fulfil their ulterior motives. Thus, by using a 'local (re)creative force' that incorporates the diverse oral and written traditions within a single framework, the African artist turns a global phenomenon into a creative novelty that serves a given purpose in a given local context.

It is obvious, therefore, that, from its inception in East Africa, *taarab* has never been a static or homogeneous body, but is instead an eclectic composite of a variety of styles with their own autonomies serving different roles and functions. Its various musical and lyrical styles have always been formed to promote the pursuit of different interests by artists: social, cultural, commercial, political and gender-asserting ones. Thus, at any point in time in the history of *taarab*, one can delineate two major categories: the 'élitist' *taarab*, often affiliated to global influences (i.e. Arabic, Indian, Afro-Cuban, Western), and 'popular' *taarab*, which prefers to take on local structures and practices.

By showing such a creative fusion between orality and literacy, between tradition and modernity, between local and transnational influences, the continuum model challenges the theoretical notion that stresses flows of influences as being 'unidirectional', from the 'center' to the 'periphery'. This may be true only in economic, scientific and technological terms, especially in the contemporary situation in which scientific and technological achievements are often regarded as virtue of the West. In culture and the arts, as Bihalji-Merin (1972:2) contends, things are different: '[I]n a certain sense, one could maintain of the highly developed great powers, highly developed that is from the viewpoint of technical civilization, that they have called forth psychic desolation and represent a menace to the life of the creative mind whenever their influence is felt ... [D]isgust with civilization, empty virtuosity and the boundless prospects opened up by the exploration of space have occasioned modern artists to look for new sources for renewal far removed from the world of technological precision.'

(Auto)biographical Approach

In explaining 'the new', one can also resort to an '(auto)biographical model' focused on the artist as the maker of a given art form. As such, s/he is in the perfect position to examine the mood(s) and psycholog(ies) of his/her audience. S/he is also cognizant of current trends, or may opt for dominant stylistic potentials waiting to be experimented on. S/he then constructs his/her work according to the modes and styles that s/he thinks may appeal to the target audience. S/he finally articulates his/her subjective Self as s/he gives shape to certain lyrical forms that may be inspired by, among other things, a certain musical framework in mind. In short, the artist proceeds with certain motive(s) and works them out to let his/her motives affect an art form s/he creates.

Although all this bears some truth, it is politically incorrect to emphasise the 'absolute subjectivism' of a poet, for we know that 'individual creativity' is not fully personal – it contains a great deal of what the artist has internalized from the world(s) s/he lives in. The (auto)biographical approach must therefore go beyond the confines of the personal. It must incorporate a sense of objectivism that challenges the contemporary orthodoxy in literary theory, namely the assumption of an objective and impersonal critical stance. It must point out the dangers of framing by challenging the ways in which identities are categorized. It must, in the words of Henderson (1995:13), '[c]onstruct a fundamentally dialogic relationship between 'author', 'text' and 'reader'. It should invite the potential reader to participate in the interweaving and construction of the ongoing conversation a criticism can be.'

The question of the poet's or poetess's motive and his/her choice of poetic strategy brings us closer to 'why' the *taarab* lyric has changed, and changed recently. It places us in a position to explain why change has taken place and what the new stands for. Within the (auto)biographical space, we are made to see that a consideration of poet's or poetess's intentions goes beyond the descriptive adequacy of the 'cultural imperialism' model, which thrives on the 'mental enslavement' or the 'principle of lulling the mind' and luring one into believing that what comes from the centre is always lustrous, attractive and superior. Instead of basing its assumption on the idea of 'polysemy', the cultural imperialism model uses the notion of a 'singular' standard of taste and of the true meaning of a work of art, i.e. from the point of view of the centre as compared to the periphery. This assumption collapses when one realizes that there are many types of art in the periphery that have resisted the temptation to take up 'the foreign' blindly. Even those art forms whose origins are traceable from the centre have undergone drastic changes to the extent of assuming a 'new authenticity', away from their sources. In the words of Appadurai (1990: 295), '[A]s soon as forces from various metropolises are brought into new societies they tend to become indigenized in one way or another.'

Certainly the composer's intentions play a crucial role in the (auto)biographical approach, but, as Nercessian (2002: 6) rightly argues, even the seemingly uncontroversial idea of the composer's intention is usually unable to impose a correct or incorrect meaning on a work. '[M]ost composers will readily admit that intention is a rather odd matter as far as composing is concerned, and meanings of artworks change considerably as they move from composer to audience to other audience perhaps in a totally different culture' (ibid: 6-7).

By examining the internal incentives that include 'credit wants', that is, the desire of some individuals to bring credit to themselves by initiating change; 'creative wants', in which individuals have the drive to creativity; 'relief and avoidance wants', prompted by the desire to change existing conditions because the individual experiences physical or mental discomfort; and 'the desire for quantitative variation', in which changes occur in society because existing mechanisms do not provide enough of something that is valued, one can gauge from which direction change has evolved and in which direction it is moving. It is only through a combination of several factors that we can plot the contours of change appropriately.

In our case, we see composers' motivations and intentions as a drive that has changed greatly with time in the making of both *taarab* music and its lyrics. In the past, *taarab* was used as a status symbol reflecting the catch phrase *kwenda na wakati* (moving with time), which incorporates a sense of 'modernity' – an idea connected with alleged enlightenment coming from outside through the mass media, especially phonograph record and sound film. *Taarab* music and lyrics were also composed as pasttimes, serving the curiosity of urban populations in plural, multiethnic, cosmopolitan settings. It also existed and flourished as a tool for expressing multiple identities – a view well put by Tadasu Tsuruta (2003), who maintains that *taarab* was used as a means of expressing not only 'pluralism' and 'cosmopolitanism', but also 'rivalry' and 'competition':

> [I]n colonial Tanganyika, popular music and football were the most important genres of popular culture in urban areas then as now. From the 1930s, these modern forms of recreation grew out of a precedent tradition of the competitive dance societies among the Swahili on the coast. In the capital Dar es salaam, various musical and sporting organizations developed in the urban community made up mainly of coast Africans, besides including the migrants from upcountry and the people of Arab descent (ibid.: 195) ... *Taarab* was exclusive and primarily limited membership to the coastal Swahili people, due to its explicitly coastal and Arabic origin. (ibid: 201)

Taarab became visibly commercialized when the audio-cassette was introduced in East Africa. But not until videos entered the market that the commercial value of *taarab* increased twofold. In the 1990s, when East African *taarab* penetrated a new public space by travelling to and being played live in the Gulf, Japan and Western Europe, a new phase of the commercialization of *taarab* began. Since then its commercial role has greatly increased, to such an extent that it has become more of a livelihood to its artists than it was in the past. A combination of sales of audio-cassettes, videos, CDs and the signing of contracts for live performances at political rallies, wedding ceremonies, bars, night clubs and entertainment locales has made it possible for more of its artists to live entirely from their music. This is a relatively new phenomenon, especially in Zanzibar.

Globalization and Post-modern Tendencies

To achieve their goals effectively, traditional and modern artists work on mass psychology, governed by a different urge of *kwenda na wakati*. Nowadays *kwenda na wakati* generally means meeting the West through globalization and its concomitants, such as political and economic liberalization, technological superiority, (tele)imagistic global collage, post-modernist tendencies, conflicts and contests – all replete with illusions and hence with local attempts to understand their elusiveness as well as their latent agendas.

Written along these lines, whether deliberately or unwittingly, the new lyric stands for a 'new era' which is post-modernist, an era that posits life as being at the same time 'real' and 'hyper-real'. Nicol (2002:5) is right in describing this kind of reality as being '[n]o longer something we can take for granted, but is something that we suspect is continually organized and constructed for us by the twin apparatuses of the mass media and the global capitalist economy.'

The post-modern condition is reflected in the text in both style and substance: the fragmentary nature of the text, the loose coherence of the linguistic structures, the fuzziness, the hybridity and intertextuality in which styles and contents negotiate a place in the same location, in which subjects engage in contending personal discourses with manipulative techniques relying on icons, tropes and images. The language used in the lyric marks a change of times so as to generate faith in the audience. Hence, the language distinguishes between the 'verbal' and the structural irony in which 'fake' is regarded as 'real'. The language itself serves as a language of psychopathology or schizophrenia, hysteria, abuse, narcissism, and paranoia. The content is personal laudation and praise. The self-praise is part of a rivalry based on sexism and alcoholism – textual and societal contradictions, permutations or the projection of alternating texts in a multi-layered narrative, self-reflexive images, parody, and linguistic play and games.

Mimi ni wa Karne ya Ishirini na Moja is a good example of the new lyric that represents the spirit of post-modern era. It is a self-eulogy written in metaphors of high-sounding jargon of modern media technology which stand for the idea of *kwenda na wakati*. The lyric itself is full of self-praise, narcissistic elements and abuses and is rendered fuzzy and fragmentary in its syntactic and semantic workings. It is a lyric that has a sense of profuse repetition of the same narratives ('pseudoevents' and spectacles), in which code-mixing recurs stubbornly in a kind of 'metalanguage' that refers to globalization through its metonyms and synecdoche: 'new Millennium', *karne* (century) 'top ten', 'maintenance', 'software', 'Microsoft style', *mepanda chati* (I have risen to the top on the chart), *nina teknolojiya* (I have the technology), *laivu kwa satalaiti* (live through satellite), *kwa sayansi ni mahiri* (I am good at science), *ninaruka kwa rocket* (I am flying in a rocket), *teknolojia ya kisasa* (modern technology).

Interrogating Gender Positions in the New Lyric

When, from the (auto)biographical perspective, one also compares the narratives of several poets or poetesses of both traditional and new *taarab* lyrics, both lyrics appear informed by men's subjective assertion of gender and their self-imposed superiority over women. A closer look at these lyrical styles, however, shows a remarkable distinction between the two. Whereas in the traditional lyric we read of a general tendency to denigrate women by often using tender and romantic images (i.e. women as angels, flowers, fruit(s), birds, gazelles, celestial bodies etc.), in the new lyric women are 'bluntly' described as being randy, satanic, or at best caught up in a vicious circle of fighting not for a man's love, but for his money.

By establishing woman's subjectivism nonetheless, we may look for alternative discourses to counter man's chauvinism, as has always been the case in the *taarab* lyric, where the 'Other' as 'woman' never writes back, but is always written 'to', 'against' and 'about' by the poet. In fact, only a handful of women have composed Swahili poems in Swahili literature. It is therefore man who monopolizes everything except for the *mipasho* dance, with its psychology of competition and rivalry, which is intensified at any performance of *taarab* today and shows negative relationships among women themselves. This is why we do not find any 'true expression' of women's plight in *mipasho*, but only of man's sense of belittling them as he himself enjoys his privileged status.

Interrogating Change through Cultural Studies

By placing ourselves within the larger project of cultural studies in order to interrogate change in the *taarab* lyric, we have a choice whether to articulate the 'critique of mass culture' or to explain the problematic within the *taarab* lyric as part of a global phenomenon. The critique of mass culture, in the words of Ross (1988: 50), is based on a '[p]rofitable opiate, synthetically prepared for consumption for a society of automatons'. The critique of mass culture has relevance in explaining the motivation behind the pervasive nature of the new lyric. For example, my interviews with *taarab* composers reveal that any lyric based on a language of *heshima* (respect) will not sell to the kind of audience who, according to the composers, have an appetite for sensationalism, sexism, abuse, wishful thinking and consumerism, which is all about *kwenda na wakati*. However, an alternative view within the framework of cultural studies holds that culture is a complicated negotiation of inside and outside, of internal and external, a battle of meaning(s), a battle within meaning(s), a crucial site for the construction of social identity, as well as a key terrain for ideological conflicts.

Especially when popular culture enters directly into the circuits of a dominant technology, it plays a pivotal role in contemporary cultural studies. Theories from cultural studies not only allow us to observe the manipulation of the technology of popular culture, but also provide a window for reinventing the 'self' in culture. It is an arena that is profoundly mythic, a theatre of popular desires and popular fantasies. It is where we discover and play with the identification of ourselves, where we are imagined, where we are represented.

The three-decade old debate on the shift from traditional prosody to modern free verse neatly fits into the cultural studies project. The debate started in the 1970s, when some poet-scholars began to compose in free verse. The reaction was immediate, as the conservationists started to assign certain criteria to Swahili poetry. For any form of poetry to be regarded as Swahili poetry, according to them, it should follow the prosodic rules that typify Swahili poetry. By imposing such rigid criteria on Swahili poetry without being overt about their statements, the conservationists are seen as making a political statement about both Swahili poetry and Swahili cultural identity. By using the divide 'self'/'other', they are drawing 'safe' and 'unsafe' boundaries highlighting their agendas and politicizing *taarab* in a special way. This reflects Anzaldúa's 'prohibited' and 'forbidden' (1987: 3), adequately described as follows: '[B]orders are set up to define the places that are safe ... A border is a dividing line, a narrow strip along a steep edge. A border is a vague and undetermined place created by the emotional residue of an unnatural boundary. It is a constant state of transition. The prohibited and forbidden are its inhabitants'.

In fact, the conservationists' claim is that Swahili poetry has 'always' been and 'must' remain different in form and content compared to the poetry of other cultures, since it is a product of interaction(s) that has taken place along the Indian Ocean littoral in a period of over a millennium. The conservationists accuse the modern poets of introducing into Swahili poetry some influences from English poetry.

Those who defend Swahili free verse, however, have responded to this accusation in two ways. Some accept that free verse has been inspired by English poetry and make no apology for having adopted this 'external cultural influence' to their own purposes. Others, according to Mazrui (1992: 68), '[p]lead innocent to the charge of having succumbed to 'Anglocentric' poetics'. In fact, they argue, Swahili's traditional prosodic forms are themselves externally inspired, for prosodic poetry is merely a symptom of Arabic cultural imperialism. Members of this camp further argue that Swahili free verse found its inspiration not in English poetry, but in an 'African' and, more specifically, 'Bantu' poetic tradition.' This is indeed true of the new lyric, whose oral features, like the presence of 'abundant repetition', 'sociolects', 'cants', 'colloquiums', 'energized local imagery' and 'certain icons', have nothing to do with English, except for code-mixing, which is not the same thing.

The debate continues to date, although with an emphasis on *taarab* in general. In his essay, Musau (2004: 175-91) shows that the ideal/traditional *taarab* has its own 'diehards' like Bakari (1999: 10), who totally rejects any idea of change in *taarab* in general or in any of its components: '[t]he authentic *taarab* must be protected and valued so that it is not destroyed by being mixed up with any other type of music and should be given a force and impetus to play its role as mother of coastal music.' [Musau's translation].

It is untenable to endow art with such protective predilections, which not only go against its existence, but are also hard to come by anyway. In the 1960s, the Zanzibar revolutionary government tried hard to subject *taarab* to strict censorship for political purposes, but failed. It is difficult to perceive how censorship can work today in a much more open and liberal political situation. However, such statements are not made to defend the purity of an art form for its own sake, but are rather an expression of what is to be positively judged as a disaster by those for whom the traditional reference points were valuable and for whom 'scientific reason' is too narrow (Musau 2004: 176). It is not only changes in instrumentation, musical structures and performance style(s) that have brought discontent among some segments of the Swahili community, but also in the form and content of the *taarab* in general and the lyrics in particular. For example, the musical lines now tend to come more from *ngoma*, the performance is based on percussion rather than on melodic rhythms, and it includes the active audience, especially women dancing on the floor instead of sitting down to listen to the music and words of the lyrics. Also there has been a relative shift in the use of language from obscurity to openness, and there is also more obscenity than before.

In this verbal exchange, the opponents of the conservationists argue their case from the point of view of the 'inevitability' of change, especially now that the world has become a 'global village' and the city more multiethnic and plural in composition today than it was in the past. The argument of the reformists is also political, as exemplified by Issa (1994: 4), who stresses the ordinance of change: '[t]he old ways will go away with the old and in its place there will be the new and modern, the latter will also come to an end and will be deemed to be nothing' (Musau's translation).

Issa's statement stresses the spirit of modernity, which relies on change as its vital force. This statement, however, creates an impression that the present is discontinuous with the past, which is wrong, since change in its many facets subsumes a number of ontological questions about 'being' itself, culture, cultural concepts, space, mobility, values, identities and differences. It emphasises the fact that identity can rarely remain singular and homogeneous and is indeed multiple, shifting both in terms of historical time and social context, and constantly being negotiated. This is especially true when we know that Swahili society is becoming more (de)territorialized, with significant numbers living in other parts of East Africa and further afield: the USA, Europe or the Gulf States, for example (Caplan 2004: 14).

A dynamic framework has been proposed by Kellner (1992: 141) and Goonatilake (1995: 232), within which cultural change can be interpreted to emphasise the fact that, in the world today, the individual self is being dynamically encroached on by many shifting cultures because of globalization. Instead of having just one culture, the mind of the individual is being 'Lebanonized', with multiple frames of reference for action corresponding to each sub-culture. Instead of having one fixed and stable identity which is a function of predefined social roles, an individual has multiple selves and identities. Identity thus becomes mobile, multiple and self-reflexive. One tends to agree with Musau (2004: 188) that '[a] *taarab* singer, or by extension a Swahili person, at one time, has the identity of the traditional Swahili area, at another time that of belonging to a larger geo-political entity (e.g. Kenya, Mombasa, Lamu, Zanzibar, Pemba, Tanzania), while on another occasions and he could have other identities. The culture of the Swahili could thus be seen as a dynamic one with multiple identities, where there is an inter-penetration of the 'local', 'national' and 'global' influences.'

If modernity means the urbanization of the mind (Schlör 1998: 16), it implies a specific urban experience, whereby cities like Dar es Salaam, Zanzibar, Mombasa and Nairobi come to be regarded as 'metonyms' for urbanity and modernity. In this view, we see the city as a social and cultural collage, the field of artistic production, the cycling of mythology that makes the city itself a permanent intertextual field. In all these attributes of the city, we might note in particular the linkage of artistic experience with a particular intersection of sexuality and urban space. The city also figures as a place around which debates over the sexualization of the public sphere have revolved. Thus, the issues of sexual desire in art and its relationship to the streets are inflected specifically by experiences of Dar es Salaam, Zanzibar and Nairobi. As Crang and Thrift (14) accurately observe: '[P]art of this orientation has been bound up [...] with its legacy of a masculine gaze, visual consumption, commodified (and, in sexualized public sphere, feminized)...' It is not therefore 'only' *taarab* music and its lyric that has been subjected to the 'postmodern frenzy' of the visible and audible, the social multiplication of images – not only the circulation but also the extension of a geographical field of the visible, but of the whole chaotic world. The whole range of arts, especially performing arts, literature, musical genres other than *taarab*, cartoon strips, newspapers, styles of dressing, fashion, night life and culture, manners and mannerisms, social behaviours etc., have all been affected by the new 'agitated space' connected with a sense of the compression of time and space created by modern media technology, which permits the rapid and errant mobility of social facts, bubbling up from inside as though influenced from the outside through the mass media.

All these pointers bespeak of how the effects of 'cultural globalisation' are penetrating every corner of the world, and yet the historical connections between nations have generally been previously understood largely in terms of an 'economic world system'. The economic content of international contact has thus been emphasised at the expense of cultural flows. Hence, the epithet 'cultural' in cultural globalization came later into use, being volatile, furtive and less amenable as a 'social fact'. Thus, whereas it is more tenable to think of controlling, as far as possible, the taste of Coca Cola, McDonald and Kentucky Fried Chicken as fast food(s) through 'patents' and 'contracts',[5] it is not so easy to impose restrictions on mobility and standards on the pieces of music, lyrics, poetic diction and images that float about through the media, transgressing national borders. The receiving artist is also not as strictly bound by any inhibition to tamper with incoming musical and cultural flows as those who deal with business transactions. Hence the artist appropriates, copies, re-combines, blends or even changes the whole paradigm of an art while retaining 'just' a name like '*taarab'*.

Concluding Remark

The shift of the Swahili *taarab* lyric from traditional prosodic form to a form that is less prosodic but freer raises a number of theoretical problems. For example, how do we now categorize the new lyric that has the features of both old and new (i.e. prosodic, free and blank verses)? Or how are we to consider a sense of syncretism that regards 'the new' as an aberration that challenges the whole notion of purity and absolutism? In this essay, we maintain that the syncretistic is the result of a simulation in which the global is only used to give a certain impression to the new. The new lyric imposes its presence simply because it is vested with the power of the global influences, though it does not substantially draw much from it. This is indeed a more open and eclectic attribute of the notion of syncretism, compared to that of a 'hotchpotch' or a 'bastardization of the authentic and pure'. It is Minh-ha's 'undoing', 'redoing' and 'modifying' the limit which ultimately creates a sense of syncretism that subverts the notion of globalization, with its flow of influences from the West to remote places. It is a new form that has a new power to defend it – the power of the local agents.

In this study I have also shown that the idea of 'self' and 'other' works not only with reference to the dichotomy centre/periphery, but

[5] Even these have to be tampered with to fit local taste, e.g. preference for Japanese taste rather than American.

also to the oppositions that emerge from local contexts. The notion of identity as a single stable location is challenged by the change from the traditional to the new lyric, which posits a sense of fragmented identity and hence leaves room for alternative discourses and negotiations over relations and positions. Since the new lyric is used as a political label in the framework of Swahili identities, gender relations must also be seen as occupying a prominent space in Swahili cultural studies.

As for 'change', our analysis shows that, although every new generic form has its heydays, stability in the internal structure of the form is not permanent. Signs have already shown how 'ephemeral' change can be in the new lyric as it is seen to lose its grasp and sense of appeal to its fans.

Bibliography

Al-Ghassany, Muyaka bin Haji (1940): *Diwani ya Muyaka*, Johannesburg: Witwatersrand University Press.

Anzandúa, Gloria (1987): Borderlands/La Frontera: The New Mestiza, San Francisco: Spinters/Aunt Lute, 3.

Appadurai, Arjun (1990): Disjuncture and Difference in the Global Cultural Economy, *Theory, Culture and Society* 7: 295-310.

Bakari, Amina (1999): *Taarab* au Nini, *Jua* 1 and 2, Cologne: 4-10.

Bihalji-Merin, Oto (1972): Art as a Universal Phenomenon, in: *World Cultures and Modern Art*, Munich: Bruckmann: 2-11.

Caplan, Pat. (2004): Introduction, in: *Swahili Modernities: Culture, Politics, and Identity on the East Coast of Africa*, Trenton: Africa World Press: 1-14.

Crang, Mike; Thrift, Nigel (1995) Introduction, in: *Thinking Space*, London: Routledge: 1-30.

Goonatilake, Susantha (1995): The Self Wandering Between Cultural Location and Globalisation, in: Pieterse, Jan Nederveen and Bhikhu Parekh (eds.): *Decolonization of Imagination*, London: Zed Books: 224-39.

Henderson, M.A.E.G. (ed.) (1995): Introduction: Borders, Boundaries and Frames, in: *Essays in Cultural Studies*, London: Routledge.

Issa, Salim Vuai (1999): Ipi *Taarab* Halisi? Mambo Yote Yamebadilika, *Jua* 4, Cologne: 3-6.

Kaminsky, Amy K. (1993): *Reading the Body Politic: Feminist Criticism and Latin American Women Writers*, Minneapolis: University of Minnesota Press.

Kellner, Douglas (1992): Popular Culture and the Construction of Postmodern Identities, in: Lash, Scott and Friedman, Jonathan (eds.): *Modernity and Identity*, Oxford: Blackwell.

Mazrui, Alamin (1992): Conservationism and Liberalism in Swahili Poetry: The Linguistic Dimension, in: *Research in African Literatures* 23.4, Indiana University and Ohio State University: 67-76.

Mazrui, Ali A (1986): *The Africans: A Triple Heritage*, London: BBC Publications.

Minh-ha, Trinh T. (1991): *Framer Framed*, London: Routledge: 218.

Musau, Paul M. (2004): *Taarab* Songs as a Reflection of the Changing Socio-political Reality of the Swahili, in: Caplan, Pat; Topan, Farouk (eds.): *Swahili Modernities: Culture, Politics, and Identity on the East Coast of Africa*, Trenton: Africa World Press: 175-89.

Nercessian, Andy (2002): *Postmodernism and Globalization in Ethnomusicology: An Epistemological Problem*, London: Lanham.

Nicol, Bran (2002): *Postmodernism and the Contemporary Novel: A Reader*, Edinburgh: Edinburgh University Press.

Ong, Walter J. (1982): *Orality and Literacy: The Technologizing of the Word*, London: Routledge.

Ross, K. (1988): *The Emergence of Social Space: Rimband and the Paris Commune*, Minneapolis: University of Minnesota Press.

Schlör, J. (1998): *Nights in the Big City: Paris, Berlin, London, 1840-1930*, London: Reaktion.

Tsuruta, Tadasu (2003): Popular Music, Sports, and Politics: A Development of Urban Cultural Movements in Dar-es-Salaam, 1930-1960s, *African Study Monographs*, 24 (3): 195.

The 'Idea' of India: Syncretism[1] or Creativity in Vodun Art and Thought

Dana Rush

> ...I grew up with two ideas of India. The first idea...was about the kind of country from which my ancestors had come.... There was a second India. It balanced the first. This second India was the India of the independence movement, the India of greatness.... This was the identity I took to India on my first visit in 1962. And when I got there, I found it had no meaning in India.
>
> (V.S. Naipaul, *India: A Million Mutinies Now*)

There are many ideas of India. As the Trinidadian author V. S. Naipaul notes above, 'India' does not always refer to the peninsula region of South Asia, south of the Himalayas, between the Bay of Bengal and the Arabian Sea, where Hindus and others live and revere their gods. In West African Vodun art and thought,[2] the idea of India

---

[1] Even though the word 'syncretism' is in the title of my essay, I am relegating its discussion to this footnote. Syncretism, whether as a concept or a heuristic device, must be recast as a historically contingent term. Its beginnings had purely positive connotations, but to this day, the term continues to raise polemical questions of 'purity', 'authenticity', 'hybridity' and 'originality', often from outside the society in question, rather than from the critical perspective coming from within. We must also be careful with postcolonial celebrations of 'syncretism' in that the possibility exists of overlooking precolonial areas that produced some of West Africa's highly dynamic, composite cultures. Rather than focusing on 'syncretism', I choose to concentrate on 'creativity' as an active ongoing process stemming from the centuries-strong experiences of people who make creative and strategic choices, either from necessity or from inventiveness and ingenuity. Lived experiences are equal to any ideology, any time, and may very well provide insights which might have otherwise been missed.

[2] There are few words in the English language as charged with evocative power as the word 'voodoo'. It derives from the West African religious system of Vodun, and means 'spirits' in the Fon language Although Vodun is one of the world's most misunderstood religions, it is nonetheless a legitimate and vital system of beliefs that

is not simply one of geography or theology. Rather, 'India' offers boundless aesthetic and spiritual opportunities in both time and space, going beyond the empirical known world into the unempirical, unknown world. Through an exploration of the origins and deployments of Indian imagery within contemporary Vodun art and thought, outside influences emerge as constituent components of it, whose origins have, at times, become lost in the eternal process of creation. In this analysis of the incorporation of Indian imagery into contemporary Vodun art and thought, the present-day concept of globalism, with its compelling notions of international boundarylessness, can be understood in a way which goes far beyond the visible, tangible, human domain into a world in which eternity and divine infinity are collapsed into the here and now.

Vodun arts document Vodun histories. For centuries, the coastline of Bénin and Togo has acted as a vortex, incorporating items and ideas from across the sea into its littoral. This ongoing phenomenon has generated a fertile mosaic of international, transcontinental, transoceanic peoples, histories, commodities and spirits, made manifest in Vodun art and thought. The present chapter focuses on a relatively contemporary aspect of this 'vortextual phenomenon', that is, the incorporation of 'India' – via chromolithographic imagery (mostly Hindu) – into the eternally organic religious system of Vodun. Although the idea of India in Vodun art and thought probably emerged no earlier than the late 1950s, it is the ancient, essentially elastic conceptual system of Vodun which has allowed it to thrive on both sides of the Atlantic Ocean. The integration of Indian chromolithographs into Vodun epistemologies is exemplary of the overall incorporative sensibilities of Vodun art and thought.

---

originated in and around the area of the Benin Republic and spread to the Caribbean and the Americas through the transatlantic slave trade.

The Essential Sea

> Coasts kept alive the dialectic between the seen and the unseen…tangible horizons making the unattainable attainable… contract[ing] time as well as space.
>
> (Paul Carter, 'Dark with Excess of Bright: Mapping the Coastlines of Knowledge,' in *Mappings*.)

In Vodun thought, India spirits invariably come from the sea, rendering 'India' and the sea synonymous; they are both known yet unknowable, a paradox mediated through art. Because the sea is as deep as one's own imagination and vice-versa, the breadth of 'India' spirits, associated 'India' arts and 'India' experiences is inexhaustible. The Atlantic coastline of Bénin and Togo simultaneously effaces and defines the meeting of land and sea: that is, where Africa and 'India' merge. It is a place where awareness can be Janus-faced, where space and time can and do alter. At the same time, this very coastline – liminal as it may be – is a gateway to centuries of intercontinental and transoceanic interactions and exchanges. This particular seaboard was a very real market place during the transatlantic slave trade (Law 1977, 1991, Lovejoy 1986, Manning 1982). As such, it qualifies as a 'diaspora space', a concept introduced by Avtar Brah as a meeting point of 'economic, political, cultural, and psychic [spiritual] processes…where multiple subject positions are juxtaposed, contested, proclaimed, or disavowed, where the permitted and the prohibited perpetually interrogate, and where the accepted and the transgressive imperceptibly mingle' (1996: 208). The idea of 'diaspora space' thus encapsulates the global position of 'culture as a site of travel' (Clifford 1992). In effect, along this West African seaboard we are confronted with two simultaneous processes in which the sea functions as both a passageway to vast cultural and spiritual potential, and an exceedingly lucrative portal to centuries of travel and commodities exchange. The idea of 'India' in Vodun art and thought thus occupies its own 'diaspora space'.

Chromolithographs in Vodun

> If images are invested with power, how then are they made to work?
>
> (David Freedberg, *The Power of Images*)

Lithography, or the process of making prints from a metal plate or a flat stone surface, was invented in 1796 by Aloys Senefelder of Prague, and color lithography was in use in Europe by the middle of the nineteenth century (Smith 1997: 6). In India, however, there was a long history of text printing before the advent and spread of lithographs. In 1556, the Portuguese planned to send the first printing press – via Goa, India – to missionaries in Abyssinia. However, the Abyssinian emperor changed his mind about welcoming missionaries, so the press remained in Goa, where the first book was published on Indian soil in 1556 (Wadley 1995: 21). From that point on, printed texts were used extensively by missionaries to spread Christianity in India. Then, in the nineteenth century, print technology became a major factor in the transmission of Hindu and Muslim religious traditions through written text. Chromolithograph presses were operating in India by the late nineteenth century, and colour prints began circulating throughout the subcontinent at around the same time. Raja Ravi Varma (1848-1906), a South Indian portrait and landscape painter, is usually cited as the principal influence in the emergence of India's popular religious poster and calendar art. He not only painted popular images of gods, goddesses and legendary episodes, he is also credited with setting up the first chromolithographic press in Bombay in 1891 (Inglis 1995: 58). In fact, before 1900 India had several chromolithographic presses, one of which is the press of Hem Chander Bhargava and Company in Chadni Chowk, Delhi, which has been continuously printing chromolithographs of religious subjects for over a hundred years (Wadley 1995: 22).

How and when did chromolithographs arrive in West Africa and become a part of the visual theology of Vodun? The potential for imported prints to have been seen in West Africa first existed shortly after the first colour reproductions were produced in Bombay in 1891 (Inglis 1995: 22). It is critical, however, to note that the presence of Indian commodities in West Africa dates back to the fifteenth century, when Portuguese sea commanders and merchants of the British and Dutch East India Company began active participation in the trading and selling of Indian cloth between India and coastal West Africa (Eicher and Erekosima 1996). Consequently, the sea bordering this coast has been associated with foreign wealth and power since the fifteenth century. Then, the institution of colonial empires and increasing trade, connecting Africa with both east and west, rapidly spread images that were incorporated into West African artistic and religious expression, beginning as early as the late nineteenth century. Since then, the contemporary appeal of Indian gods to West Africans has led to a burgeoning African market in Indian prints. According to Henry Drewal, around World War I, when Indian merchants set up firms along the West African coast, West African peoples began observing aspects of Hindu religious practice such as those of Gujaratis, devotees of Lakshmi, the Hindu goddess of wealth and patroness of merchants (1988b: 174-6).

Elaborately detailed Indian chromolithographs have been incorporated into the religious system of Vodun precisely because of their open-ended structures and richly suggestive imagery, which allow them to embody wildly diverse ideas, themes, beliefs, histories and legends in Vodun art and thought. The prints themselves both teach and serve as vehicles of divine worship, suggesting rules of conduct, recounting legendary narratives and acting as objects of adoration. The specific animals, foods, drinks, jewelry, body markings and accoutrements within these chromolithographs have become sacred to the Vodun spirits represented. Although, at some point, these images were newly seen, they have been approached in Vodun as something that was already known and understood, as something already familiar within the Vodun pantheon. These Indian gods have not been *combined with*, but rather *are* local gods.

Henry Drewal has documented the earliest evidence to date of the incorporation of a foreign printed image into a local religious vocabulary in West Africa. He has traced the history of the most popular representation of the water spirit-*cum*-seductress, known as Mami Wata, which was based on a late nineteenth-century chromolithograph of a snake charmer in a German circus from an original European painting (Drewal 1988a, 1988b, 1996; Salmons 1977). Dating from circa 1885, the chromolithograph was reprinted in large numbers in India and England and distributed widely in sub-Saharan West Africa. The edition that Drewal illustrates (1988b: 169, Fig. 7) was printed in Bombay by the Shree Ram Calendar Company in 1955 to copy an earlier version provided by a trader in Kumasi, Ghana. During 1955-1956 twelve thousand copies (10' x 14') were sent to this trader and another trader in Kumasi (Drewal 1988b: 183, fn. 6). The image has since been reproduced *en masse* and has been found in the Dominican Republic and Haiti (Houlberg 1996: 30-5, 101), as well as in *botánicas* throughout the United States in the form of printed images, statues, candles and pendants.

Although by far the most popular chromolithograph, the image of the snake charmer is by no means the only print to be found in West African religious practice. Chromolithographs from an ancient Indian epic, the *Ramayana*, and other Hindu lore are available for purchase in local markets. There seems to be a quick turnover of the chromolithographs of Hindu gods at the market stands: as images are sold, new ones become available. Some chromolithographs are wrinkled and slightly torn older images straight from India, while others are newly printed in and imported from Nigeria and England. A wide repertoire of chromolithographic imagery is available, including prints of Rama, Sita, Hanuman, Shiva, Dattatreya, Hare Krishna, Shirdi Sai Baba, the Buddha, Guru Nanak and al-Buraq, as well as the Pope, Eve, Jesus Christ, the Virgin Mary and various Christian saints.[3] Other prints, available from Indian stores in the form of decorative promotional calendars, express a clear first-order advertising purpose within the Indian community. These same prints, however, have second- and third-order significances within Vodun artistic and spiritual sensibilities. The superabundance of flowers, gold, jewels, coins and other luxurious items surrounding the spiritually charged deities depicted in these prints function as links into particular Vodun sensibilities, especially those of Mami Wata, the Vodun of wealth and beauty, who commands the sea and is known for her allure as a source of potential wealth, both religious and economic.

Even though the exact arrival date of Indian chromolithographs in coastal West Africa is unknown, the images themselves have become quite significant in contemporary Vodun practice. Though in demand, Indian prints are no longer as readily available. Within view of the Atlantic coast, a particular market stand in the Asigamé Market in Lomé, Togo, was a 'hot spot' for purchasing Indian prints in the 1990s. People used to travel there from the bordering countries of Bénin and Ghana to seek out India spirit prints from Mama Sikavi, the very discerning market woman who kept her stand full to overflowing with wide varieties of constantly changing images. She refused to sell these prints at a reasonable price, and some people would save money for up to a year just to purchase one, that is to have access to 'India' and the powers within. After working the same market stand for close on twenty years (early 1980s until 2004),

---

[3] Chromolithographs from non-Indian cultures have also been incorporated into Vodun shrines and temple paintings, but with nowhere near the frequency of Indian images (especially in Mami Wata). For example, I have documented Jesus, the Virgin Mary and Pope John Paul II in a handful of Vodun temples. However, Christian persona are not regarded as nearly as powerful as those associated with India.

Mama Sikavi is no longer selling prints.[4] However, a print seller round the corner continues to sell India prints, though his selection is still nowhere near as comprehensive as that of Mama Sikavi. Another likely source for Hindu imagery is the popular Hindu movie corpus shown throughout Africa.[5]

The Use of Images

Most Vodun art forms are forever unfinished, and the seemingly static nature of a mass-produced image such as a chromolithograph is indeed misleading. Although a chromolithograph used in Vodun may appear 'finished', it continues to change in terms of both form and meaning. It can expand in form from a two-dimensional image into three-dimensional spiritual and artistic presences in shrines, sculptures, and temple paintings; and a three-dimensional shrine can be represented by a chromolithograph as an ethereally collapsed, ready-made, two-dimensional shrine. The appeal of the chromolithographic image in Vodun art and thought is its visual and spiritual saturation in an economical and portable equivalence.

Chromolithographs in this 'diaspora space' exist in an infinite aesthetic and spiritual synesthesia in which the visual impact itself induces godly presence. For much Vodun art, 'completion' is not the point. Hard as one tries, one will not find a positivist rationale behind

---

[4] Personal communication, market sellers at Asigamé Market, Lomé, Togo, January 2005.

[5] In my quest to learn the origins of the Hindu images I found in Vodun temples, I visited Hindu temples in Togo and Ghana, attended services, and talked to practitioners and priests. The walls of the Hindu temples were covered with a wide variety of Hindu chromolithographs, and large, active Hindu shrines were bedecked with statues of the same Hindu gods. People attending the services –Togolese, Beninese, Ghanaians, and resident Indians – were devout and learned practitioners of Hinduism. The priests I spoke with concerning the incorporation of Hindu gods into Vodun worship felt that the images were obtained through market stands and calendars, and then shared among fellow Vodun adepts, which accounted for their frequent 'misinterpretation'. The priests seemed very certain that no one in any of their congregations was a Vodun adept.

the perpetually unfinished Vodun shrine, ever growing, changing, accumulating, continually transformed and transforming. Following the same line of thought, even though the outward form of a mass-produced chromolithograph may seem complete, the name or meaning can change, as can the power residing within it, depending on how it is used. A chromolithograph which appears ostensibly complete may, in fact, never be complete: not only its uses but its visual form when reproduced in temple paintings, shrines and sculptures actualizes this eternal potential creativity to adapt in response to any new problem or situation that arises needing spiritual guidance or intervention, and/or in acknowledgement of the changing demands and desires of the spirits.

Clearly, chromolithographs are outwardly mobile in that they are easily transported, copied and reproduced. It is precisely this quality that permits their quick external proliferation. Equally important is the fact that chromolithographs are inwardly mobile: their inherent forms and meanings do not remain stationary, but accumulate multiple readings. The same chromolithograph easily attracts a second and third audience and a new range of interpretations and conventions beyond, for example, the first-order Hindu reading of the same image. Although various gods in separate Vodun compounds may be derivatives of the same Hindu image, they take on lives of their own. Similar images appear in different Vodun settings with different names. In most cases, the images are unrelated in any way except that they look alike. Arguments among Vodun priests and priestesses in different Vodun compounds arise over the 'correct' appellations and use of images in religious practice, even though the images in dispute are hardly, if ever, local in origin. Admittedly, there is overlap and grounds for potential confusion. However, what appears at first glance to be confusion can, in a 'diaspora space', become multi-layered fusion.

Ramayana Remix

The monkey king, Hanuman, is a popular Indian hero who became a god in the ancient Hindu epic, the *Ramayana.* Dedicated to Rama, the seventh incarnation of Vishnu, the epic narrates the trials and tribulations of Rama and his wife Sita as they go into exile, accompanied by Rama's brother Lakshmana. Sita is abducted by Ravanna, the demon-king of Lanka (now Sri Lanka), and is rescued by Hanuman, the faithful servant of Rama (Narayan 1972).

Attingali is a powerful witch-fighting Islamic Vodun concentrated in and around Abomey-Calavie, Bénin.[6] The strongest soldier in the Attingali pantheon is known as Foulani[7] Agbokanli, i.e. 'Fulani cow-animal'. One Attingali temple painting of Foulani Agbokanli resembles a chromolithograph from the *Ramayana,* illustrating a victorious Hanuman with a diminutive Rama and Lakshmana on his shoulders. The demon king Ahiravana (Ravanna's son or, in some versions, his brother) is shown prostrate under Hanuman's foot as at the end of the *Ramayana* episode in the netherworld of Patala Loka (Lutengendorf 1995: 3-8). Yet, in Abomey-Calavie, the same small figures are known as Ablewa, or the 'angels' of Foulani Agbokanli, who help him fight witchcraft. Another Foulani Agbokanli shrine, a five-minute walk away, displays the same Indian chromolithograph, but here Foulani Agbokanli has captured a second witch. Thus, the

[6] Attingali originated in northern Ghana and spread to Nigeria. It is also known by abbreviated names such as Attinga and Tinga in Bénin, Alatinga (*al* = owner of in Yoruba) and Tingare in Nigeria, and Tigare in Ghana. Although the idea of 'Islamic Vodun' may seem to be a contradiction in terms, it is not. Vodun, as a religious system, incorporates and embraces foreign elements which appear, at first, antithetical in nature. Vodun thrives on apparent contradictions. Within the Attingali Vodun, Islam relates to its geographical origin in the predominantly Islamic northern Ghana. Within various Islamic Vodun (Attingali and Thron, for example), Islamic symbols, such as the crescent moon and the star, are incorporated into their arts, and their practitioners observe holidays such as Ramadan and Tabaski, though the ceremonies themselves are Vodun-ized in interpretation.

[7] I use the French spelling 'Foulani' for paintings on Vodun temples for this particular Vodun. Otherwise it will be spelled 'Fulani'.

chromolithographic image is ever-evolving. Although they look identical, there is no relationship between Foulani Agbokanli, the Fulani cow-animal, and Hanuman, the Indian monkey king.

An image photographed along the coast of Ghana, between Cape Coast and Accra, represents neither Hanuman nor Foulani Agbokanli, but a hero in a Fante belief system.[8] The breadth of chromolithographic influence becomes even more evident in an Ibibio shrine sculpture like that found in a Kalahari Ijo shrine in the Eastern Delta region of Nigeria, which dates from the last half of the nineteenth century. William Arnett suggests that the sculpture quite likely comes from a southern Ibibio group, such as the Anang (illustrated in Arnett 1978).

Hindu Images in Mami Wata Vodun

Along coastal Bénin and Togo, Mami Wata is much more than a single spirit: she is an entire pantheon. With creativity as a strong ally, any new problem or situation that arises needing spiritual intervention or guidance is accounted for in that a new Mami Wata spirit inevitably arises from the sea. Life's recently introduced or previously unfamiliar uncertainties (such as birth control, abortion, prostitution or homosexuality, for example) often are embraced and made sense of through Hindu imagery used in Mami Wata religious practice.

The Mamisi (wives or devotees of Mami Wata) not only worship their own demanding spirits from the sea and new spirits addressing the needs of a quickly changing society, they must also venerate the principal gods found in most Vodun houses, such as Gu, Sakpata, Xeviosso, Tohosu and Hohovi. Mamisi have found an ingenious way to do this, with the aesthetic and spiritual flair that has come to be expected of Mami Wata: they have incorporated parts of the Hindu pantheon into the worship of these main gods, who are represented

[8] Another Ghanaian example of this image of Hanuman, the Indian monkey king, is illustrated in *Africa Explores* (Vogel 1991: 127).

by lavish Hindu chromolithographs reproduced on temple walls and placed in Mami Wata shrines.

Ghanaian artist Joseph Kossivi Ahiator is the most sought-after India spirit temple painter in Bénin, Togo and Ghana. He consults his own array of chromolithographs when commissioned to paint Vodun temples, and then elaborates the images based on his own dreams, coupled with the dreams and desires of the temple owner. Ahiator is closely connected to the sea. He was born with India spirits and he visits 'India' often, sometimes in his dreams, sometimes on the beach. These travels thoroughly inform his art.[9] In a Vodun temple in Cotonou, Bénin, he has envisioned and executed representations of a particular set of spirits within the Mami Wata pantheon that are recognizably derived from Hindu chromolithographs. Ahiator has placed this particular set of spirits within the Mami Wata pantheon under the protective arch of the paired rainbow serpent Dan Aida Wedo, often associated with Mami Wata. Such conflation is based on the iridescent rainbow-like serpent, which encircles Mami Wata's neck and arches over her head in her most common depiction, based on the snake charmer chromolithograph. A discussion follows of some of the local-*cum*-India spirits illustrated on this large mural.

Hanuman and Gniblin

Hanuman is often referred to as Gniblin in various Mami Wata Vodun in Bénin, Togo, and Ghana. Featured prominently in the centre of the mural is a painting of the powerful half-animal, half-human super-being called Gniblin Egu, which can be translated as 'cow-person' of Egu in Mina.[10] Gniblin is famous for his power of

---

[9] Ahiator is much sought after as an artist, especially by Mami Wata priests and priestesses. I have documented and written about his temple paintings in coastal Bénin, Togo, and Ghana. See Rushforthcoming 2007.

[10] The relationship between Gniblin and Egu remains unclear. Aguessy (n.d.: 58), in a list of Vodun from the Mono province in Bénin, writes that Gniblin is the Vodun of the sacred forest. Aziamblé (1981) describes Nyigble (presumably just a different spelling of Gniblin) as the protector of the Sacred Forest of Bé and an important

Egu, the Mina cognate of the Yoruba Ogun, and the Fon Gu, deities of iron, war and technology. Gniblin Egu is credited with teaching humans iron technology. Hanuman is interpreted as bovine rather than simian, as is Foulani Agbokanli in Attingali. Although Gniblin Egu comes from the sea, Mami Wata adepts hold that he lives on the road and is associated with traffic accidents. He can travel anywhere his fiery tail being seen as he flies through the air. If he is angry, he can burn a whole city, and he can use his tail to beat witches.

In the *Ramayana*, Hanuman is revered as Prince Rama's loyal servant and protector, who carries the essence of Rama (and sometimes Rama and Sita) with him wherever he goes. A popular chromolithograph shows Hanuman responding to the challenge that he does not have the power to do so. Hanuman tears open his chest and, to the bewilderment of his onlookers, reveals Rama and Sita within. Similarly, Gniblin Egu tore open his chest to demonstrate that he carries his deceased parents with him at all times, thus proving his eternal respect for them. Given the importance of ancestor veneration among the Fon and Mina, Gniblin Egu is both a Vodun spirit and an ancestral shrine.

Ganesh and Tohosu

To the right of Gniblin Egu is Tohosu Amlina. Tohosu is the Fon Vodun of royalty, human deformations, lakes and streams. Amlina means 'strange' in Mina. The painting of Tohosu is based upon a chromolithograph of Ganesh, the elephant-headed, pot-bellied Hindu god of thresholds, beginnings and wisdom, remover of obstacles. Although he has only one tusk, he has four arms in which he holds a shell, a discus, a club and a water lily. His means of transportation is a rat, usually depicted as going before him. In Hindu belief, Ganesh

---

Vodun in the history of the quarter of Lomé called Bé. Chesi describes Gniblin as the most powerful fetish who came from Adja and rules over the holy forest (1979: 26). His symbol is a stone, but he has the shape of a panther.

is always called upon before the beginning of any new venture, from taking a trip to opening a business.

The image of Ganesh visually encapsulates the Fon spirit of Tohosu: royal (surrounded by wealth, corpulent from luxurious eating) and super-human (a human with an elephant's head and four arms). Although Ganesh is not known to be associated with lakes or streams, Mamisi often recognize the blue background of many Ganesh chromolithographs as representing a watery abode (cf. Drewal 1988b: 171). The chromolithograph of Ganesh has directly influenced the Mami Wata worship of Tohosu Amlina. A Mamisi with the spirit of Tohosu Amlina may never kill rats, for this creature, which is always depicted with Ganesh, has become sacred to the spirit's devotees. Thus, not only do Hindu chromolithographs suggest and reify characteristics already inherent in local gods, they also introduce, influence and change already established, albeit organic, religious practice, attesting to the profundity of 'visual piety'(cf. Morgan 1998).

Shiva and Mami Dan

To the right of Tohosu in Ahiator's mural is Mami Dan,[11] also called Akpan, whose job it is to clear the path for Mami Wata. Mami Dan was born with snakes draped around his neck and always appears that way. He is known to be old as the sea, and his job is to clear the path for Mami Wata. This depiction of Mami Dan comes directly from one of the best known illustrations of Shiva, called Shiva-Dakshina-Murti or Mahayogi, one of the oldest gods of India. In Brahmanical theology, Shiva is the third member of the Divine Trinity of Creator-Preserver-Destroyer, and, although Shiva means

---

[11] Although this would appear to mean 'the mother of Dan Aida Wedo', the term 'Mami' is not gendered. Thus a spirit who is a 'Mami' is a mother, but is not necessarily female. Similarly, the suffix *-si* (from *asi*) means 'wife'. Mamisi or Sakpatasi, although literally 'wife of Mami' or 'wife of Sakpata', thus refers to an adept of either gender.

'the friendly one,' he is also the Lord of Destruction. Similarly, the Mina name Akpan means 'the one with the bad temper'.

The Indian chromolithograph shows Shiva as an ascetic in deep meditation atop the Himalayas. He is wearing a simple loincloth and is seated on a tiger skin, which Mamisi say is the panther who clears the path for Mami Dan, and in turn, Mami Wata. In northern India, Shiva always has a cobra around his neck and a trident, drum and water jug nearby, all of which also surround Mami Dan in the Mami Wata temple painting. Mamisi call the trident *apia*, which is reproduced as a protective tattoo pattern and drawn on the earth with sacred powders. *Apia* tridents are also carried as ritual paraphernalia, which, when not in active use, are stored in Mami Wata shrines.

Hindu influence extends well into Nigeria and Togo. Joseph Nevadomsky photographed a chromolithograph of Shiva in a Mami Wata shrine in Benin City, Nigeria (Gore and Nevadomsky 1997: 63, Figure 4). Other available prints, including those of the snake charmer, Dattatreya, and Jesus, may have influenced a Benin City temple painting, also photographed by Nevadomsky, of a two-headed, double-haloed female Jesus with a snake around his/her waist held up in two of four arms. Jesus' foreheads are graced with Indian *bindi* spots (Nevadomsky 1997: 58, Fig. 6).[12]

Two new Indian images have been incorporated into Ahiator's India spirit Vodun corpus: a nineteen-headed Indian god known as the King of Mami Wata, and his wife, the nine-headed NaKrishna, based on Ravanna. Unfortunately, Ahiator does not remember the name of the nineteen-headed god, as it was first shown to him in 1977. In January 2005 he saw this image in his dreams, then he saw

[12] Gert Chesi has photographed many Mami Wata shrines in southern Togo in which Hindu chromolithographs are found, but unfortunately he gives very little information concerning these images (Chesi 1979: 67-8, 85, 97-9, 159).

it while swimming in the sea and was therefore compelled to paint it.[13]

Aneho's 'India'

Aneho, Togo, a coastal town known for its high concentration of Mami Wata devotees, also boasts a strong 'diaspora space' of India. Upon entering the compound of a renowned Vodun priest, Gilbert Attissou, one is greeted by bas-reliefs of Shiva and Lakshmi flanking the other side of the doorway. Inside his compound, 'India' becomes even more profound, and again, Shiva prevails. Through the doorway facing the compound is a shrine room called 'India.' From left to right on only one of the four fully decorated walls are depicted Mami Wata and Lord Shiva, with below them Lakshmi, and on the right another Mami Wata with a statue and chromolithograph of her triple-headed husband Densu (from the Hindu Dattatreya). In this shrine room called 'India,' Attissou explained that the walls were blue because we were below the sea. Another doorway, which led further into an even more sacred space, was brimming with more posters of Indian gods, perfumes, powders, alcohol, candles, statuettes, stuffed, plastic and ceramic animals, and other offerings.

This shrine room – filled with mass-produced lithographs, plastic flowers and dolls – may appear too obvious, repetitive and artificial to be taken seriously. However, this imported object-filled site is actually both subtle and powerful to Vodun aesthetic sensibilities. The primary colours and glossy surfaces of things may seem gaudy, but in comparison to the vibrant colour and noises of a West African

---

[13] In January 2005, I commissioned a mural on cloth of the nineteen-headed King of Mami Wata for the exhibition *Sacred Waters: The Many Faces of Mami Wata and Other Afro-Atlantic Water Spirits*, to open at the UCLA Fowler Museum of Cultural History in March 2007. This commission was based on a suggestion Ahiator had made to me in 1999 when I was working with him. Because he knew of my strong desire to learn about India spirits, he suggested that he paint wall murals for me on cloth to hang in my bedroom so that I could study during my sleep. He feels that viewers of the exhibition will be able to travel to 'India' if they study his painting.

market these images and objects become pale, yet remain potent. They have power and presence, and most importantly they work – they make things happen. Rather than being just 'kitsch', therefore, these items are spiritual status symbols. This is religious imagery has also certainly reached a high level of commodification, but on two very different levels: first, it represents a considerable financial investment on the part of the devotee; and secondly, it offers access to powers unattainable through any other means. This is a spiritual marketplace, and India spirits themselves reflect the arbitrary nature of power and wealth.

When he works with what appears to be a very typical Vodun shrine arrangement, Attissou likes to wear his favourite Shiva cloth. However, the shrine is dedicated to Nana-Yo, one of the many Vodun names for Shiva, in front of whom is a carved *yoni* receptacle representing the female principle and the origin of Hindu creation, placed there to receive Vodun offerings. In the shrine Attissou keeps his Shiva trident, which he found in an Indian boutique in Lomé, Togo, in the early 1960s. He says that he was always drawn to Indian gods and their power to control the sea. He bought whatever he could afford in these Indian boutiques and forged friendships with the Indian merchants.[14] During the 1960s, Gilbert spent hours upon hours on the coast, where he would journey to 'India' and find himself surrounded by beautiful things. He would spend months in 'India' during a few hours at the beach. His family worried about his obsession with the sea and his curious behaviour, so they brought him to a Christian Celeste church in order to exorcise these 'demonic' spirits from his system. Christian Celeste, however, deemed these India spirits so powerful that they advised him to nurture them

---

[14] Indian art and artefacts, outside the Vodun context, are primarily found within the Indian expatriate communities in large cities such at Lomé, Togo, and Cotonou, Bénin.

rather than eliminate them. Thus he began incorporating Indian items into his own Mami Wata worship.[15]

Transatlantica: Chromolithograph as Crux

In conjunction with deep spiritual conviction, chromolithographs have been a central and critical feature in the maintenance and proliferation of African-derived religious systems throughout the Americas. The spread of chromolithographic imagery in African diasporic communities is commonly attributed to the strategem of masking the identities of proscribed African deities. This explanation has proved limiting, and recent scholarship asserts more. Writing of Haiti's Vodun Sen Jak, represented by Catholic chromolithographs of St. James, Cosentino states that 'chromolithographs constitute the single most important contemporary source for the elaboration of Ogou [Sen Jak's African counterpart] theology' (1995: 253).

More than simply a ubiquitous phenomenon in response to oppression, a means of solving problems under the difficult circumstances of enslavement, chromolithographs offered a mechanism for articulating deep-seated, centuries-old African religious sensibilities. Chromolithographs represented, and continue to represent, Vodun's potential as a means of expression, assertion, creativity and faith. They are adoptable and adaptable to all circumstances, from the worst to the best, on both sides of the Atlantic.

Within the conceptual 'diaspora space' of 'India', the late Haitian master assemblage artist, Pierrot Barra (1942-1999),[16] was one who incorporated chromolithographic imagery into his work. In one piece of his marketable shrine art, Barra honored Ezili Freda, famous in Haiti and throughout Haitian diasporas as 'the goddess of love and luxury...a flirtatious Creole woman who adores fine clothes, jewels,

[15] See Chesi (1979) for an earlier photograph of Gilbert Attissou's 'India' objects.
[16] For an obituary, see Cosentino, Donald, 'In Memoriam, Pierrot Barra, 1942 - 1999,'African Arts Winter 1999, Volume XXXII, Number 4, pp. 16-17.

perfumes, and lace' (Cosentino 1995: 240-1). She is represented by the Catholic chromolithograph of Mater Dolorosa, Our Lady of Sorrows, which graces the background of the piece. In the foreground, however, is another representation of Ezili Freda: a miniature statuette of clearly Indian origin, recognizable by the tell-tale Hindu *bindi* spot on her forehead. Hindu imagery may have played an even greater role in the artist's work. In his description of Barra's doll-assemblage creation of the Vodou spirit Ti Jean Danto (with two extra legs and feet extending from her shoulders), Cosentino writes that the artist 'has further reconfigured his doll to mirror lithographs of Shiva or Lakshmi, in whose many limbs Hindu worshippers recognize the polydexterity of their gods' (1998: 19, 53, Plate 9).[17]

Other examples suggest that Eastern imagery seems to have a relevance and resonance in a large segment of African diaspora communities. The centre of Haitian flag-maker Clotaire Bazile's Petwo altar (illustrated in Cosentino 1998: 21) features a white ceramic figurine of a clearly Asian god (probably Chinese), which unquestionably fits into the 'diapsora space' of a Haitian shrine. A Gede shrine of *oungan* Saveur St. Cyr in Port-au-Prince, Haiti, has various statues of multilimbed Hindu deities, one of which (probably Lakshmi) St. Cyr identifies as the Virgin Mary.[18] Similarly, in his article on Catholic chromolithographs in Haitian Vodou, Michel Leiris describes Ezili as represented by an image of 'Our Lady of Monserrate', which he correlates with what he witnessed a month earlier in a chapel near Carangaise, an area of Guadeloupe known for its Dravidian population. The chapel, which he reports is occasionally visited by Guadeloupeans of African descent, houses a statue which in Haitian Vodou would represent Ezili. In this Guadeloupean context, however, it represents Maryemen (or Madeyemin or

[17] A strong Indian presence in the Caribbean began after the abolition of slavery in 1838, when African slaves were replaced by indentured labourers, mostly from India (Bettelheim and Nunley 1988: 120).
[18] Personal communication, Eileen Moyer, July 1997.

Mayêmé or 'Marie aimée'), a female Indian deity conflated here with the Virgin Mary. The white cloth that cloaks the figure, except for its face, hides four arms holding a sword, a gold disc, a branch and a trident, all of which remind Leiris of the accoutrements found in Haitian shrines dedicated to Ezili (Leiris 1952: 206). Although obscure, Leiris' observation is worth pondering over. In this 'diaspora space', the Catholic Virgin, the Hindu Lakshmi and the Vodou Ezili become one and many, moving from two to three dimensions and back, literally and conceptually, and blurring them.

This Indian-African phenomenon is in no way unidirectional. For some Afro-Trinidadian Indians in Brooklyn, for example, an image of Yemoja, the Yoruba goddess of the river Ogun, represented in a popular chromolithograph by a fair-skinned, long-haired, crowned female figure emerging from the water, may represent Lakshmi, the Hindu goddess of wealth and beauty.[19] In Trinidad, the Indian deity Kali may merge with Shango, the Yoruba god of thunder, lightning and associated elements.[20] Statues and images of Indian gods are also found in *botánicas* in major US cities.

The potential of Hindu chromolithographic imagery continues to be recognized as something already familiar within transatlantic Vodou. In her introduction to *Mama Lola: A Vodou Priestess in Brooklyn,* Karen McCarthy Brown recounts how she and a friend visited Mama Lola. Upon seeing for the first time Hindu chromolithographs of Krishna and Kali which Brown's friend had with her, the priestess cried 'Let me see.... You gonna get me some for my altar?' (Brown 1991: 13). Mama Lola recognized instantly that there was a place for these richly suggestive images in her spiritual and religious sensibilities.

[19] Personal communication, John Peffer, August 1997.
[20] Personal communication, Pamela Franco, April 1998.

Transatlantic Vortextual Momentum

Chromolithographs in the 'diaspora space' of 'India' do more than just echo an aesthetic precedent in a quickly changing world: they are, and always have been, essential to the process. The visual theology of chromolithographs in 'India' – enhanced in its pervasiveness – reifies mass-production subsumed by inventiveness and faith. Take the truly authentic 'aura' of God, multiply it in the Age of Mechanical Reproduction, and find the omnipotence of Indian chromolithographs framed in a 'diaspora space' that Walter Benjamin never imagined (1968). Clearly, the integration of Indian images into Vodun epistemologies, in conjunction with deep spiritual conviction, attests to the ongoing, globally incorporative sensibilities of 'creativity' in Vodun art and thought.

Bibliography

Aguessy, Honorat (n.d.): *Cultures Vodoun: Manifestations-Migrations-Métamorphoses (Afrique-Caraibes-Ameriques)*, Cotonou: Institut de Développement et d'Echanges Endogènes (IDEE).

Arnett, William; Wittmer, Marcilene K. (1978): *Three Rivers of Nigeria*, Atlanta: The High Museum of Art.

Aziamblé, Abbé G. Kodjo (1981): Les Prêtres du dieu Nyigble dans la Forêt Sacrée de BE, Responsable de Culte en Mileu Traditionnel, *La Voix de St. Gall,* 38: 22-6.

Babb, L. A.; Wadley, S. S. (eds.) (1995): *Media and the Transformation of Religion in South Asia*, Philadelphia: University of Pennsylvania Press. Benjamin, Walter (1968): *The Work of Art in the Age of Mechanical Reproduction*, New York: Schocken Books.

Bettelheim, Judith; Nunley, John (1988): *Caribbean Festival Arts*, Seattle and London: University of Press.

Blier, Suzanne Preston (1995): *African Vodun: Art, Psychology and Power*, Chicago: University of Chicago Press.

Brah, Avtar (1996): *Cartographies of Diaspora: Contesting Identities*, London: Routledge.

Brown, Karen McCarthy (1991): *Mama Lola: A Vodou Priestess in Brooklyn*, Berkeley: University of California Press.

Carter, Paul (1999): *Dark with Excess of Bright: Mapping the Coastlines of Knowledge*, in: Cosgrove, Denin (ed.): *Mappings*, London: Reaktion Books.

Chesi, Gert (1979): *Voodoo: Africa's Secret Power*, Worgl (Austria): Perlinger-Verlag.

Clifford, James (1992): Travelling Cultures, in: L. Grossberg, C. Nelson; Treichler, P. (eds.): *Cultural Studies*, New York: Routledge.

Cosentino, Donald J. (1995): *Sacred Art of Haitian Vodou,*. Los Angeles: UCLA Fowler Museum of Cultural History.

Cosentino, Donald J. (1998): *Vodou Things: The Art of Pierrot Barra and Marie Cassaise*, Jackson: University Press of Mississippi.

Cosentino, Donald (1999): In Memoriam, Pierrot Barra, 1942-1999,' *African Arts*, Winter 1999, XXXII, 4: 16-17.

Cosgrove, Denis (ed.) (1999): *Mappings*, London: Reaktion Books.

Drewal, Henry J. (1988a): Interpretation, Invention, and Representation in the Worship of Mami Wata, in: Stone, Ruth M. (ede.): *Performance in Contemporary African Arts*, Folklore Institute, Indiana University: 101-139.

Drewal, Henry J. (1988b): Performing the Other: Mami Wata Worship in Africa, *Drama Review* 32, 2: 160-85.

Drewal, Henry J. (1996): Mami Wata Shrines: Exotica and the Constitution of Self, in: Arnoldi, Mary Jo; Geary, Christraud, Hardin, Kris L. (eds.): *African Material Culture*, Bloomington: Indiana University Press: 308-333.

Eicher, Joanne B.; Erokosima, Tonye V. (1996): Indian Textiles in Kalabari Funerals, in: *Asian Art and Culture*, 9, 2: 68-79.

Freedberg, David. (1989): *The Power of Images: Studies in the History and Theory of Response*, Chicago: The University of Chicago Press.

Gore, Charles; Nevadomsky, Joseph (1997): Practice and Agency in Mammy Wata Worship in Southern Nigeria, *African Arts*, 30, 2: 60-9, 95.

Houlberg, Marilyn (1996): Sirens and Snakes: Water Spirits in the Arts of Haitian Vodou, *African Arts*, 29, 2: 30-5, 101.

Inglis, Stephen R. (1995): Suitable for Framing: The Work of a Modern Maste, in: Babb, L. A.; Wadley, S. S. (eds.), *Media and the Transformation of Religion in South Asia*, Philadelphia: University of Pennsylvania Press: 51-75.

Law, Robin (1977): *The Oyo Empire c. 1600-c.1836: A West African Imperialism in the Era of the Atlantic Slave Trade*, Oxford: Clarendon Press.

Law, Robin (1991): *The Slave Coast of West Africa 1550-1750: The Impact of the Atlantic Slave Trade in an African Society*, Oxford: Clarendon Press.

Leiris, Michel (1952): Notes sur l'usage de chromolithographies catholiques par les vodouisants d'Haiti, in: *Les Afro-Americains*, Dakar: IFAN.

Lovejoy, Paul E. (ed.) (1986): *Africans in Bondage: Studies in Slavery and the Slave Trade*, Madison: University of Wisconsin Press.

Lutgendorf, Philip (1995): *Another Ravanna, Another Rama*, XIIth International Ramayana Conference. August 28-30. Leiden, Netherlands.

Manning, Patrick (1982): *Slavery, Colonialism, and Economic Growth in Dahomey, 1640-1960* Cambridge: Cambridge University Press.

Morgan, David (1998): *Visual Piety: A History and Theory of Popular Religious Images*, Berkeley: University of California Press.

Naipaul, Vidiadhar Surjprasad (1990): *India: A Million Mutinies Now*, New York: Viking Press.

Narayan, R. K. (1972): *The Ramayana*, New York: Penguin.

Nevadomsky, Joseph (1997): Contemporary Art and Artists in Benin City, in: *African Arts*, 30, 4: 54-63, 94.

Peffer, John (1997): *Personal communication.*

Rush, Dana (2007) 'Somewhere Under Dan's Rainbow: Kossivi Ahiator's India Spirits in the Mami Wata Pantheon,' in *Sacred Waters: The Many Faces of Mami Wata and Other Afro-*

Atlantic Water Spirits, Los Angeles: UCLA Fowler Museum (forthcoming 2007).

Salmons, Jill (1977): Mammy Wata, in: *African Arts*, 10, 3: 8-15.

Smith, H. Daniel (1997): Introduction: The Impact of 'God Posters' on Hindus and Their Devotional Traditions, in: Lawson, G.J.; Pal, P.; Smith, H.D. (eds.): *Changing Myths and Images: Twentieth-Century Popular Art in India*, Bloomington: Indiana University Art Museum

Vogel, Susan (1991): *Africa Explores*, Munich: Prestel for The Museum for African Art, New York.

Wadley, Susan (1995): No Longer a Wife: Widows in Rural North India, in: Harlan, Lindsey and Courtright, Paul (eds.): *From the Margins of Hindu Marriage: Essays on Gender, Religion, and Culture*, New York: Oxford University Press: 92–118.

The Pot and the Kettle: 'Hybrid' Discourse in Swahili Literature

Farouk Topan

> '... [The] cross-fertilization of cultures has been endemic to all movements of people ... and all such movements in history have involved the travel, contact, transmutation, hybridization of ideas, values and behavioural norms.'
>
> (Ahmad 1995: 18)

Some processes, like some diseases, exist and develop without being identified, although their effects are beyond doubt. The process which emerges from a state of hybridity has only been identified and labelled as such relatively recently; as Fludernik puts it, hybridity and syncretism 'have recently established themselves as new luminaries on the horizon of critical terms' (1998: 19). I will discuss syncretism later in the paper, but it is noteworthy that the term 'hybrid' and its derivatives ('hybridity', 'hybridization') have expanded in usage, particularly in literary discourse, from their initial meaning denoting a subject of mixed race to a cultural state, process or even site that describes the effects of an interaction between two peoples, the ruler and the ruled, from two different (usually racial) backgrounds. The main exponent of this alternative meaning in its various guises has been Homi Bhabha, whose *Location of Culture* (1994) is acknowledged to be a seminal corpus in which different facets of this phenomenon are explored.

Bhabha is not easy to read, as his treatment of hybridity seems to take one through a labyrinth of ideas in which one sees the focus shift, as in a kaleidoscope, on to different sites. Fortunately, the works of Fludernik (1998) and Young (1994) provide an excellent insight into Bhabha's theory while making a contribution of their own in this field. I draw mainly on them in attempting to understand the phenomenon in relation to the Swahili, a people inhabiting the east coast of Africa.

Hybridity has been studied, elaborated and applied mainly in relation to colonial and post-colonial situations. In this context, 'colonial' is usually taken to refer to the era of the reign and rule of Western powers over the peoples of Asia and Africa. However, as is now being increasingly acknowledged, hybridity transcends the colonial experience back in time. Its patterns and cultural underpinnings can be discerned in Asian and African societies long before the onset of the European incursion. One finds that such has been the case among the coastal Swahili, for example, when one explores their history, particularly in terms of Braudel's concept of the *longue durée*, which I have explored briefly elsewhere with regard to the Swahili (Topan 2000).

In this sense, then, the Swahili could be said to have gone through a double process of hybridity – the pre-colonial on the one hand, and the colonial and the post-colonial on the other. The first occurred when the 'indigenous' East African coastal culture – itself probably hybrid in some ways – interacted with certain dimensions of Arab culture over a period of at least twenty centuries (if we base ourselves on the accounts in the *Periplus of the Erythrean Sea*). Clearly, what we call 'Arab culture' was itself not constant over this period, its greatest catalyst for change being the introduction of a new *Weltanschauung* in the Makkan society of the seventh century.

The second process of hybridity for the Swahili – as indeed for millions of other people the [Third] world over – was initiated by European colonialism. The powers which occupied the coast brought their own values and ways of thinking to the people. How they imparted these values and inculcated their thinking depended largely on the pre-conceived attitudes the colonials brought with them or developed towards the colonized during their rule.

These two types fall almost neatly into the two categories of hybridity postulated by Bakhtin for languages (1981: 358). There is, first, the unconscious, 'organic' hybridity which is a feature of the historical evolution of all languages. When we apply this model to culture and society more generally, we find, as Werbner explains, that, 'despite the illusion of boundaries, cultures evolve historically through unreflective borrowings, mimetic appropriations, exchanges and interventions' (1997: 4-5). With organic hybridity, there is no disruption to the sense of order and continuity in society: 'new images, words, objects, are integrated into language or culture unconsciously' (ibid.).

The second type, the conscious intentional hybridity, ironically builds on the foundations of the organic. It builds 'to shock, change, challenge, revitalise or disrupt through deliberate, intended fusions of unlike social languages and images' (ibid.: 5). It is this type of hybridity which has been the focus of studies on colonial interventions and their postcolonial impact.

The two – the unconscious and the intentional (as applied to culture) – find expression in a Swahili text of superb craftsmanship. *Wakati Ukuta* ['Time is a wall'] is a short play by Ebrahim Hussein written, remarkably, when he was a student at the University of Dar es Salaam in the late 1960s (though published in 1970). The dynamics of the plot involve a clash between characters whose differing world-views are conditioned by the cultural hybridities they espouse, or, perhaps more correctly, which envelop them. Tatu is a young woman of 21 who wants to go to the cinema with her boyfriend, Swai, an immature lad of equal (or younger) age. Her mother, Asha, is a woman who believes strongly in the correctness of 'tradition': she wants to raise Tatu the way she was raised and accordingly expects Tatu to behave as she herself had behaved when she was Tatu's age, particularly in public. To Asha, the public image of herself and her family matters a great deal, and 'what people say' therefore is important to her. She wants to avoid *aibu,* 'shame', at all costs. So when Tatu announces that she is going to the cinema with Swai, Asha reacts vehemently against the idea, is shocked that her daughter should even entertain such a thought. When Tatu persists with her idea, saying that she does not care what people say, Asha tells her sternly:

> Mimi najali – sitaki aibu mimi. Unalofanya wewe sio aibu yako tu, bali ya wote, mimi, baba yako, ukoo mzima. Mimi nimelelewa na wazee wangu, nilipokuwa mkubwa wakanipa mume. Sikumjua, hakunijua, lakini mpaka sasa tunakaa vema. Nami nitakufanyia hivyo hivyo. Mpaka nikupe nyumba yako halafu hapo tena shauri yako. Kama huyu Swai anakupenda mwache alete posa.
> I care – I do not want shame [upon me]. Your action will bring shame not only on yourself, but on all of us, me, your father, the entire family (lit. clan). I was brought up by my parents, [and] when I was of [marriageable] age, I was given your father [in marriage]. I did not know him, he did not know me, and yet we have lived together well [since getting married]. And I shall do the same with you. [I will do this] until I give you your own home, and then it will be up to you [how you behave]. If this [man] Swai loves you, let him bring a proposal of marriage for you.[1]
>
> (Hussein 1970: 12)

The passage contains significant Swahili cultural traits, both explicit and implicit, which the mother deems to be under threat through the behaviour of her daughter. Respect for parents and the purity of the daughter are two among the implicit traits; explicitly, there is discussion of the proper way of bringing up a girl to the age of marriage, the responsibility of the mother in doing so, the relationship between husband and wife, and the accepted way for a boy to demonstrate his love for a girl, i.e. by sending a proposal of marriage, and, perhaps above all else, the fear of shame *(aibu)* sanctioned by gossip. Interestingly, Asha does not lay the blame on herself for Tatu's behaviour; it does not even cross her mind that she

---

[1] Unless otherwise stated, Swahili texts have been rendered into English by me.

might have gone wrong somewhere for Tatu to turn out the way she has. Instead, she blames *uzungu*, 'Europeanness', 'to behave like a European'. In fact, in the very first lines of the play, the mother chastises Tatu for wearing a tight 'mini', accusing her of aping European manners:

> Sio uzungu! Ndio kuiga uzungu tena. Basi sisi si Wazungu. Mzungu na Mwafrika mbali mbali. Mila zetu mbali mbali. Wao hawana haya, anaweza kwenda na mume huyu na mume huyu isiwe kitu.
> Isn't that being European! That is indeed aping 'Europeanness'. So [do understand that] we are not Europeans. A European and an African are two different [people]. Our customs are different. They have no shame, she could go with this man and this man and nothing happens [i.e. without any sanction or consequence].
>
> (ibid.: 12)

Swai calls at Tatu's home to take her to the cinema. The mother refuses to give her permission, but Tatu goes with him defiantly anyway. The mother then asks Tatu not to come back, in effect throwing her daughter out of the house. When her husband returns home, he becomes angry with her at first and is puzzled, as her actions are sure to cause the family precisely what she has been desperate to avoid, namely shame (*aibu*). But he then looks at the situation rather philosophically, drawing an interesting lesson from Swahili history:

> Mwarabu alitutawala sisi, na sisi tukafuata tabia zake na mila zake. Nitazame mie, navaa kofia na kanzu. Kwani jadi yangu mimi ni kofia na kanzu – au asili yako wewe, au watani wako, walivaa buibui au mtandio? Sisi hatukuwa kama wazee wetu. Basi na hawa sasa watoto wetu vile vile. Wanasoma kizungu, tunawavalisha kizungu, wanakwenda shuleni kusoma kizungu – Na wataiga kizungu katika kusema, mavazi, mila hata na

> tabia. Sisi tunaona mabaya, wao wanaona mazuri. Hakuna mtu anaweza kushindana na wakati.
>
> The Arab ruled over us, and we followed his habits and his customs. Look at me, I am wearing an [Arab] cap and *kanzu [long dress-like shirt]*. Did my ancestors wear (such) a cap and *kanzu* – or [consider] your origins or [those of] your friends/compatriots – did they wear the [black] veil and scarf? We have not grown up like our parents. It is thus the same with our children. They learn in a European way, we make them wear [their clothes] in a European fashion, they go to school to learn a European language – and they will [therefore] imitate European ways in their speech, clothes, customs and even (personal) habits. What we see as bad [ways], they consider good. No one can compete with time.
>
> (ibid.: 17)

To Tatu's father, the episode was a logical outcome of the European incursion; it is to him inevitable that children like Tatu will embrace *uzungu* ('Europeanness') the way his forefathers had absorbed *ustaarabu* ('Arabness'). He goes on to say that time is like a brick wall. If you fight it you will hurt yourself, implying that time is on the side of *uzungu*, a term which stands for things European and, by extension, for Westernisation and, in that sense, for globalisation as an ideological underpinning of hybridity (and vice versa). For the mother, however, *uzungu* is disruptive, divisive and disintegrating. The implication of what she says is clear enough: that *ustaarabu* was a seamless process which worked always in favour of the Swahili, empowering them with moral and ethical values by which to live and behave in society. The social system generated by *ustaarabu* facilitated the fulfilment of Swahili aspirations and developed their self-consciousness as a cultured people who 'plugged into' – to use de Vere Allen's phrase (1979: 11) – a wider, global system of thought. The Swahili did this not as 'Arabs' but as a people with their own identity who adopted some of the cultural traits of the other. Abdulaziz captures well this syncretic mode when he writes:

> The Arab-Islamic component did not superimpose itself but acted as a strong cultural stimulus to the development of this urban form of African culture. [...] In any given period the Arab population element must have been very small, compared to the population of the local inhabitants. Indeed the trend on the Coast has always been the Swahilizitation of the Arabs rather than the Arabization of the African Muslim inhabitants, in such facets of culture as language and mode of living in general. This trend has been so forceful that most Arabs on the Coast, who have settled here within the last two centuries or so, have lost their original culture and language and completely adopted Swahili culture.
>
> (Abdulaziz 1979: 8)

Islam played a crucial role in this process. It is a characteristic of Islam, as indeed of other world religions, that, in its interaction with pre-established cultures, it introduced ideas which people gradually adopted and then adapted to make their own. But the 'package' conveyed as 'Islamic' also included customs and traditions which belonged more to native Arabia than to the message of the Revelation. These two entities, the message and the traditions, interacted with yet a third, the existing coastal culture, to forge what then gradually emerged as Swahili culture. Other influences, mainly Persian and Indian, also fed the cultural cauldron of the East African coast. It is thus difficult today to disentangle the threads and categorically state their origins. But even so, the perception among the Swahili is that Islam provided an ethical framework for Swahili morality through which human relationships were conducted with propriety. As both Mama Tatu and Baba Tatu would acknowledge, this framework effected the smooth running of the family in which a consciousness of respect permeated the domestic environment. Mothers, fathers, wives, husbands and children knew what was expected of them, and each knew his or her place.[2] Children accepted as a matter of course the status of their parents – and of the elders in the extended family – as their moral mentors (cf. Swartz 1991: 189-208)

But things change. Vasco da Gama's voyage of 1498 opened the door for Western contact with the coast. Another system of values, sanctioned by the power and might of yet another race and underlined by another world religion, gradually exerted its presence among the Swahili. To the Portuguese, chronologically the first Europeans to interact with the Swahili, religion seems to have been one of the main ingredients that underpinned their attitude. Mazrui and Shariff quote a powerful directive of Pope Nicholas V 'granting the King of Portugal the monopoly of trade with African peoples, provided they were brought willingly or by force to baptism' (1993: 22). And yet it is largely true to say that, despite this, the Portuguese made little impact on the Swahili in terms of the conversion of faith. True, they have contributed many loan-words of almost daily usage to the language – *meza* (table), *karata* (playing cards) and *nanasi* (pineapple) among them – and they have left behind architectural legacies. However, they did not succeed on the coast to the extent they did in Angola, Mozambique and in Goa, for instance, where they effected a deep transformation of local communities, with religion as a focal point.

The story is, of course, different with the other three European powers, the German, the French and the British, whose proselytizing abilities met with huge success on mainland East Africa, with significant inroads on the coast itself. This is symbolized by the fact that early Western scholarship of Swahili was conducted by missionaries whose works and names have now become 'classic'. Krapf, Sacleux, Taylor and Steere are among the foremost examples of

[2] A testimony to such relationships, mainly between husband and wife, may be found in a poem by Mwana Kupona (Allen 1971; Topan 2004).

scholars whose work generated the publication of dictionaries, grammars, collections of tales, proverbs and poetic manuscripts, with the next generation of missionaries building upon their achievements. These scholarly activities took place in tandem with the entrenchment of a colonial system of education whose ethos was based inevitably on Western ethics. Western influence trickled into society and then permeated it, through other means such as fashion, dress, films, cigarettes, beverages and drinks, food, etc. Language was, of course, the most significant. The list is admittedly familiar, but I repeat it here to underscore a point not usually made in such surveys, namely that these factors moved some Swahili on to the site of hybridity, where the old 'high culture' from the Middle East was replaced in their eyes by a new one from Europe. And it is not inconceivable that, in this process, a few 'educated' Swahili even weighed in their minds some aspects of the 'new' faith which they might have found attractive.

An example of this thought comes again from the works of Ebrahim Hussein (Topan 1974: 180-2).His poem *Ngoma na Vailini* was written at about the same time as *Wakati Ukuta* and actually 'performed' by him in 1968 at the University of Dar es Salaam, where he was a student at the time. I quote from a description of the performance I have written elsewhere:

> He [Hussein] played back a tape of his recitation of the poem and he danced to it with movements of his body, standing on the same spot throughout the performance with arms outstretched on either side. He swayed to one side and then the other – symbolizing the pull towards the drum and the violin respectively – as the poem progressed. His costume consisted of a black and white *kanzu* (with patches removed) and a cross of considerable size hung from his neck. When he reached the end of his poem, he bowed his body, hung his head, and let the cross swing before him.
>
> (ibid.: 162)

The poet – or the narrator – goes through an excruciating experience of having to make a choice between the outcomes, as we might say, of the two processes of hybridity, symbolized by the (African) drum on the one hand, and (Western) violin on the other. The drum offers him a throbbing, almost erotic pleasure, the violin a calm, soothing joy. He feels he has to make a choice between the two. The metaphor is then extended to include Christianity, represented by the cross, on the side of the violin, and a torn, patchy *kanzu* representing Islam, on the side of the drum. The choice is a hard one to make, and his recourse in the end is to prayer:

> Lazima niswali, lazima niabudu
> nimuabudu Allah
> I must pray, I must worship
> I must worship Allah

And it is here that doubts generated by his position assail him. The poem ends with an incisive question, born directly out of the feeling of being 'in between':

> Lakini ataisikia sauti yenye panda
> Sauti inayotokana na mwenye kuvaa
> kanzu na msalaba?
> But will He listen to a divided voice
> the voice of someone who wears
> both a Muslim *kanzu* and a Christian cross?
>
> (ibid.: 180-1)

Lest this gives rise to some speculation (as it did in the case of Mohamed Kijuma and, before him, Liyongo), I should state that, as far as I know, Ebrahim Hussein has not converted to Christianity. All the same, it is interesting that the son of a well-known sheikh of the Shadhiliyya order should have posed this question, albeit during the turmoil of youth. Thus, the process of hybridity could also be painful for those caught up in its throes, though (as Bakhtin noted in another context) the subject could well then be placed on the cusp of a new world, or at least, a new way of looking at the world.[3]

What arc the other characteristics of hybridity, what factors are concomitant with its presence? Bhabha identifies three: liminality, ambivalence and mimicry. Again, as these are articulated by Fludernik in a far more comprehensible manner (1998: 32-46), I draw on her essay but project them according to my own interpretation of the East African situation.

Liminality is a central concept of hybridity, referring to the 'in between' space [the site] where one stops in a move from being totally 'original' towards being like 'the other'. The perception of the other prompts and generates certain actions, both simple and complex, on the part of the subject as he moves through the period of liminality. In most cases of hybridity, however, the transit stage of liminality itself becomes a terminal stop.

The Swahili have occupied such a liminal site for centuries, 'basking' – if I may borrow Parkin's word [1994 : 1] – in the paradox of their identity generated by the move. For the Swahili, the 'high culture' of the Arabs was the first and enduring 'other' to emulate. It is significant that the word for 'civilization' is *ustaarabu*, 'to be like an Arab', captured so pointedly in the title of Salum Kombo's booklet, *Maendeleo ya Ustaarabu wa Mwafrika*, 'The Development of African Civilization [literally, 'of the African']'. Mimicry, or perhaps more properly imitation, is implied in the term. But, as Bhabha points out (1994: 86, quoted in Fludernik 1998: 45), such imitation (or mimicry for him) renders the subject 'almost the same, but not quite' as the object of that action. This, to my mind, is an extremely crucial distinction for the Swahili that characterizes the independence and autonomy of their identity. Far from being a

[3] It is interesting to note that the form of the poem was itself new part of the innovative experiment in 'free verse' which gave rise to interesting debates among the innovators and the 'traditionalists' on the definition of the Swahili poem and the identity and status of those who compose it.

negative attribute of their status, liminality has become a positive, effective hallmark of their existence. And, as Abdulaziz pointed out earlier, it is the Swahili who accommodated the 'Arabs' and Swahilized them.

This bears out another point made by Bhabha: that the colonizers too become hybrids in that same process of hybridization. The colonial administrator or official is affected by the process and undergoes a change in his attitude towards the world around him. For instance, the Englishman or -woman abroad is not the same as those at home (cf. *A Passage to India*). One could say the same about the so-called 'Arab' in Swahililand.

The status of the 'nation' in Africa is another example of an entity that occupies a liminal status in the process of hybridity. It too was a colonial creation, in many instances with arbitrary boundaries. The retention of the Westminster model of governance in the case of the former British colonies, with all its regalia, highlights this hybridity, as does the regalia of the judiciary. Some leaders, Nyerere amongst them, have attempted to modify the system to suit African needs. His policy of *ujamaa* ('African socialism'), as Blommaert notes, aimed to create one single classless society within the boundaries of a nation that considered itself 'a family', with Swahili as the national (family) language among the *wajamaa*. Such a move, as Bhabha would say, also created an 'internal liminality'; as the nation moved, so did the communities within the nation in relation to one another, creating interspaces of liminality and hybridization. Although the policy of *ujamaa* has since been abandoned, its effects, especially on the linguistic front, have lasted. There are today far more speakers of Swahili as a first language within Tanzania than on the coast and the islands. These individuals, born between two ethnic cultures, have been reared for over a generation now within the cultural milieu of the hybrid nation. The definition of Swahili identity has acquired a newer paradox for scholars to ponder over.

In relation to Swahili literature as such, the question posed in terms of its identity was similar to that posed for English when the latter was used by others to produce excellent works.[4] The answer for Swahili, as for English, has now long been settled in the same way (see Bertoncini 1994: 205-13 for a discussion of the issue). Mainland and coastal or island writers, both groups hybrids in their own way, have produced fine literature and have grappled with the same issues in their works. They have noted the rise of the *wazungu weusi* ('black Europeans') and *wabenzi* (the newer classes, symbolized by possession of Mercedes Benz) during the pre-*ujamaa* phase of Tanzanian history; the uses and abuses of political office during and after *ujamaa*; the suffering brought about by corruption; the inhumanity of over-zealous Youth Wingers; and the amassing of wealth and indulgence in pleasures by ministers and government officials. There is also an expression of hope for the future, but the overwhelming focus is on the present.

Quite a few of these issues have been discussed in the Swahili novel, itself – as Geesey would probably say – a hybrid genre (Geesey 1997: 134). Two good examples of novels which discuss the outcomes of hybridity for Tanzania (and African nations in general) are Gabriel Ruhumbika's *Miradi Bubu ya Wazalendo* (1992) and Said Mohamed's *Babu Alipofufuka* (2001). Ruhumbika specifically targets Tanzania, and even more interestingly, draws Nyerere as a President under whose watch corruption rises while the economy falls. He seems to be blissfully unaware of both while continuing to exhort the *wananchi* (citizens) to higher ideals.

Mohammed's novel posits a framework of magical-realism in which the older generation attempts to correct the follies of the young. K is an arrogant young member of the elite, a hybrid who is forever moving in liminal spaces that are devoid of his roots. But

---

[4] This comparison was not lost on Nyerere, who once remarked that English is the Swahili of the world.

then his dead grandfather appears to him (rather like Mzee Jabiri in *Miradi*) as an apparition, and through dialogue, fantastic expeditions and death, K comes to realize what he could have been and what he could have done for his country and his family.

Both novelists are part of the Swahili diaspora in the West, where the experience of the 'immigrant' is conditioned by attitudes whose forces of interplay are both local and global. He or she is placed on a continuum of liminality with the expectation (and sometimes promise, or perhaps threat, as some view it) of moving towards 'acceptance' and 'integration' in the wider community. Tanzanian writers in English have recorded such experiences, notably Gurnah (*By the Sea*) and Vassanji (*No New Land*). With the exception of a novel called *Lwidiko*, part of which is set in Scotland, there is an almost total absence of reflections in Swahili writers on this dimension of life, of such importance for the younger generations who have been born or at least bred in the West. As they move in and out of two cultures – one at home and the other 'outside' – perhaps their experiences in the West will be more syncretic than hybrid. They will learn to fuse the better aspects of the two and move in a circle that also transcends both: 'a confluence of different traditions which are homogenized into a new culture' (Fludernik 1998: 20).

Conclusion

But to return to the Swahili coast, the main question which has arisen in my mind as this brief essay has taken shape is whether becoming aware of the process of hybridity and the experience of syncretism make it easier to understand the Swahili. Theirs is, after all, a complex situation. They are a people who have undergone a double process of hybridity, first with the Arabs, and then with the Germans and the British (or Europeans). Their lands in Kenya became part of a larger national entity and have since been acquired by others. They themselves own hardly any land today and have become largely marginalized. The situation is slightly better in Tanzania, where the

Swahili still have some control over their land, though the forces of tourism and the multinationals are now denuding them of that control. In one respect, then, one can view the Swahili as a people who have always had to negotiate their space with other people. The Swahili perception of these others is expressed in songs and poems of *taarab*, spirit possession cults, wedding celebrations, etc., and in the names and organisation of clubs and societies (Ranger 1975, Topan 1974).

Today, the focus of identity for the majority of Swahili has shifted inwards within the countries themselves. The futures of Kenya and Tanzania respectively will decide how the Swahili are viewed, and perhaps even how they view themselves. The political affiliations now being forged might well plant seeds of future perceptions. The discourse of the clubs and social gatherings *(baraza)*, the market place, the parliament (*bunge)*, the streets, the beaches and other public and private spaces need to be captured by literature, including also those of the mosques, the churches and the marginalized neighbourhoods and wards (*mitaa)*.

Bibliography

Abdulaziz, M.H. (1979): *Muyaka: Nineteenth Century Swahili Popular Poetry*, Nairobi: Kenya Literature Bureau.

Ahmad, Aijaz (1995): The Politics of Literary Postcoloniality, in: *Race and Class*, 36, 3: 1-20.

Allen, James de Vere (1979): *Swahilisation: A Cultural Concept and its Significance in Kenya Today*, Nairobi: The Institute of African Studies, University of Nairobi. Paper No. 125 (mimeographed).

Allen, John W.T. (1971): *Tendi: Six Examples of a Swahili Classical Verse Form with Translations and Notes*, London, Heinemann Educational.

Bakhtin, Mikhail (1981): *The Dialogic Imagination.* Austin: University of Texas Press.

Bertoncini, Elena (1994): Inland Tanzania: Swahili Literature or Literature in Swahili?, in: *Continuity and Autonomy in Swahili Communities: Inland Influences and Strategies of Self-determination*, Parkin, David (ed.), Wien: Beiträge zur Afrikanistik: 205-13.

Bhabha, Homi K. (1994): *The Location of Culture*, London: Routledge.

Blommaert, Jan (1991): Some Problems in the Interpretation of Swahili Political Texts, in: Blommaert, Jan (ed.) *Swahili Studies. Essays in Honour of Marcel Van Spaandonck*. Gent: Academia Press: 109-35.

Blommaert, Jan (ed.) (1992): *Swahili Studies*, Ghent: Academic Press.

Fludernik, Monika (1998): *Hybridity and Postcolonialism*, Tübingen: Stauffenburg Verlag.

Geesey, Patricia (1997): Cultural Hybridity and Contamination in Tayeb Salih's Mawsim al-hijra ila al-Shamal (Season of Migration to the North), *Research in African Literatures*, 28, 3: 128-40.

Hussein, Ebrahim. (1970): Wakati Ukuta, in: Topan, F. (ed.): *Michezo ya Kuigiza*, Nairobi: East African Publishing House.

Kombo, Salum Mohamed (1950): *Ustaarabu na Maendeleo ya Mwafrika*, Nairobi: Eagle Press.

Mazrui, Alamin; Shariff, Ibrahim Noor (1994): *The Swahili: Idiom and Identity of an African people*, New Jersey: Africa World Press.

Mohamed, Said A. (2001): *Babu Alipofufuka*, Nairobi: Jomo Kenyatta Foundation.

Parkin, David (ed.), (1994): *Continuity and Autonomy in Swahili Communities. Inland Influences and Strategies of Self-Determination.* Wien and London: Beiträge zur Afrikanistik, School of Oriental and African Studies.

Ranger, Terence (1975): *Dance and Society in Eastern Africa, 1890-1970: The Beni Ngoma*, London: Heinemann Educational.

Ruhumbika, Gabriel (1992): *Miradi bubu ya wazalendo*, Dar es Salaam: Tanzania Publishing House.

Swartz, Marc J. (1991): *The Way the World Is: Cultural Processes and Social Relations among the Mombasa Swahili*, Berkeley: University of California Press.

Topan, Farouk (1974): Modern Swahili poetry, *Bulletin of the School of Oriental and African Studies*, London, XXXVII, 1: 175-87.

Topan, Farouk (2000): Being Muslim in East Africa: A Swahili perspective, in: Salter, Thomas, King, Kenneth (eds.): *Africa, Islam and Development*, Edinburgh: Centre of African Studies, University of Edinburgh: 283-97.

Topan, Farouk (2004): From Mwana Kupona to Mwamvita: Female Representations in Swahili Literature, in: Caplan, Pat and Topan, Farouk (eds.): *Swahili Modernities*, Trenton N.J: Africa World Press: 213-227.

Topan, Farouk (1995): Vugo: A Virginity Celebration Ceremony among the Swahili of Mombasa, *Journal of African Languages and Cutures*', 8: 87-107.

Werbner, Pnina (1997): Introduction: The Dialectics of Cultural Hybridity, in: Werbner, Pnina; Modood, Tariq (eds.): *Debating Cultural Hybridity: Multicultural Identities and the Politics of Anti-racism*, London: Zed Books.

Young, Robert J.C. (1995): *Colonial Desire: Hybridity in Theory, Culture and Race*, London: Routledge.

Syncretism and Anti-Syncretism in Marriage Matters in Kumasi: The Role of Pentecostal Charismatic Churches

Astrid Bochow

Syncrestism and Antisyncretism: talking about social change

The rise of new Pentecostal charismatic churches[1] in the past fifteen years in Africa has been subject to many academic writings. By introducing a new discourse on wealth, economic success and access to consumption, such churches have been treated as institutions offering coping strategies with modernity and the liberalisation introduced by structural adjustment programmes in the mid-1990s (Meyer 1998, Gifford 2004). Recently they have also been analysed for their influences over popular culture, as in Birgit Meyer's studies of Ghanaian videos (1999, 2004).

The influence of images, produced in popular media on social praxis, has been highlighted by Appadurai (1997). However, what role do these popular images play in social realities? In other words, how are these discourses translated into social praxis? What role do they play in social change?

This chapter attempts to examine the question of how discourse and praxis relate to each other by examining changes in marriage and matrimony in Ashanti, especially Kumasi,[2] which have been pro-

---

[1] The term has been suggested by Birgit Meyer (2004: 448).

[2] Kumasi is situated in the centre of Ghana. It is known for having been the capital of the Ashanti kingdom since the eighteenth century and for accommodating the oldest market in West Africa. With its approximately one million inhabitants, it is now a modern town with Internet cafes and electronic shops, even though in Ghana itself it has the image of being 'culturally conservative' for accommodating the seat of the Ashanti kingdom and for having a predominantly Twi-speaking population. In contrast, the capital Accra is considered to be more cosmopolitan, modern and

moted by charismatic churches as global agents in introducing new ideas of marriage and the family.

The new Pentecostal churches are exerting a vast impact on social life in South Ghana's urban environment. They attract a predominantly young audience, who attend the services in large numbers to sing, clap and dance, accompanied by a band and dressed in their best clothes. I rarely met people who did not claim to be a member of a church, which in most cases meant specifically a *charismatic* church.[3] Membership of a church is so much part of the identity of the social person in Kumasi that it became unthinkable *not* to be a member of a church. In addition, taking somebody to one's church is an act to create and demonstrate commonness and, last but not least, is a legitimate way to approach a girl or to be approached by a boy.

Marriage and matrimony are dominant subjects in the discourses of the new Protestant churches, which have been quite successful in launching a strong normative discourse postulating the purity of these norms and rejecting any compromise. In this text, two Pentecostal charismatic churches (PCCs) I regularly visited exemplify the policy of such churches towards marriage. The churches have different approaches to marriage, but their overall discourse about marriage, promoted in the public media, is very similar. As a result, I will talk about PCCs' discourses in general, but will specify my data when I talk about their procedures.

Using 'syncretism' and 'anti-syncretism' as descriptive tools for social change, I will explore the changes in the Ashanti marriage ceremony that have been encouraged by PCCs, as well as their effects on discourses on sexuality. Charles Stewart and Rosalind

innovative. During 2004 and 2005 I conducted research for about seven months in Kumasi and for about three months in an Ashanti-speaking village in Assin District. In this chapter I refer mostly to my experience in Kumasi. I thank the German Research Council for their financial support.

[3] Most of the former mission churches have introduced charismatic branches to prevent their members leaving.

Shaw have criticized the use of the term 'syncretism' in religious studies as essentialising and de-historising the (religious) tradition out of which syncretic praxis resolves: 'Religions are frequently treated as analogous to 'rivers of traditions' which flow free of human agency' (Stewart and Shaw 1992: 25). Rather than using 'syncretism' as merely a metaphor for the mixing of two or more 'cultural elements', therefore, I will follow up Steward and Shaw's suggestion that processes of syncretisation should be examined within historically specific situations and power relations (see also Ferme 1992, Meyer 1992).

Syncretism has been described as a cultural practice that combines already known elements from different contexts. It might be perceived by actors themselves or by the researcher as mixing or merging. This perspective stresses the constructive character of any syncretistic situation by stressing that either actors or researchers may regard it as a puzzle of various elements not combined formerly. Following up this position on syncretism, all social praxis is syncretic – a merging of various influences – and thus, syncretism becomes a metaphor for social change in general. Anti-syncretism, then, is the artificial manufacture of purity as commonly found in religious movements.

In my text I will indicate changes. I will use the terms 'new' and 'old' as well as 'traditional' and 'customary' which are labels that people in Kumasi themselves have applied. 'New' denotes points on which church policy is different from the 'old'. In defining what is 'old', 'customary' or 'traditional', I consider descriptions which have been given congruently by *all* interviewees between the ages of 40 and 80. 'Formally' this is not a clearly distinctive period. Those interviewed refer to their own experiences in the past, between 20 and 60 years ago.

During this time I lived in two households, observed family matters in everyday life, conversed with people inside and outside the churches about courtship and life-views, visited services and witnessed marriage counselling at two churches: the Assemblies of God in Kwadaso, and the Lighthouse Chapel International in Asafo, both in Kumasi.[4] I conducted interviews with their members and pastors, of which thirty have been recorded and fully transcribed. Others are recorded in my field diary.

Discourses of Pureness: The Imperative of Holiness

In their agenda, the church authorities produce a discourse of purity about their doctrines which they derive from the *imperative of holiness*. Representatives of the churches place a lot of emphasis on rules of proper conduct rooted in this imperative of holiness. This includes the rejection of polygamy, extra- and premarital sexual intercourse – the keyword is fornication – and divorce, precisely re-marriage, as well as the consumption of alcohol. Here I analyse the discourse surrounding the imperative of holiness as opening up a discursive space in which to negotiate the old and the new.

In his booklet *All about Fornication*, Dag Heward-Mills, the founder and bishop of the Lighthouse Chapel International, writes in the first paragraph of the first chapter: 'Fornication is sexual intercourse before marriage.' Even though in the following text he also speaks about the situation of adultery, it is obvious that in his discourse against fornication he is especially addressing young people who are not yet married (Heward-Mills 2002: 1). The reasons given for not entering into pre-marital relationships are in the first place spiritual ones. Generally, and also here in Dag Heward-Mill's writing, the prohibition of pre-marital sex draws support from the

[4] The Assemblies of God arrived from the US in the 1930s with the puritan movement. The Lighthouse Chapel International (LCI) was founded in the mid-1980s by a Ghanaian with a Swiss background. Whereas the Assemblies of God is very popular among young people of the lower middle class, that is, young people learning a trade or being in some sort of tertiary education such as a polytechnic, the LCI attracts people with an academic background, since their authorities are university degree holders and their services are held in English.

famous sentence in 1. Corinthians 6:19: 'The body is the temple of God.' This prohibition is justified by constructing sexual intercourse before marriage as a spiritual and physical violation of the self and the body, which do not belong to the individual but to God.

This principle of not becoming involved in pre- or extra-marital sexual relationships is one which is always mentioned by pastors as well as born again Christians. Especially young pastors preach against fornication. In the case of the Assemblies of God it is part of the church's doctrine. But young people in church too stress the importance of not entering into sexual relationships before marriage, since they have learned to understand their abstinence as a process of building trust in a relationship. This is taken as evidence that one's partner is strong enough to resist adultery *within* a marriage.

Whereas the ban on pre-marital sexual contact may be familiar to many Western readers from the history of Christianity in Europe, the demand for abstinence of alcohol makes sense in the cultural context of Ghanaian society more specifically. This is particularly because the claim not to be using alcohol is made with reference to the assumption that alcohol accommodates 'bad spirits' and therefore is considered powerful and destructive.

In the Akan context, alcohol is important for any decision made when chiefs and elders – family elders as well as community elders – are hearing cases concerning conflicts or the signing of contracts and agreements. They legitimise their decision by 'pouring a libation', which consists in a little of an alcoholic drink with a high percentage of alcohol such as *schnapps* or *akpeteshie* (local gin) being poured on the ground to pacify the gods. A larger sip out of the glass which makes the rounds among the participants is, consumed by the men in power. Given that *akpeteshie* has a very high percentage of alcohol, between fifty and seventy percent, participants in this ritual drinking often become quite drunk. This procedure is also performed during the marriage ceremony: two bottles of *schnapps* and two bottles of *akpeteshie* form a fixed part of the marriage payment.

The men in power, the chiefs and elders, who are associated with the sacred use of alcohol, are easy to meet in Ashanti as well as other Akan societies. Under the main chief of a community are about thirteen sub-chiefs in a single village, not all of whom are equally present in community affairs. In addition, every matrilineage or *obusua* has its elders, who have quite a responsible function since land used for agriculture is in the possession of the matrilineage. Their function is to administer investments and profits from the harvest (for instance, of cocoa) and distribute them to the other members of the matrilineage. Elders are both nominated through their position due to kinship (ministries are inherited matrilineally) and selected by the other members of the *obusua*. In general, chiefs and elders are known to demonstrate their power, or at least their influence, by insisting on symbolic actions to fulfil 'tradition'. A teacher in Assin Endwa, of the Central Region, for instance, commented on the 'attitude of the *obusua panin*', as he expressed it, while telling me the story of a complicated marriage. He mocked:

> 'And then another *obusua panin* came up and requested schnapps for something, and then another one, and another one. They always find something to make life difficult for you.'
>
> (Field diary, 8 April 2004)

Given the great number of chiefs and the restricted influence they have,[5] it is likely that their position does not guarantee all of them influence and access to resources. However, advocating that things should follow the right agenda according to 'tradition' is a sure means for them to claim influence.

The discourse of born-again Christians reacts to the elders' interpretation and use of alcohol as a symbol of the exercise of power by treating alcohol as a carrier of evil spirits which has to be avoided by

[5] Chiefs have the power to decide over small-scale conflicts, mostly family-related matters, as well as land disputes.

every Christian. Just to use alcohol for the performance of the customary rites is forbidden, even though the church authorities insist that the parents must agree to the marriage.

These claims are often part of a public debate, for instance on phone-in shows on the radio about the use of alcohol during the customary rites. On this subject, the imperative of holiness conflicts with so-called traditional values, and hence with traditional authorities like the chiefs or the *obusua panin*.

I argue here that the debate over the use of alcohol represents a symbolic struggle between two domains of power: of the churches of Born Again Christianity,[6] associated with modernity (Meyer 2004), and of the chieftaincy, which leans on tradition as its source of power. In the social history of Ghana, alcohol has long played a role in the transition of power structures: in his social history of alcohol in Ghana, Akyeampong (1996) shows that its consumption in the colonial and post-colonial societies of the coast was an instrument for young men to rebel against the authority of older men. Drinking and possession of alcohol had been the privilege of old men. With the introduction of paid labour first in the gold mines and later in the cities, young men could afford to buy alcohol with their own money, which quite early, in the 1920s and 1930s, encouraged the creation of some sort of youth culture associated with drinking alcohol and night life (ibid.: 53-62).

The relationship between the church authorities and the political authorities of communities, as well as those of the *obusua*, is itself one of conflict. Theoretically, marriage could be an occasion for these conflicts to manifest themselves, since customarily the ceremony requires the pouring of a libation. I did not, however, witness

---

[6] Only the Catholic Church still allows their members to consume alcohol. They also tolerate polygamous marriages. Hence all chiefs and elders are members of the Catholic Church. The division between different elites by church membership became very visible in Assin Endwa, a village in the Central Region: Whereas chiefs and elders were members of the Catholic Church, the teachers, all around the age of thirty, were members of the Pentecostal Church.

any such conflicts myself, and when I asked about them, pastors could not describe any actual case in which there have been arguments surrounding this practice. In an actual case the spouses, their families and the pastors would come to a compromise: instead of presenting *schnapps* or *akpeteshie* as marriage payments, the Christian groom would hand over their value in cash. Whether the pastors really had been as successful in their aims as they claim or whether they simply chose to understate these conflicts is hard to judge. Rijk van Dijk reports some conflicts in which *obusua panins* had exerted their influence over the ceremony by insisting on the proper use of alcohol (van Dijk 2004: 449).[7]

My observations indicate that actual conflict tends to shift to the virtual space of TV and radio shows, where the question is debated as to whether it is legitimate to substite money for alcohol in the marriage payments.[8] Here, only supporters of the purist position insist that a Christian should not substitute money for *akpeteshie* since un-Christian items such as alcohol will be bought with it, and non-Christian acts, such as the pouring of libations, done with it. In the discourse of purity, there is no compromise on this position.

Whereas the procedure of courtship recognises and integrates family authorities here, in the public debate, the antagonism between the family elders and the church authorities becomes obvious. This debate is one of the very few moments in which the replacing of an old order by a new one is actually articulated. It is remarkable that this negotiation is purely symbolic and merely found on the discursive level.

---

[7] Unfortunately he does not mention where he observed these conflicts. I suggest that the low level of recognition of potential conflicts in my data from Kumasi reflects first the broad acceptance that PCCs enjoy today, and secondly, that families in general are so happy that their daughters are marrying that they avoid any confrontations that might upset the ceremony.

[8] As it was done, for instance, in a debate on the TV show *Ye di kɔmo* ('We are Talking') at TV3 in June 2004.

The Problems of Status and Community, the Promise of Success of Changing Celebrations: 'Customary' Rites and Weddings in Kumasi

With their demand that young people abstain from sex before marriage, pastors are also impinging on a field which has, according to the literature, never clearly been distinct before (Fortes 1975; Manuh 1995: 190-2; Allman and Tashjian 2000: 50-60). From what point in their relationship a couple are regarded as 'married' is a matter of interpretation. The less formal situation would be the case of a man and a woman living together in the same room: they will be regarded by both neighbours and friends as being married, and nobody would question their actual married status. Customarily, however, there are some requirements which couples have to meet before they gain the status of being fully married. For women especially, it is always desirable to be considered married, since prestige and respect are linked to this status. Unmarried women are referred to as 'small girls', just as unmarried men are called 'small boys'. For men, however, it is easier to compensate for one's unmarried status by obtaining a respectable position or earning enough money from a job. Being a 'small girl' has the unpleasant effect that everybody can send one on errands and that men can approach one, whatever the situation, as Regina from Endwa, 29 years old and still unmarried, explained:

> 'When you are not married, they don't respect you. Even a small boy on the street can call you and tell you 'I want to marry you'.'
>
> (Interview, 24 March 2004)

In the following paragraphs I will first discuss different statuses of marriage before going on to describe changes in the celebration of marriage. In my last paragraph, I will show why weddings in church became popular. What are they offering with their 'new' celebration, and how does the 'new' match the 'old' in it?

The anthropological literature of the colonial period discusses the different ways in which the married status might be obtained by treating it as actually consisting of different *forms* of marriages (Rattray 1929/1969: 23-31) that exist at the same time. More recent literature, however, talks about different stages of marriage and emphasises that marriage is a process in which not only the spouses, but also the families of both are involved (Allman and Tashjian 2000: 78).

To be fully recognised as husband and wife, the husband's family or relatives must make marriage payments (*aseda*) to their future affines. These prestations are actually a combination of various separate payments – one for instance, called *akontasekan*, for the brother so that he may protect his sister from dangers and the harassment of other men – which today has been merged into a single sum handed over to the father of the bride, who then redistributes it. These payments not only ensure the husband's sexual rights to the woman and their children: most important in the Ghanaian context, even today, is that this status obliges him to contribute to his wife's funeral expenses in case of her death.

The first stage, which can be seen as a preparation of this final stage, is the so-called 'knocking' (*kɔkɔɔkɔ*), in which the husband introduces himself with a bottle of *schnapps* to the family, today usually to the girl's father or a representative if he is absent. On this occasion, the man introduces himself as a prospective spouse and acknowledges his responsibilities if 'something happens to the girl', namely if she becomes pregnant.[9]

---

[9] These different modes of marriage were first described by Rattray (1929/1969) as different *forms* of marriage. However, in their social history of gender relations, Allman and Tasjian claim that these forms are rather to be thought of as different *stages*. By doing so, they stress the idea that marriage is a process and does not imply an immediate change of status as has been the case in the West (Allman and Tashjian 2000: 78). Even though the 'knocking' is perceived as a provisional arrangement, in everyday praxis it often replaces the 'final' form. Given this, I

The literature agrees on the point that although formally the 'knocking' allows sexual intercourse, it is not regarded as a demarcation of the full marriage status and therefore does not transfer all the sexual rights over the woman and the couple's children to the man (Fortes 1975: 279; Manuh 1995: 190-1). In contrast to Manuh, Allman and Tashjian (2000: 52-7) point out that in the first colonized generation in Asaante, a relationship might have been considered a full marriage in its knocking stage, provided it was accepted as such by the parents. Even today the knocking can at times still replace the actual customary rites.[10] In this case, the knocking is mostly performed with the promise to 'finish everything' later, as it is popularly put. This may be demonstrated by a case study, the marriage of Kwame Mensah.

Now 73 years old and a Twi teacher in Kumasi-Kwadaso, 'Master', as Kwame Mensah is popularly called, has been married just once. His relationship with his future wife started after she approached him, and he went to her parents to present the *schnapps* and ask their permission to marry their daughter. Later she moved into his room, and they had two daughters. His wife was a beautiful woman, he recalls, but was troublesome and 'was taking men'. As a result, he decided not to perform the rites and also not to marry her in church, which would have been more important since he is a strong Catholic. One day she left for Côte d'Ivoire. Some years later she came back and died soon afterwards. Even though, according to custom, he was not obliged to, he did attend her funeral and contributed to the costs. According to his explanation, the fact that they both came from the same home town and that their families' houses were

---

would suggest that Rattray's earlier view of different *forms* of marriage existing next to each other be rehabilitated.

[10] Another piece of evidence for the varied use of the terms can be found in Rijk van Dijk's reference to the 'modern engagement', which requires a payment of money as well as of gifts and is at times also celebrated as a 'knocking', which is, however, a pre-stage for the 'engagement' (van Dijk 2004: 247). Today the modern engagement usually contains all three stages of courtship.

next to one another obliged him to do so, even though the full rites had not been completed.

Kwame Mensah's shows that the various stages of acquiring married status are clearly distinct from each other in the *model* of custom, though in practice the knocking can be regarded as a full stage in marriage, either through habit or for reasons of prestige. For a couple to be recognized as married, family acceptance as well as communal expectations is stronger than the actual formalities required for the marriage.

Among Ashantis, the marriage *ceremony* is customarily not a big celebration, unlike funerals, in which the *obusua*, the matrilineage, puts itself in scene. As I observed in the rural context, the occasion on which the marriage itself is contracted is merely a meeting of the *obusua panin* (elders of the family) and the parents of the spouses, at which they drink a lot of *akpeteshie* and negotiate the marriage payments. The bride and groom are not necessarily present themselves.

Some elderly people still recall that they celebrated the moment at which the bride moved into the groom's household, a practice unknown to today's younger generation. In the urban environment, a new form of celebration was created in the 1990s. This celebration is commonly referred to as an 'engagement' and consists mostly of all three stages of the marriage process: the knocking, the introduction of the suitor to the family and bride, and the final payment). For this celebration both families will be present, as are the bride and groom, who sit under canopies facing each other. The ceremony itself brings together various symbols, some of them borrowed from the West, like the veil and the ring, while others come from different regions of Ghana. The costs of the celebrations are relatively low. These ceremonies are colloquially referred to as 'engagements', even though *de jure* they have the same legally binding consequences as weddings or registered marriages. But a new celebration has also arisen within the Christian churches, namely the wedding. There are various opportunities to celebrate the wedding, depending on the financial means of the spouse, for instance the option of serving refreshments in church for everybody present, or of going to lunch or dinner at a restaurant for invited guests only. Obligatory is the white wedding dress for the bride and the black suit for the groom.

Historically the wedding is not a new celebration. The archives of the Basler Mission contain pictures of brides in white and grooms in a wedding suit from the beginning of the last century.[11] Furthermore, 'white' marriages have been common among urban elites since the1970s. In this period, a new model of family in which the nuclear family has priority in terms of care and expenditure, for instance for education, had become a symbol of status and prestige for the urban elite (Oppong 1981: 1-27).

To date, these celebrations and the values attached to the Christian marriage have gained a good deal of normality. Among young people in an urban context like Kumasi, it has become a common goal to marry in church, as can be seen from the case of Nana Owusu. This 23-year-old member of the Assemblies of God works in a shop and is one of the better off young people, since he can afford to live on his own:

> 'I would want our wedding to be like the *normal* one. She will put on the wedding gown and march inside, then I meet her and we go and sit down.'
>
> (Interview, 16 February 2005, my emphasis)

In general, it is the pride of the groom to be able to have *many* people at the wedding. Common phrases such as 'people came in their number' indicate that the celebration was a success.[12] But generally it is more important for women to be married in church, as became very clear from two interviews I carried out with a young couple

[11] See www.bmpix.org, picture number D-30.20.022.

[12] Not only weddings, but also, and more importantly, funerals are judged by the numbers of people attending.

about their plans for their wedding. Talking about the wedding Isaac, 26 years old and working in the service sector, said:

> 'I have a lot of friends. I am going to invite all of them [...] and I will make some food for them but not at the church premises. I will take them to some place [...] to a restaurant.'
>
> (Interview, 28 February 2005)

In talking with him, I found that the question of how to celebrate the wedding was not a particularly big issue, but we did speak in length about the amount of money he had been able to save for the wedding. In addition, whether he communicates with Isabella, his fiancée, about money issues was very important to him.
Isabella, however, whom I interviewed separately, imagines their wedding as follows:

> 'As for the dress, I want to be simple and smart. I want to look gorgeous because this is the first and the last so I want to look gorgeous,' and explains further: 'As for that day, it will be a great day in my life because it is once, because you give the woman the privilege to look glorious, so it's a very great day and [the] happiest day [in my life].'
>
> (Interview, 5 March 2005)

The dream of a wedding that honours her by displaying her beauty, as articulated by Isabella, might just as well have been expressed by any woman in the Western world. The congruence between the Western idea of the wedding as honouring the bride as described by Bulcroft et al. (Bulcroft et al. 1999) and Isabella's dream of her wedding is perfect. Weddings in church have become a commonly pursued ideal for young people, a commonly desired good.[13] This

---

[13] Here I am relying on Bourdieu's theory of the various types of capital which are important for processes of defining and establishing one's status (Bourdieu 1983, 1998). In Kumasi many debates go on about how much money should be spent or rather not spent on weddings, which promotes the association with 'goods' (items bought with money) and refers to the idea of the market.

trend can be seen as a continuation of popular notions of the wedding as a carrier of the values that represent a middle-class or elite life-style.

Not only are the ceremony and the celebration a goal that young people want to achieve in life, but so are the values which are attached to it by the churches, and even more so. The combination of three particular principles promoted for Christian marriage makes it very attractive. First, there is a great deal of emphasis on the patri-central shape of the family. Secondly, the principle of *care* is a core concept, meaning that men must cater for their wives and children in a way that cannot be taken for granted in the traditional matrilineal context. Economic preconditions and household management during a marriage are highlighted by church authorities, and sometimes even considered an obligatory requirement, so that marriage becomes a successful enterprise with which to provide the church's members with basic needs, food, medical care and basic education. A third principle which makes a Christian marriage attractive – especially for women – is that polygynous marriages and taking girl- or boy-friends are prohibited. The models that PCCs offer together with this new wedding celebration can be seen as a continuation of what the mission churches introduced earlier. Whereas in colonial times as well as earlier in the postcolonial period the Christian wedding was an exclusive status marker of the educated elite, it has now become not only desirable, but also accessible for a broader population, holding out the promise of success and well-being in life.

Syncretistic Praxis: Marriage Procedure in the Assemblies of God

PCCs watch over this ideal of Christian marriage, popularly associ-ated with the imperative of holiness. Here they stress the opposition to 'fornication' rather than the ban on the use of alcohol. Their statements and procedures, criteria for a good Christian marriage, should also be assessed against the background of the fluid nature of

Akan customary marriage. They not only promote the criteria for a good Christian wedding in particular, but also define strict criteria for the boundary between married and unmarried statuses in general.

In this section, I shall show how, in their *social praxis*, PCCs are incorporating old-established patterns of courtship. Whereas in their discourse they promote purity and thus engage in a politics of anti-syncretism, in their praxis they are instead rather syncretising. In spite of the antagonistic nature of relations between the church and family authorities, churches tend rather to co-operate with family elders or parents, with whom they mostly deal directly. Customarily parents are the authority that actually approves the marriage. In church too, one of the most important pre-conditions for marriage is that the parents agree to it, and usually they even insist that the 'customary' rites have to be performed. As a result, the wedding can never *replace* custom but can only be added to it. Concerning matters of marriage, therefore, churches rely on the authority of the family rather than encouraging a 'complete break with the past' as had been prominently described by Meyer (1998) for deliverance sessions in a charismatic church.

However, the Assemblies of God have invented a new process of courtship in which they have created new authority to watch over the reputation of those wanting to marry. Pastors as well as lay workers in church devote a lot of their time to this procedure of testing and teaching the candidates. Before a couple can be married, they have to go through from five to fifteen sessions of marriage counselling, in which they are taught knowledge about the institution of marriage.[14] Depending on the couple, the church and the marriage counsellors, these courses will start between three and six months before marriage. Candidates are examined as to whether they fulfil the necessary pre-conditions for marriage. This practice seems to have been

---

[14] Most PCCs now have this kind of marriage counselling before marriage, but the first church to come up with the idea was the Catholic church.

successful among their clients: to acquire a certain standard of living before marriage was important for all young people. Whether they find the *right* partner, a subject that belongs to the romantic discourse about love, was not a question they were concerned about.

Potential spouses are also tested by the church on their mental and social maturity, which can be seen as a continuation of old-established practises of courtship.According to custom, when a couple expressed a desire to marry, their families would launch an investigation into the other family and the prospective spouses by asking around in the community about the spouse's character (*suban*), whether he or she was known as a respectable person, was not a thief, a liar or a womaniser, or, in the case of a woman, known to be 'troublesome'.

In the church the pastor or members of the marriage committee have taken over this function, and not only by 'testing' the candidates in marriage counselling. Their activities go far beyond this and require time-consuming activities outside the church, for instance, when they visit the families in order to check whether the two people are planning to marry with the consent of their families, and in order to receive a positive impression about the prospective tie. If the bride and groom are not from the same church, the pastor requests a letter of recommendation from the other spouse's pastor, in which an evaluation of the candidate's qualities as a Christian and a church member are requested. Only with this letter of recommendation will permission to marry be given.

The second enquiry a family will start concerns the family and health backgrounds of the prospective spouse. It is of importance whether there are chronic diseases like epilepsy or frequent deaths in a family, which are commonly seen as witchcraft. To marry a family in which there are said to be witches would mean endangering one's own family because, according to customary beliefs, witches can only operate within their own families. Any marriage into such a family, however, would also make one's own vulnerable to it.

Health questions are still an important issue, now watched over by church authorities. It is obligatory for both partners to undego a health check, which includes a test for the sickle cell anaemia status and recently also an HIV/AIDS test.

In sum, the new authorities for controlling the process created by the churches have taken over the role of the family. The most important feature of this newly installed ceremony is that they must co-operate with the 'traditional' authorities, like the family elders, instead of confronting them. They both support and gain the support of these more traditional authorities, but also have created new authorities and structures of control, which today have a stronger impact on courtship than the fomer authorities did, namely parents and family elders.

Talking about Sexuality: Silence, Jokes and Power

How successful are the churches with this rigid policy of regulating premarital and extramarital relationships? In fact, 90% of all those interviewed between the ages of 20 and 40 wished to marry or recommended marrying a good Christian.

In addition, the churches have been quite successful in watching over the ethics of relationships so that having boyfriends or girlfriends becomes an issue of morality. Most particularly, they have influenced the discourse about relationships. At an initial stage of my research and my relationships with people, even with people of my own age it proved very difficult to talk about 'love matters'. Sexual relationships and sexuality are talked about in a secret language which insinuates actual facts rather than clarifies the situation and opens up a space for a great deal of guessing and speculation.

In addition, church doctrine encourages arguments and negotiations in relation to 'former times' and 'today' in which these questions of morality are projected into time. Older people stress that today young people have sex before the actual rites are performed, which had not been the case in their own youth. Almost every time I introduced the topic of change in Ashanti marriages, the old people reacted with this strong talk about the 'loose youth'. Young people, however, sometimes perceive their 'mother's time' as having been 'loose'.[15] Likewise tradition can at times be considered to be marked by many predicaments over sexual activities (Bochow 2001).

Since probably all societies have figures of speech in which the older generation condemns the younger generation, we may consider talk about a morally upright past to be coloured by collective projections. Nonetheless studies in the social history of Ghana do suggest that sexual matters became more marginalised from the public sphere through colonisation and the missions. Sources from the seventeenth century tell us about 'public women', slaves bought from rich men and women in the community for the sexual needs of bachelors. Before they were allowed to start acting in this role, however, they were instructed in their duties as well as introduced to the community by receiving an initiation. In addition, their position gave them certain communal rights (Akyeampong 1996: 147-9). The existence of this institution suggests that the sexual needs of the bachelors of the community were commonly recognised and not at all tabooed in the seventeenth century and later. This raises the possibility that the rejection of sexual relations before marriage 'in former times' has become a taboo *a posteriori*, possibly as a reaction to the 'new' discourse.

In discussing the looseness of young people, older persons I interviewed refer to the drinking of beer. As well as listening to music and hanging about in the streets, drinking was associated with loose living. At the same time, they observed that the old children's games of clapping and singing, which they themselves played in childhood, have been forgotten. These perceptions reflect deeper transforma-

---

[15] 'In our mother's time, you see, people were loose', said Aysha (interview, 14th August 1998, Accra), speaking about Christian marriages which are popular among this generation.

tions in society, like the adaptation of youth life-styles, from which, for example, puberty rites have entirely disappeared.

Elderly persons above fifty also used this hidden language to camouflage sexual contacts. Talking about the knocking, for instance, they would point out the importance of letting a girl's parents know where to find her. Not only do parents relinquish here a part of their control over the girl's movements, but also possible sexual contacts could be hinted at by remarks from men, such as: 'The parents have to know you, otherwise they might think you are a thief when they see you with the girl.' Thieves are usually considered to go around by night. This remark relies on the common sense in Ghana that a boy and girl being either alone together in a room or alone at night, hidden in the dark from outside glances, are always considered to have been sleeping with each other.

In spite of the ban on sexual relationships in the official discourse, everyday talk provides discourse patterns to remind, insinuate and communicate people about sex nonetheless. These are 'juicy jokes': just like the existence of any heterosexual relationship outside of marriage, jokes with sexual connotations of various kinds can be heard all day long. Especially in the women-dominated domain of the Central Market in Kumasi, sexual matters are expressed in an almost rude manner, sometimes at the expense of the few men around. Teasing interrogations about the duration and quantity of sexual intercourse belong to this discourse, as well as 'language games' using self-created words to describe the act itself. Permanent jokes in the street in which people call each other girlfriend or boyfriend, or ask a third person whether he or she is the girlfriend or boyfriend of someone else, or teasing men over the number of girlfriends they have, as well as girls calling each other 'rivals', are common in everyday communication.[16]

---

[16] I suggest that 'boyfriends and girlfriends' constitute a new type of relationship between young men and young women, a friendship developed out of the range of parental control, and without the knowledge of the church authorities. One indica-

Asymmetrical power relations between men and women, as well as power games among women themselves, are thus detected and tested playfully, questioned and taken back. But talking about sexual matters in public is a matter of age and status. Married women who have given birth and show by their voluminous bodies that they are mature and experienced enough are allowed to talk about sexual matters more than young women or even young men.

In the realm of the female-dominated Central Market in Kumasi, these language games eventually turn into a discourse of *confidentiality*. Here having a partner was not so much a concern of economic stability or social recognition, but rather an expression of the wish for company to counter their loneliness, sexual matters themselves being discussed under the aspect of pleasure. Here women complain about their loneliness because their husbands have gone abroad and their families will not allow them to divorce them. They therefore complain about their limited degree of mobility and the fear of their becoming a victim of gossip. However, the same people who reveal their desires during a confidential conversation in the market may nevertheless stress the importance of Christian values when advising younger people to abstain from premarital sexual relations. Here they are presenting themselves as gate-keepers in respect of moral issues. Recalling the churches' position, older women, especially when they are married, are thus able to assert their authority in cross-generational relationships.

Talk about sexual matters and relationships offers a discursive space in which to negotiate and demonstrate power relations. It often reflects power relations between men and women, old and young, educated and non-educated. Here, the PCCs offer a strong narrative which may be called on as a resource to justify one's position. In creating or just strengthening social pressure with moral arguments,

---

tion of this is the adoption of the terms 'boyfriend' and 'girlfriend' into the local language Twi. I heard it used even by Twi speakers who did not use common anglicisms such as 'doctor' or 'hospital' in their language.

their discourse patterns dominate everyday discourses, and everyday talk about sexuality becomes a taboo. As a result, the Pentecostal discourse encourages the emergence of the classic mechanisms of double ethical standards.

Conclusion

Although hard evidence is missing, I suggest that Pentecostal Churches have *created* the problem of sexual activity or rather premarital sexual relationships.[17] The fluid nature of marriage suggests that pre-marital intercourse was, if not encouraged, nonetheless accepted.

Three consequences can be observed coming out of the marriage policies of the PCCs. First, they are continuing a trend started by the mission churches: Christian marriage as an exclusive good for the colonial and early post-colonial elites. Their discourse upholds Christian marriage as a rare good – only achievable by those who abstain – which has become very much part of the everyday life for most young people in south Ghana's cities, including Kumasi, since it provides a model for success in society. Christian marriage is no longer part of a foreign exotic life-style followed only by a small elite but has become part of *normality* in Kumasi.

Secondly, with their courtship procedure, the churches are not only promoting the criteria for a good Christian marriage, but also introducing clear, distinct boundaries between the married and unmarried statuses. The wedding serves as the marker of this change of status. Outside church this boundary very much depends on the acceptance of parents and family and on communal expectations, as we saw in the discussion of the meaning of the knocking ceremony (see above), so that the churches are filling a gap in social norms and

[17] In Ghana, it is not only churches that introduce sexual matters into the public discourse, but also newspaper and magazines and also the Internet, which promote 'sex' as an issue to talk and learn about.

praxis outside themselves. With the wedding as a celebration that clearly marks a change in status, together with the norms of Christian marriage; they are offering something which cannot be found outside the church.

Thirdly, by producing a discourse of purity concerning not only sexual relationships but also abstinence from alcohol and its use in customary rites, the PCCs have opened up a symbolic space in which social relations of power can be negotiated. Here, the 'old', i.e. the chiefs and elders as traditional authorities, and the 'new', i.e. the church authorities, have became polarised. In practice, however, potential conflicts rarely arise. Indeed, the church authorities tend to rely on the traditional authorities when it comes to marriage, especially in legitimising a new marriage. We have seen how various actors – church authorities, chiefs and elders, radio show producers, young people about to establish themselves, old people in the village, already established market woman – rely on, refer to and/or sneak around this discourse, using it in the everyday praxis of marking positions in society (*Positionierungsprozesse*) (Bourdieu 1998).

Even though these Pentecostal churches are promoting something 'new', the imperative of holiness, and promoting also its purity, in their praxis of courtship they are therefore relying on old established patterns of courtship which they have reformed. This skilful playing with the 'old' and the 'new' may well explain a good deal of their success.

Bibliography

Akyeampong, Emmanuel Kwaku (1996): *Drink, Power, and Cultural Change: A Social History of Alcohol in Ghana, C. 1800 to Recent Times*, Oxford: James Currey.

Allman, Jean; Tashjian, Victoria (2000): *'I Will Not Eat Stone': A Women's History of Colonial Asante*, Oxford: James Currey.

Appadurai, Arjun (1997): The Production of Locality (Chapter 9), in: *Modernity at Large: Cultural Dimensions of Globalizazion*, Delhi etc.: Oxford University Press: 178-99.

Bochow, Astrid (2001): 'Europe Is Charming, Right?' Vorstellungen von Modernität, Wandel und dem guten Leben in Gesprächen über Europa in Accra, Berlin: unpublished MA thesis.

Bourdieu, Pierre (1983): Ökonomisches Kapital, kulturelles Kapital, soziales Kapital, in: Kreckel, R. (ed.): *Soziale Ungleichheiten*, Göttingen: Verlag Otto Schwarz: 183-98.

Bourdieu, Pierre (1998): *Die feinen Unterschiede: Kritik der gesellschaftlichen Urteilskraft*, Frankfurt am Main: Suhrkamp.

Bulcroft, Kris et al. (1999): *Romancing the Honeymoon: Consumating Marriage in Modern Society*, London: Sage Publications.

Ferme, Mariane (1992): What 'Alhadji Airplane' Saw in Mecca, and What Happened When He Came Home: Ritual Transformation in Mende Community (Sierra Leone), in: Shaw, R. and C. Stewart (eds.): *Syncretism/Anti-Syncretism: The Politics of Religious Synthesis*, London, New York: Routledge: 27-44.

Fortes, Meyer (1975): Kinship and Marriage among the Ashanti, ed. A.R. Radcliffe-Brown, D. Forde, *African Systems of Marriage and Kinship*, London: Oxford University Press: 252-85.

Gifford, Paul (2004): *Ghana's New Christianity: Pentecostalism in a Globalising African Economy*, Bloomington: University of Indiana Press.

Heward-Mills, Dag (2002): *All About Fornication*, Accra: Parchment House.

Manuh, Takyiwaa (1995): Changes in Marriages and Funeral Exchanges among the Asante: A Case Study from Kona, Afigya-Kwabre, in: Guyer, JI (ed.): *Money Matters: Instability, Values and Social Payments in the Modern History of West African Communities*, London: James Currey: 188-99.

Meyer, Birgit (1992): Beyond Syncretism: Translation and Diabolization in the Appropriation of Protestantism in Africa, in: Shaw, R. and C. Stewart (eds.): *Syncretism/Anti-Syncretism: The Politics of Religious Synthesis*, London, New York: Routledge: 45-68.

Meyer, Birgit (1998): The Power of Money: Politics, Occult Forces and Pentecostalism in Ghana, *African Studies Review* 41, 3: 15-37.

Meyer, Birgit (1999): Popular Ghanaian Cinema and 'African Heritage', *Africa Today* 95, 2: 93-114.

Meyer, Birgt (2004): 'Praise the Lord': Popular Cinema and the Pentecostalite Style in Ghana's New Public Sphere, *American Ethnologist* 31, 1: 92-110.

Oppong, Christine (1981): *Middle Class African Marriage: A Family Study of Ghanaian Senior Civil Servants*, London: George Allen & Unwin.

Rattray, Robert S. (1929, 1969): *Ashanti Law and Constitution*, Oxford: Clarendon Press.

Stewart, Charles; Shaw, Rosalind (1992): Introduction, in: Shaw, R. and C. Stewart (eds.): *Syncretism/Anti-Syncretism: The Politics of Religious Synthesis*, London: Routledge: 1-27.

van Dijk, Rijk (2004): Negotiating Marriage: Questions of Morality and Legitimacy in Ghanaian Pentecostal Diaspora, *Journal of Religion in Africa* 34, 4: 438-68.

Expanding the New

The New and its Temptations: Products of Modernity and their Impact on Social Change in Africa

Elísio Macamo and Dieter Neubert

Introduction

An underlying assumption in the discussion of modernisation and globalisation is the opposition between universalising processes on the one hand and the tendency to maintain traditional – or better still, local – life-worlds on the other, most pointedly captured in the slogan 'Jihâd versus McWorld' (Barber 1996). However, this opposition has been bridged or even dissolved by concepts like *glocalisation* (Robertson 1995) or *hybridisation* (respectively, creolisation or syncretisation) (for an overview, see Weißköppel 2005). Throughout these debates, we have come to know that local and global processes are interwoven and that people make their own sense of them and may appropriate outside influences in their own terms. Many studies focus on this process of interaction and theorize about the ways in which people come to terms with global influences, as well as about weather the outcome should be described as local, with some domesticated global elements, as in *glocal*, hybrid or, more bluntly, globalised and homogenised. We have the feeling that two issues have not yet been adequately addressed in this debate.

Firstly, in this debate it seems that modernity and globalisation are somehow perceived as being interchangeable and the choice of either concept merely draws from the discourses in which authors take part. We think a study of local life-worlds and global forces should differentiate between these interlinked concepts.

Secondly, the process of transformation at the local level has still not been understood in detail. We are faced with two contradictory approaches. Classical modernisation theories (e.g. Inkeles and Smith

1974, Smelser 1973) and some of their current followers (e.g. Oesterdiekhoff 2006) imply that modernity is a teleological movement. The corresponding process of modernisation is leading up to an almost automatic creation of a homogenous modern world society which is only mildly shaped by local cultural features.

However, classical modernisation theories have been dogged by their inability to explain cases where development does not materialise given their assumption that development is the result of the transition from tradition to modernity. In such cases these theories would refer to persistent 'tradition', a statement which is more of an observation (that does not necessarily have to be correct) than an analysis.

Their opponents criticise this assumption of an automatic development with a predetermined end and underline the agency of people who create their own way of innovation as well as their own future; this way does by no means lead to a universalised future, but rather to radicalised diversity in which modern equals contemporary because everything is or can be modern. Seen from this perspective, transformations are the result of local agency and the appropriation of outside influences according to local criteria and orientations. While we sympathise with this understanding we think that agency is neither almighty, nor should it be constructed to mean that anything can happen. Additionally, this way of looking at things might lead to the loss of the analytical quality of the notion 'modern'.

For an understanding of the transformation of local life-worlds we must take a closer look at how people react to outside influences which appear to them as 'the new'. As far as people are concerned, at least at the beginning, it does not matter whether the new is 'modern' or 'global'. The main question is whether it is attractive, a threat or even unimportant. This approach will require us to develop an understanding of the nature of 'the new', for the way people react to it is intimately linked to its properties.

We propose to study how specific innovations come into local life-worlds and how people react to them. To approach this question we start with the simple observation that industrial technology and engineering and their products are attractive. Additionally, at least for a considerable number of people, ideas like freedom and democracy are tempting, too. We propose to understand these types of innovations as 'products of modernity', a term that encompasses material artefacts, techniques, institutions or ideologies. While these products of modernity are from a local perspective just something new and tempting, we think that given their very nature dealing with them may have a specific impact on people and their society. Furthermore, this impact may be of relevance to an understanding of social processes. We hope that an analysis of the appropriation, rejection, mastering or transformation of these products will open up paths to the understanding of change in local life-worlds under the conditions of globalisation and under the influence of modernity. We think that this gives us an opportunity to place local agency in a context that is open to the consideration of structural influences without walking into the trap of structuralist or classical modernisation theories and their shortcomings.

Before we develop our concept of products of modernity and present some examples of its empirical-analytical relevance, we would like briefly to go back to the first issue and clarify the concept of modernity as we use it here as well as its relation to globalisation. To be more specific, in this chapter we are not concerned with the empirical description of change, but rather with the development of an analytical perspective for the empirical description of social change.

Modernity and Globalisation: A Brief Clarification of Concepts

By modernity we understand a historical period marked by a specific structural figuration which had its origin as well as initial development in Europe but subsequently spread all over the world. Moder-

nity is characterised by a qualitatively new relationship among people and between them and nature. This relationship manifests itself in special political and societal projects as well as in the technological mastering of or dominion over nature.
This conceptualization of modernity is based on Anthony Giddens. He sees three dynamic forces that drive modernity (Giddens 1990: 17-45):

- The separation of space and time.
- The development of social mechanisms through which certain societal functions are wrestled free from their localized 'bed' and are restructured over wide distances in space and time.
- The reflexive appropriation of knowledge and its feedback on society.

Modernity is organized around four interlinked institutional dimensions (Giddens 1990: 55-63):

- capitalism
- industrialism (production process based on machines driven by sources of inanimate energy)
- surveillance capacity and information control (national administrations)
- control of the means of violence.

These institutional dimensions developed against the background of the Enlightenment and of what Weber called the rationalization process.

Whereas the economic institutions of capitalism and industrialism reach across borders and are withdrawn from complete political control, the political institutions of control are executed within the borders of a territorial state which is itself part and parcel of modernity.

We should bear in mind that these institutional dimensions have not been universally implemented. To put it differently, there is no necessary link between capitalism and modernity. Socialist countries, for instance, were, and some of their heirs still are, part of modernity without necessarily being capitalist. What would (have) happen(ed) if socialism had dominated the whole world is only a hypothetical question.

For the development of our argument one element of Giddens' theory of modernity must be stressed here, particularly his ideas on 'disembedding mechanisms' drawn largely from Karl Polanyi and Georg Simmel. 'Disembedding mechanisms' allow social relations to detach themselves from a local context. Giddens mentions two such mechanisms, namely on the one hand, symbolic tokens (money and political loyalty) that organize impersonal exchange, and, on the other hand, expert systems. In this paper, we will focus on expert systems, as these play a crucial role in giving products of modernity properties that are relevant to an understanding of social processes.

> Expert systems bracket time and space through deploying modes of technical knowledge which have validity independent of the practitioners and clients who make use of them. Such systems penetrate virtually all aspects of social life in conditions of modernity…
>
> (Giddens 1993: 292)[1]

In expert systems, expert knowledge is integrated within a system of organisations and works continuously. Examples are house construction and the production and operation of cars or airplanes. The appropriate knowledge is held by experts only. The remaining members of society can only assume the effects of this knowledge, as they trust the underlying expert knowledge. The existence of expert systems underlines the fact that modernity is based on a complex institutional network which is essential for its functioning and development.

[1] This quote is originally from Giddens (1991) modernity and self-identity. A similar formulation is used in Giddens (1990: 27).

Modernity driven by a capitalist economic dynamic and the political interests of modern territorial states spread itself over the whole world. Its technical achievements improved the possibility of worldwide communication and traffic extremely and accelerated the process of its own extension.

The result is what we can arguably call globalisation which was based on modern achievements.[2] In fact, globalisation can be understood as "... the intensification of worldwide social relations which link distant localities in such a way that local happenings are shaped by events occurring many miles away and vice versa (Giddens 1990: 64).

However, globalisation in the sense we understand it here brings forth a radical change. For one thing, it makes modernity available all over the world, while at the same time modernity ceases to be under the control of 'the West', or even linked to the West. In other words, modernity detached from its regional origin does not equate with the West. Rather, it is a global phenomenon. At the same time, though, globalisation is not just an extended modernity. Globalisation opens up new options for communication, traffic and trade that are not predetermined by modernity. Any idea, action or item can use the new global linkage whether they are intrinsically modern, anti-modern or completely oblivious to modernity at all.[3]

It is important to see the difference between modernisation and globalisation. This is not, as implied by the public debate, their historical focus. Globalisation is not a very new process that only just started in 1980s or 1990s. In fact, globalisation theories underline the historical process of globalisation whose starting point is placed in the seventeenth century or even earlier (Robertson 1992, Osterhammel and Petersson 2003).

---

[2] This relation between technical progress and globalisation is very well shown by Robertson (1992).

[3] In a way, this open structure of globalisation, which highlights the new structural conditions set up by modernity, goes beyond Giddens' concept.

The difference lies in their perspective. The concept of modernity focuses on a dynamic structural figuration of the already mentioned dynamic forces (separation of space and time, disembedding and reembedding mechanisms like expert systems, the reflexive appropriation of knowledge) and the interlinked institutional dimensions (capitalism, industrialism, surveillance capacity and information control, the control of the means of violence) that fuel an extremely dynamic process of overall change. Globalisation highlights a spatial dimension in underlining that the whole world (or globe) is interlinked and connected without a generic centre. Many studies on globalisation are, in fact, studies of change triggered off by modernity. These studies use the term globalisation to distance themselves from the simplifying classical modernisation theories.

Another difference can be seen in the ascribed importance of states. Whereas in the concept of modernisation the territorial state is a crucial element of political organisation, globalisation theories postulate its dwindling role and some speak of the end of the nation state (Albrow 1998). Seen from this perspective, at an international level supra-national institutions and regimes limit the independence of national states and, as a result of better communication, transnational relations at the level of individuals and social movements are intensified leading to an international civil society. According to this concept, the study of change cannot be focussed on nation states and their societies any longer. We are confronted with *ethnospaces* that cut across national borders. Flows between the once contained states and societies are at least as important as between states and societies (Appadurai 1998). The thesis of a fading nation state and fading national societies helps to highlight the shortcomings linked to a narrow understanding of nation states and national societies, a core unit of social science research. However, all approaches to global governance and global regimes are still based on the decisions of nation states, and states with political and military power cannot be brought under international control. At the level of people and movements we observe networks, group formation and movements with both national and cross-national orientation. But the thesis of the dwindling nation state reflects, in fact, new developments that strengthen linkages across borders. This does not contradict the concept of modernity. The compression of time and space is a core element of modernity, just as the resulting change in political and social relations is. Whether the territorial states are key actors of international politics and whether we find social movements also claiming national goals, the world remains still modern. Changes do not so much point to a post modern era as to the development of modernity itself which is an open process that cannot come to end. As long as the driving forces work and have an effect we are still in the age of modernity.

Up to now we have not mentioned democracy, human rights or the rule of law which drawing from classical modernisation theories have often been labelled 'modern'. However, they are explicitly not included in Giddens' concept of modernity. He makes clear that modernity is not a normative goal, but a process that creates typical institutions and structures. As such, it is full of ambiguities in its outcomes.

However, in Europe the emergence of modernity was intertwined with the quest for democracy and human rights. These were social and political answers by social movements in European societies to the challenges of capitalism, industrialism and the creation of territorial states. Modernity succeeded in Europe not in a mysterious dynamic process behind actors' backs. Rather, it came to fruition as an emancipatory societal project which combined its own dynamics and the new institutional dimensions which it spawned with socio-political visions of progress. Indeed, it was such promises of modernity as freedom, welfare and prosperity that mobilized the social forces that sustained modernity in Europe (Wittrock 2000). The social movements fighting for this emancipatory project referred to each other, some were interlinked and supported their fellows in other countries, but the main focus of their political action was their specific territorial state. Whereas the dynamics of modernity in the sense of Giddens were extremely successful all over the world, the emancipatory project of modernity is still a deeply contested issue. While it is true that the political program which it entails underpins ideas of human rights, freedom and democracy, it has always had to contend with many defeats and setbacks.

Totalitarian ideologies are the other side of the same coin. Just like emancipatory societal projects, totalitarian ideologies try to link modernity with an ideal normative vision. These seek to set a point of orientation that replaces the disenchanted transcendence of religion. Analytically, we must sharply differentiate between modernity as a dynamic structural setting as conceptualised by Giddens, and the substantive socio-political project. Neither the emancipatory project, nor totalitarian ideologies are part of this dynamic structural figuration, but both emerged against the background of modernity.

The modernisation theories of the 1960s mixed two elements together and postulated the realisation of the socio-political project under the conditions of the structural figuration of modernity as the 'goal' of modernisation. They assumed that modernisation would lead inexorably to the achievement of this socio-political project.

Developments in the real world hardly matched these expectations. The structural setting of modernity turned out to be an open-ended process. Different historical conditions in different parts of the world, unforeseen consequences of modernity itself, and random events shaped and reshaped modernity. Modernity came in different guises to different localities, indeed so much so that it is legitimate to draw from Eisenstadt (2000a, 2000b) and speak of 'multiple modernities'. To put it differently, the modernities we face today are a result of that interaction between the structural figuration of modernity, which first emerged in Western Europe, and its refractions in numerous local settings. With the exception of the influence of the structural features of modernity the outcome is neither standardised nor homogenous. Robertson's concept of 'glocalisation' captures this interaction between overall features and different local structures, as it posits a process of reflexive interaction (Robertson 1995). In a different way, Eisenstadt shows the power of different historical trajectories in a process of modernisation (Eisenstadt 1979, 2000a).

Two possible misunderstandings should be avoided. Firstly, those who postulate a radicalised diversity of modernity without a set of common characteristics refer also to Eisenstadt's notion of 'multiple modernities' despite the fact that Eisenstadt sees common elements between modernity as such and his own notion of multiple modernities. He mentions modern constitutional states, industrial capitalism, new forms of relations between state and society represented by a civil society and changes in political processes (Eisenstadt 2000a: 24). Secondly, the common features of modernity in Eisenstadt's concept include civil society with an element from the above mentioned emancipatory project. Because of these common elements Eisenstadt's understanding of multiple modernities is much narrower than the diversity thesis to the point of even contradicting it. Our use of the term multiple modernities following Gidden's concept is not based on elements of the cultural program like civil society and allows more diversity than Eisenstadt's does.

We would like to stress in connection with this view of modernity – and in that way attempt an escape from the conceptual difficulties of classical modernisation theories – the fact that modernity is an open-ended process. Classical modernisation theories of the sixties assumed that the process of modernisation, which engulfed developing societies, would necessarily produce the same type of societies as were produced in Europe.

According to the concept developed here different historical conditions in different parts of the world, unforeseen consequences of modernity itself, and random events shaped and reshaped processes of modernisation and led to multiple modernities. This modernity is reflexive in nature, first because the impact of modernity has an effect on modernity itself – the process of globalisation is a very good example for this – and secondly, because people who live in modernity reflect on it and its consequences and their agency shapes the manner in which it manifests itself (see: Beck, Bonß and Lau 2001).

Our concept of modernity differs in its basic assumptions from the conventional modernisation theories of the sixties:

- It does not assume established ideas of an evolutionary progress or even of a teleology.
- It does not assume established phases of modernisation.
- It does not assume that modernisation is a purely endogenous process.
- It acknowledges that modernisation is a reflexive process with consequences; these can include the formation of institutional rules.

The Temptations: Products of Modernity

In some parts of the world people may be critical against the West, its political goals, its form of society or styles of life. But modernity with its Western origin has spread over wide parts of our globe. To understand the impact modernity has inside a society and what reactions are triggered off by it we would do well to focus on the local level.

At the local level modernity as such, or the dynamic structural figuration with its driving forces and institutional dimensions, is usually not an issue. People are fascinated by specific things or ideas that create a desire and which, once they are there, have an effect in everyday life. For example, modern technologies may promise a more comfortable life with more affluence. The emancipatory project of freedom, democracy and human rights may represent the utopia of a just society. In this sense people want to take part in modernity, but often on their own terms.

We propose to analyse processes of change in local life-worlds by focussing on the concrete things which we call 'products of modernity'. The kinds of things we have in mind are material and ideational.
Products of modernity are:

- industrial products (produced by machines driven by inanimate power sources) like consumer products, tools, weapons, vehicles etc. and the aspects of industrial processes themselves,
- technical elements like tools, machines, production plants,
- the processes and know-how and the organization of production (including capitalist wage labour),
- the technical infrastructure needed for production (e.g. roads, water and power supply),
- (other) science based techniques, processes and knowledge (e.g. in medicine, agriculture, communication),
- secular ideas and ideologies that offer orientation within the dynamic process of social change unleashed by modernity like emancipatory societal projects or totalitarianism.

The first two groups of products may be seen as part of a complex of scientific-technical achievements and can be separated from the third group of ideas and ideologies. The latter are related to modernity, but are not directly linked to the institutional dimensions of Giddens' modernity. We will come back to these two groupings and their relationship later.

'Products of modernity' should not be seen as a synonym for Western or Northern. There are Southern products of modernity like software programmed in India, computer components designed and produced in China, instant soup bags from Thailand. There are products of the 'West' that are globally available without being products of modernity like hot dogs, crafted glass from Venice, or the habit of wearing ties. The origin of a product may be an interesting issue for research, but the origin as such does not tell us anything on whether a product is modern or not.

Even if people are not interested in modernity as such, it becomes relevant to people's lives through the intensive use and appropriation of the products of modernity. The widespread use of products of modernity is extremely momentous as far as social change is concerned. Once products of modernity become available and are used in given social settings, the dynamic structural configuration of modernity may come to the fore. Such settings may be challenged to adjust to the need to get, use, maintain and make products of modernity. One analytical task ensuing from this observation concerns the appraisal of the ability of a society to master products of modernity independently.

Additionally, there were and still are political and economic forces that push modernity forward, also against resistance. Bruno Latour's work on the pasteurization of France (Latour 1984) shows that Pasteur's innovative ideas were not widely accepted because he could justify his theses through convincing scientific evidence, but rather because of a complex discursive social process which favoured their acceptance. In addition, James Scott presents some evidence that the modern state and its notion of counting and standardizing as well as devaluating local knowledge is established through power and not because people want to modernize themselves (Scott 1998).

Modernity and its Consequences

Let us now take a closer look at how societies interact with the products of modernity and what follows from these interactions. We can identify four interdependent types of consequences:

- complexity and the need for expert systems
- ideological load
- access and the risk of dependence

- social challenges and societal restructuring

Using complex products of modernity: the need for expert systems

Products of modernity are not all of the same quality. A bicycle is different from an airplane; a hoe is different from a tractor, a car or an aircraft. Especially complex technical products of modernity are not only the result of complicated processes of research and development and elaborate systems of production, but also demanding in their use. They require for their protracted use what Giddens calls expert systems. Such systems ensure that the products are operated and can be maintained. The existence of expert systems implies a whole set of institutional requirements. The use of cars, for example, requires the existence of petrol stations and garages for their repair. Health centres and drug distribution systems are necessary for the use of modern medicine.

Our argument here is that in order to be able to describe and understand the impact of certain external products in local settings it is necessary to take into account their dependence on the availability of expert systems. Those who accept the products of modernity must also accept going down the road paved by the dynamic structural setting of modernity, i.e. accepting the challenges posed by the intrusion into their lives of expert systems and all that they require. This intrusion bears directly on social relations, as it can lead to social differentiation, conflicts between different forms of knowledge and knowledge production and producers as well as resource use.

Ideological load: The entanglement of technical modernity and ideal and ideological concepts

The analytic distinction between scientific-technical and ideal products of modernity follows our concept of modernity and excludes specific social and political programs like the emancipatory project from the basic elements of modernity. At the same time, this distinction suppresses manifold linkages between scientific-technical and ideal products of modernity. Technical products bear ideational elements. Vaccines, for example, are material products which protect individuals from disease. They are also, however, commentaries on the value of human life and their use is often connected to such considerations. For example, decisions have to be made on who gets access to vaccines and under what circumstances. These are issues that structure the use of vaccines.

A further, extreme, example is provided by machine-guns. Fighters hold them in high regard because they are easy to handle and very effective. They may serve the fighters' specific 'respectable' causes or may help them to protect their families from enemies. But as violent and often very brutal conflicts show in Africa, machine-guns can devalue human life. They have the potential to disrupt social hierarchies, challenge norms and make trivial what may have been of extreme importance.

The entanglement of material products of modernity with their ideational elements is analytically relevant to us to the extent that it allows us to ask questions concerning the respective roles played by these dimensions in the adoption or rejection of products of modernity. These examples show that technical modernity is entangled with ideas, ideologies and especially with the emancipatory project of modernity. Therefore, the use of technical products of modernity may open the back door for emancipatory ideas and may trigger off ideological debates.

Access to products of modernity: and the risk of dependence

There are several ways in which a society can acquire products of modernity. First, a society can take part in their development, production and maintenance. Access to these products is therefore autonomous and defines the society concerned. This is the case for OECD states and many transformation states.

Another way in which a society can acquire products of modernity concerns countries which are not able to produce and maintain products of modernity, but can afford them. This was the case with

Arab oil countries in the late twentieth century, for instance, which basically purchased the comforts of modernity. Their relationship to other societies was (perhaps still is) structured by the extent to which they were willing, and able, to purchase the comforts of modernity.

A third way concerns those countries which do not have the capability to produce and maintain the products of modernity on their own.[4] They are dependent on other countries for access to such products. Most African societies can be found in this category. Their relationship to the wider world can be described with regard to how they gain access to the products of modernity, given their lack of capability to produce and maintain them as well as their inability to acquire them on their own terms. Such ways involve, for example, privileged ideological alliances to certain countries, development and humanitarian aid. This fragmented take on modernity brings with it the danger of a protracted dependence from other territorial states or economic carriers of modernity.

We can observe similar differences at the local level. Even if products of modernity are there, people may neither have access to them nor control their use. In fact, access to products of modernity is often linked to social differentiation. Sometimes it is simply money that offers access to products of modernity, or sociologically speaking 'socio-economic difference'. In other cases the use of products of modernity needs specific capabilities that have to be acquired through schooling and training. Additionally, the interest in products of modernity as well as adequate dealing with more complex products of modernity is linked to specific values and norms. This includes the simple interest in new ways of medicine despite the existence of traditional cures. More complex is the systematic treatment and maintenance technical products need for their protracted functioning. Especially ideological products of modernity are

---

[4] In a more differentiated typology we could put those countries that may maintain products of modernity but are not able to participate in their development and autonomous production.

by their nature linked to new values and norms. This dimension of values and norms of products of modernity shows that their use is linked to socio-cultural differentiation, too.

Early modernisation theories mixed up these dimensions under the general concept of 'the revolution of rising expectations'. They assumed that the contact which individuals in a traditional society had with goods of modernity would necessarily lead them to want them, and through that, unleash a modernisation process. This excludes cases where people resist the temptations of modernity and simplify the process of modernisation itself, which cannot simply be unwound. Modernity makes its way into local settings through products of modernity. Acceptance and rejection of products of modernity is not necessarily directed at modernity from an individual perspective, but rather it constitutes a reaction to the features that such products have. Understanding modernity, therefore, requires us to understand the manner in which people come to terms with features of products of modernity. This occurs in many different ways, including different ways of appropriation and forms of syncretism. Exactly these processes have to be described and understood in detail. Access to products of modernity offers us the opportunity to describe the changes which occur in a society as a result of the presence of products of modernity without necessarily assuming the inevitability of modernity or changes.

Products of modernity may intensify or even create social differentiation and social inequality which contradict the promises of the emancipatory project which is often presented as one crucial product of modernity.

Social challenges and societal restructuring

Products of modernity are a challenge for every society. This challenge goes far beyond the question of access and the consequences we already described.

The use of products of modernity calls for a process of adjustment of everyday life to the new constraints and possibilities brought about by the products. On the individual level, for instance, this adjustment can mean the routinised use of products of modernity.

Expert systems require the training of experts whose numbers within a society may rise dramatically. Linked to the rise of experts may be the growth of trust – as Anthony Giddens, Niklas Luhmann and even Max Weber before them all – pointed out as a unique feature of modern society. This is one of the consequences of reliance on experts and expert systems, all of which are premised on the trust which must be placed on them because of our inability to know everything.

A further consequence of the presence of products of modernity in local settings is the promotion of the type of rationality that is consistent with the production of such products. Often, however, scientific-technical rationality enters into a collision course with established forms of knowledge production. This is so because scientific-technical rationality comes not only with its cognitive forms, but also with a set of institutions such as schools, teachers and, to a certain extent, a commitment to a scientific worldview.

Vasavi (1994) gives a telling example for South India. The introduction of new agricultural techniques of the green revolution changed the understanding of cultivation completely. In the past agricultural decisions followed the notion of appropriateness which varied according to season or soil quality and included the need for rituals. This was replaced by the notion of systematic action according to an externally induced set of guidelines for 'modern' agriculture. This change was described in the local language as *systam*, a neologism drawn from the English word 'system'.

As already mentioned, the development and maintenance of expert systems has far reaching consequences. Expert systems constitute a completely new set of institutions, like the institutions of modern medicine or like services of all kinds (garages, services for electronic devices, modern communication services). They also need specialized institutions for training and schooling and create numerous new social positions and roles.

These changes are well known and have been the main object of sociology since its birth in nineteenth century. Why do we mention this again? We think that we need a new way to address these processes and the problems triggered off by them in order to overcome the misunderstandings of classical modernisation theories which inhibited access to the multiplicity of social processes exactly at the local level.[5] This led to the empirical turn in development sociology at the end of the 1980s (Neubert 2003: 113). The overall question of modernisation was out of sight or even abandoned. With the globalisation debate the interest in social change triggered off by outside influences came alive again. This brought the local reaction on products, ideas, political structures and economic changes again on the agenda and led to empirical studies in anthropological and sometimes in sociological research (e.g. Schuerkens 2004).

Many of these studies were not so much concerned with globalisation as such as with questions of modernisation. Therefore, we think it is necessary to bring modernisation back in, albeit with a new access to empirical reality at the local level. Our concept of products of modernity should help us link modernity to observable changes in everyday life at the local level.

As already indicated, at the local level people do not react to globalisation or modernity as such or even as a complex set of institutions and ideas. People are confronted with specific products of modernity. Those who are tempted by these new products try to

---

[5] The Latin-American 'dependencia' school criticised modernisation theories because of the postulate of automatic development and their ignorance towards international dependence and inequality. But they shared with modernisation theories an interest in theorizing and the use of socio-economic data at a macro level as a kind of illustration. Both schools lacked an empirical foundation for their theory, especially at the micro level and were not interested in local agency and local processes of change.

come to terms with them, be it a bicycle, car, modern medicine or ideas of freedom and democracy. They may appropriate products and ideas according to their need, they might be forced to accept certain institutions or products and they might even reject others.

Products of modernity are like a 'Trojan horse'; once people try to use them even on their own terms these products may unleash far-reaching social challenges. What the classical theories of modernity saw as 'the process of modernisation' were and still are differentiated reactions of people to outside changes. These reactions are neither fixed, i.e. set and dependant on the agency of people involved, nor are they completely open or arbitrary. The figuration of modernity described above sets a kind of core challenge people have to react to.

It is against this background that we hope to better understand the differentiated reactions of people. Much resistance to products is not so much the simple hostility to them as the problems connected with the adjustments a society has to make in order to accommodate their structural features. More often than not, opposition to products of modernity is not a rejection of their practical and functional elements which are often highly valued. The opposition may be directed against the ideational elements that accompany their use or are related to the fundamental social changes which accompany the impact of their structural features.

Additionally, in focussing on the access to products of modernity either at the macro (country) or at the micro (local) level we can better understand that modernisation is a process linked to differences in power. These differences manifest themselves in access to and control over products of modernity with far reaching consequences on the trust that may be placed on these products.

The Reception of Modernity: Some Examples

In order to illustrate the empirical-analytical relevance of 'products of modernity', we would like to present two empirical examples drawn from two different research projects. The first gives an example for a typical industrial product, a diesel engine. It is based on Kurt Beck's (2001) description of a case in the Sudan.

The second is an example of an elaborate complex product, the organization of medical services, and is based on our research on local perceptions of, and coping with hazards (or threats) in the everyday life of farmers in the Limpopo Valley (Southern Mozambique).[6]

We will use for this purpose aspects of the interdependent types of consequences we have just discussed. To recall, these were complexity and the need for expert systems, ideological load, access and the risk of dependence and the social challenges and societal restructuring.

The appropriation of the diesel engine

Modernity came to Africa not only via the colonial state but at the same time, and in some regions also earlier via industrial products like weapons or cloth. Current anthropological studies show how Africans make use of industrial products in their everyday life on their own terms. Examples for widely used industrial products are plastic bottles and dishes, enamel or iron pots; these products replace former calabashes or wooden pots without major changes in the way they are used. A paper by Hans Peter Hahn (2004) gives a striking example of the use of bicycles in West African everyday life. The bicycles open new opportunities for mobility and may be markers of status differences. One reason for the dissemination is their comparative simplicity in use and maintenance. The typical African bicycle is simply constructed with a robust and strong frame without fragile gear shifting devices. This product travels both from its European

[6] The research is part of a collaborative research project on 'Local Action in Africa in the Context of Globalisation' funded by the German Research Foundation (Deutsche Forschungsgemeinschaft, DFG). Further material on the research in the Limpopo Valley can be seen in: Macamo and Neubert 2004).

origin and from China to Africa and can be appropriated on local terms.

A more complex case is the use of diesel engines as an irrigation device in the Nile Valley in Sudan (Beck 2001). In the 1950s farmers in Sudan started to use pumps driven by diesel engines instead of their traditional *saquia*, an oxen-drawn wheel. The attraction of the new technology was the impressive hauling capacity. The potential gains in productivity make a diesel driven pump cost-effective and once the initial capital is raised an economically sound technology. However, diesel engines could not just substitute the old *saquia*. Diesel driven pumps are a much more complex technology than the use of iron pots or bicycles. One of the simpler demands was the need for fuel, which at the time was already available for trucks. The next challenge was the multiplied volume of irrigation water that exceeded the capacity of the old irrigation canals and led to their reconstruction. We know from numerous development projects that the maintenance of diesel pumps is the crucial factor for the adoption of this technology. This includes the regular servicing and repair, access to spare parts and their use. In industrialised countries service and maintenance is delegated to an expert service system while minor repairs are handled by farmers themselves.

The farmers of the Nile Valley are an example of how this technology can be mastered in Africa without a formal servicing system and even without well-meaning development assistance. Kurt Beck shows how the technology of the diesel driven pump is appropriated and domesticated. Access to spare parts is insecure and complicated. Therefore service, maintenance and repair is based mainly on improvisation. Typical solutions are the use of older engines as spare parts' suppliers. Sometimes parts are only borrowed and assembled afterwards in the original engine. Often parts of other types of engines are integrated, or those parts not essential for the functioning of the engine are left away. The closed cooling circuit is replaced by flexible tubes that use fresh Nile water. This innovative solution is even better adapted to the high temperatures of the Nile Valley and stabilizes the cooling system. The lack of original seals is compensated by the covers of exercise-books tailored into the right shape; tubes are linked by ropes made of palm leaves and sealed with plaster made of mud. The resulting minor leaks are accepted and do not really hinder the functioning of the system. Kurt Beck points out that the diesel technology is deconstructed, leaving only the indispensable core and a newly reconstructed engine in a different way. The main result is the development of a detached service system which is directly run by the users. The expertise for the use and maintenance of diesel driven pumps is integrated into everyday life without the development of an elaborate and specialized expert system. The technologies used are developed out of the already existing skills of Nile Valley farmers and extended through experience with the diesel driven pumps.

These pumps are integrated into the Nile Valley farming systems. This creates an obvious dependence from the new technology. However, the farmers managed to guarantee the access to technology for fifty years. This was possible because the engines are potentially long lasting (some of them are more than thirty years old and are still functioning) and the localized maintenance system offers a certain independence from outside support. Yet engines and mechanical pumps have to be bought, in fact imported, and are not produced by the farmers themselves. In spite of the successful appropriation and mastering of this product of modernity, Sudanese farmers remain dependent on others who develop and make products of modernity.

The above mentioned entanglement of products of modernity with ideals or ideologies (ideological load) is in this case completely absent. What is observable are processes of social change. At the beginning only richer entrepreneurs had the means and were willing to take the risk to invest in the new technology. This led to social differences and conflicts. However, once the technology proved to be cost-effective and manageable it was widely adopted and integrated in the traditional cooperative structures of water management. Sustainable changes were mainly in the agricultural systems. Thanks to access to better irrigation and limited agricultural land agricultural production was intensified which led to a change from the use of the plough to gardening techniques and more manual labour based on the hoe. Without ox-driven water wheels and the reduction of ploughing, ox keeping lost importance and fodder production was reduced. However, these changes did not challenge basic social structures or the organization of work.

This case stands for one type of the use of products of modernity which are appropriated into the local culture on local terms. They led to innovations and changes – in this case in the farming system. The product of modernity is locally mastered and maintained, but it is still produced outside. The overall influences are limited, social changes are restricted to certain social fields (in this case farming) and the expert system which in industrial countries is used for the development, production and maintenance of the product is still missing. The basic functions of the expert system to keep the product (here the diesel engine) working is integrated in an innovative, but simplified way into everyday life. The use of the product is not quite like it should be when the context from which it emerged is taken into account.

Medical services

Medical services were one of the first expert systems to be transferred to developing countries, for example through missionary hospitals. The bio-medical system is a typical product of modernity linking medical and pharmaceutical research with a complex service system which includes medical doctors, technical support staff (nurses, para-medicals), a system of drug production and distribution, the production and maintenance of medical technical devices, and the establishment of public health policy. To provide the system with its qualified staff a network of training institutions is needed (e.g. universities, medical schools).

The first access to this system was offered to people in the Limpopo Valley by missionaries in the form of a hospital in the early twentieth century. Since then medical services have become an option alongside local forms of healing present in local everyday life. Because of organisational and financial shortcomings the availability of drugs and services is uncertain and people have no means to influence the decisions of the health institutions. More efficient private medical services are unaffordable and out of reach for the farmers. Under these conditions the medical services which are present remain distant from everyday life.

The complex nature of the expert systems upon which medical services are based reveals itself in the organisational structure and the type of human resources on which it depends for its functioning. Given the precarious economic situation of Mozambique in general and of local communities in particular, medical services constitute a huge challenge. In fact, available medical facilities hardly meet minimum standards. They are understaffed, ill-equipped, sparse and are simply overwhelmed by an enormous demand. On the practical level, this means that they cannot live up to the expectations which people have developed towards them. These shortcomings have implications on the level of trust people can place in the services. From the local perspective medical services are seen as very powerful and efficient. However, practical access is problematic.

A further feature of medical services is their ideological load. By definition the healing knowledge upon which medicine rests is not discriminatory. It applies to everyone independently of their personal circumstances and position within the social structure. This feature of the medical services stands in conflict to local ideas about when healing is possible and desirable. Partly because of the shortcomings of traditional healing methods, partly because of deep-seated cultural beliefs, local communities account for the failure of healing through explanations that have no place within bio-medicine, but which structure their relationship to it. The increased dependence on technology – e.g., motorized vehicles for locomotion – has led some people to believe that there is an intrinsic relationship between medical treatment provided to pregnant women and children and the reduced ability of the current generation to walk long distances as their forefathers used to do in the past. It is believed that medical treatment weakens people on purpose. What people observe as the decline of traditional medicine is partly linked to a better diagnosis provided by the modern medical services which allows the identification of a specific illness. Besides, we can understand this decline as a consequence of the ideological load of the modern medicine system. The power of the modern medical system awakens expectations and promises the control of sickness. This allows new statements on the value of human life and sets a radical normative claim for the protection of human life against all rigours. Therefore, diseases and health hazards linked to childbirth are no longer accepted as given. And the treatment of malaria should lead to healing. Against this new normative background traditional medicine becomes weak. Compared to a glorified past traditional medicine has lost power. The existing system of modern medicine in the Limpopo Valley cannot fulfil these expectations either. In fact, it disappoints them. When villagers complain that medicine weakens them on purpose, they are not providing examples of irrationality as a simplistic view would assume, but rather documenting points of tension arising from the ideological confrontation between medical services and local communities struggling to come to terms with their expectations of healing.

Another feature is access and the risk of dependency. From the local perspective medical services are seen as very powerful and efficient. However, practical access is problematic. Because of organisational and financial shortcomings the availability of drugs and services is uncertain and people have no means to influence the decisions of the health institutions. More efficient private medical services are unaffordable and out of reach for the farmers. Under these conditions the medical services which are present remain distant to everyday life. At the same time, however, people have become so accustomed to the bio-medical option that their inability to access it becomes relevant for the manner in which they perceive their own social structures and how they relate to external influences. The medical system is seen as an expropriation of local skills. In interviews people complained that with the arrival of medical services their ability to treat diseases had diminished. Traditional healers lost power, midwives and pregnant women became weak. This system is thought to have brought new diseases such as AIDS or to have made old ones such as malaria more resistant to treatment. The medical explanation of the world which is linked with products and institutions of modernity appears alien and impenetrable, modern medicine itself is perceived as another form of magic or witchcraft resisting within the local worldview.

A final feature of the medical system is its challenge to local social structures. The expert system upon which it rests introduces forms of social differentiation within local communities which call into question established social hierarchies. This does not mean that the new forms gain primacy over the older ones. Rather, the presence of new roles, professions and distribution of knowledge imply shifts in social recognition, status and hierarchy which have to be negotiated. The same goes for the ideological content of medical services. Those who might locally be considered unfit to live get a new lease of life through the presence of medical services. This has the effect of challenging local communities to rethink their own ideas about humanity and the value of human life. Problems of access and the risks associated with dependency also bear directly on social structure by bringing social differences and divisions into the fore and perhaps unsettling established notions of priority and social status.

The attempt to describe the presence of bio-medical services in local contexts yields questions that are concerned directly with how individuals organize their social relations. These issues relate in particular to the structural features which bio-medical services have as a product of modernity. An adequate description of local life-worlds must be able to take these features into account if it wants to gain a deep understanding of what is at stake in local social relations. In doing this, it is not of course mapping out the road to modernity. Rather, such a description is basically stating the issues that confront those who give in to the temptations of the new. The notion of products of modernity offers a heuristic tool to formulate relevant questions. The complex nature of products of modernity and their articulation with expert systems raises the problem of trust and how this manifests itself in everyday life. The ideological load of these products forces individuals and communities to rethink their own ideas about prestige, equality and human dignity. Access to products of modernity raises the problem of power and the social distribution of resources. Finally, the combined effect of the presence of products of modernity in local settings constitutes a massive challenge to local social relations and structures.

What the brief description of the presence of the bio-medical system on the Limpopo Valley shows is that while the system can be easily adopted into everyday life, its presence can potentially unleash social processes of interest to an understanding of the structure of everyday life and how people ultimately relate to modernity. Under the conditions of a rural area in a developing country the efficiency of the expert system is extremely limited. The medical impact cannot keep pace with rising expectations resulting from the ideological load of the system. Nevertheless, its presence is extremely momentous and inheres into norms, values and social hierarchies.

The empirical-analytical implications of the concept 'products of modernity'

These examples show that products of modernity penetrate into local life. Some can be appropriated easily and become part of local strategies. Others, however, can remain alien. They might be used, but their legitimacy and their reference to science is not accepted locally and the institutions that offer these products are far beyond the scope of local agency. Products of scientific-technical modernity that may be present on the local level but which are beyond local control and act according to concepts that are alien to local thinking remain isolated elements of modernity. At the same time the example of medical services shows that local norms may be changed according to the still not fulfilled promise of modernity.

Conclusion: Products of Modernity as a Concept for Empirical Research

While classical modernisation theories present modernisation as if it were an automatic process, our examples show the complex process of interaction between (complex) products of modernity and local everyday life. Complex products of modernity may be used in local contexts even when the institutional prerequisites are incomplete, unstable and fragile. This may also lead to processes of social change. However, this does not trigger automatically off a (comprehensive) process of modernisation as assumed by classical modernisation theory (e.g. Oesterdiekhoff 2006, Smelser 1973).

At first sight this observation might imply that modernity may advance according to local needs and interests, and products of modernity may be used in any combination as long as this is consistent with local possibilities.

We propose a different perspective. Looking at specific complex products of modernity the reception of modernity is neither set in an automatic process of an established modernisation process, nor completely unstructured and open in the sense of 'anything goes'.

Appropriation and syncretization may influence the institutional dimensions of modernity, but people cannot escape its dynamic processes. Especially products of technical modernity show that products are deeply linked to institutions, especially expert systems, and a scientific world view. These features of modernity may be shaped, but cannot be ignored completely.

The crucial question is whether and how products of modernity and the expert systems linked to them are accessible for local agency. As long as access is precarious and expert systems cannot be influenced by the local people, modernity appears strange and somewhat out of reach.

Once products of modernity are accessible not only as isolated items but also as a whole environment and expert systems and the institutions linked with them penetrate everyday life, modernity triggers off changes which society must take into account. The ideological load influences norms and aspirations, and people have to decide whether and how they adapt to the new situation. Sometimes they are pressed or even forced to comply with new rules and systems of order. They have to undergo specific training to use or control products of modernity or to take part in the use and management of expert systems. In this change formal education is of extreme importance. It provides not only knowledge, but socializes people to organize their agency according to the scientific-technical rationality of modernity.

Against this background the arrangement of the institutional dimensions (capitalism, industrialism, national administration, means of control of violence) varies considerably. We observe a wide range of societal and ideological understandings of modernity, some of which are easy to combine while others contradict each other. The question as to how to accommodate oneself in modernity is a constant discursive element inside modernity. When we look at modernisation we find processes of syncretization and appropriation, especially in the sphere of the discourse on accommodating modernity. This is not just a peripheral phenomenon that decorates modernity. It reaches into the core of societal organization. The emancipatory project of modernity is still (and will be) debated. Even when technical modernity in Western democracies, in Stalinist, fascist or authoritarian fundamentalist Muslim states follow the same scientific principles, their societies show fundamental differences. This is one reason why we opt for Eisenstadt's concept of multiple modernities.

In a curious sort of way, products of modernity remind one of evil spirits, because some people might find them attractive because of their promise and their efficiency in the delivery of the promise. Evil spirits, just like products of modernity, however, require degrees of care that are often beyond the ability of the people who engaged them in the first place. Once they are there, however, one has to come to terms with them. These are the temptations we think that we should be talking about.

Bibliography

Albrow, Martin (1998): *Abschied vom Nationalstaat*, Frankfurt: Suhrkamp.

Appadurai, Arjun (1998): Globale ethnische Räume, in: Beck, Ulrich (ed.): *Perspektiven der Weltgesellschaft*, Frankfurt: Suhrkamp, 11-41.

Barber, Benjamin (1996): *Jihad Versus McWorld*, New York: Ballantine.

Beck, Kurt (2001): Die Aneignung der Maschine. Eine Geschichte, die davon handelt, wie der Dieselmotor von Bauern im Niltal so gezähmt und zugerichtet wurde, daß er aus seiner neuen Heimat nicht mehr wegzudenken ist, in: Kohl, Karl-Heinz (ed.): *New Heimat*, New York: Lukas & Sternberg, 66-77.

Beck, Ulrich; Bonß, Wolfgang; Lau, Christoph (2001): Theorie reflexiver Modernisierung – Fragestellungen, Hypothesen, Forschungsprogramme, in: Beck, Ulrich und Bonß, Wolfgang (eds.): *Die Modernisierung der Moderne*, Frankfurt: Suhrkamp, 11-62.

Eisenstadt, Shmuel (1979): *Tradition, Wandel und Modernität*, Frankfurt: Suhrkamp.

Eisenstadt, Shmuel (2000a): *Die Vielfalt der Moderne*, Weilerswist: Velbrück Wissenschaft.

Eisenstadt, Shmuel (2000b): Multiple modernities, in: *Daedalus. Journal of the American Academy of Arts and Science*, 129, 1: 1-30.

Giddens, Anthony (1990): *The Consequences of Modernity*. Standford: Standford University Press 1990.

Giddens, Anthony (1991): *Modernity and Self-identity*, Cambridge: Polity Press.

Giddens, Anthony (1993): *The Giddens Reader*, edited by Philip Cassell, London: Macmillan.

Hahn, Hans Peter (2004): Die Aneignung des Fahrrads, in: Beck, Kurt; Förster, Till; Hahn, Hans (eds.): *Blick nach vorn. Festgabe für Gerd Spittler*, Köln: Rüdiger Köppe Verlag, 264-281.

Latour, Bruno (1984): *The pasteurization of France*, Cambridge Mass.: Harvard University Press.

Macamo, Elisio and Neubert, Dieter (2004): Die Flut in Mosambik – Zur unterschiedlichen Deutung von Krisen und Katastrophen durch Bauern und Nothilfeapparat, in: Bierschenk, Thomas and Schareika, Nikolaus (eds.): *Lokales Wissen: ethnologische Perspektiven*, Münster: Lit, 185-209.

Neubert, Dieter (2003): Entwicklungssoziologie: empirische Wende und Ansätze zur neuen Theoriebildung, in: Orth, Barbara and Schwietring, Thomas and Weiß, Johannes (eds.), *Soziologische Forschung: Stand und Perspektiven*, Opladen: Leske and Budrich, 111-124.

Oesterdiekhoff, Georg (2006): Modernisierungstheorie und Wandel der Weltgesellschaft, in: *Soziologie*, 35, 1, 26-41.

Osterhammel, Jürgen; Petersson, Niels (2003): *Geschichte der Globalisierung. Dimensionen, Prozesse, Epochen*, München: C.H. Beck.

Robertson, Roland (1992): *Globalization: social theory and global culture*, London: Sage.

Robertson, Roland (1995): Glocalization: Time-Space and homogeneity-heterogeneity, in: Featherstone, Micheal; Lash, Scott and Robertson, Roland (eds.): *Global Modernities*, London: Sage, 15-30.

Inkeles, Alex and Smith, David (1974): *Becoming Modern. Individual Change in Six Developing Countries*, London: Heinemann.

Schuerkens, Ulrike (ed.) (2004): *Global Forces and Local Life-worlds. Social Transformations*, London: Sage.

Scott, James C. (1998): *Seeing Like a State: How Certain Schemes to Improve the Human Condition have failed*, 4th edition, London: Yale University Press.

Smelser, Neil (1973): Toward a theory of modernisation, in: Etzioni-Halevy, Eva and Etzioni, Amitai (eds.): *Social Change. Sources, Patterns, and Consequences*, 2nd edition, New York: Basic Books, 268-283.

Vasavi, A. R. (1994): 'Hybrid Times, Hybrid People': Culture and Agriculture in South India, in: *Man*, 29: 283-300.

Weißköppel, Cordula (2005): Hybridität: die ethnografische Annäherung an ein theoretisches Konzept, in: Loimeier, Roman; Neubert, Dieter; Weißköppel, Cordula (eds.): *Globalisierung im lokalen Kontext: Perspektiven und Konzepte von Handeln in Afrika*, Münster: Lit, 311-354.

Wittrock, Björn (2000): Modernity: One, None, or Many? European Origins and Modernity as a Global Condition, in: *Daedalus. Journal of the American Academy of Arts and Science*, 129, 1: 31-60.

Spiritual Terrorism beyond Borders: African Pentecostalism, Cultural Synthesis within Local-Global Space

Afe Adogame and Selome Kuponu

African Pentecostalism: Syncretism and its Malcontents

The Redeemed Christian Church of God (RCCG) and the Living Faith Church, also known as Winners Chapel (LFC) are among the most widespread and popular neo-Pentecostal churches in Nigeria. Both churches, which fall under the third wave of Christian independency in Africa, suggest a tendency that can aptly be described as anti-syncretism. African indigenous churches of various persuasions emerged partly as a direct response and reaction to the syncretized forms of Christianity introduced to their shores by European and American missionaries. These new indigenous brands of Christianity have had their religious messages packaged and branded in a way that repudiates European Christianity as far too dressed up in western cultures and thus failing either to countenance or to comprehend African worldviews and realities. On the other hand, these churches also vehemently reject any rapprochement with occultism and traditional religious cultures. Castigating indigenous African Christianity for being syncretistic involves a question of power, being a strategy to advance the hegemony and cultural superiority of colonial missionaries. Thus, dubbing another religious group as syncretistic partly involves maintaining the status quo. As Chitando (2003: 241) aptly notes about the African Instituted Churches (AICs) in Zimbabwe, 'With mission churches being taken as the standard bearers of 'authentic' Christianity, AICs gradually found themselves marginalized in both the colonial and postcolonial periods'. Syncretic appropriation may be seen as both responses to external domination and discourses of reciprocal domination (Stewart and Shaw 1994:

22). Religious syntheses emerge in two ways, being made either by those who create meanings for their own use out of contexts of cultural or political domination, or through the imposition of religious syntheses upon others by those who claim the capacity to define cultural meanings. (Kiernan 1994: 70) argued that the Zulu Zionist synthesis arose from multiple instances of agency and power. Meyer (1992) demonstrates that syncretism can be a practical result of processes of translation and diabolization. Pato (1990: 26) best describes these contexts of European domination and of the hegemony of mission Christianity. It is this critique of AICs, such as Aladura, as syncretistic that has generated an anti-syncretistic backlash in which the AICs explicitly oppose the incorporation of African ritual elements and also totally reject the syncretic forms of European Christianity (cf. Peel 1968: 133-4). Peel has argued, though controversially, that Aladura forms of prayer healing and possession are not in fact syncretic as they have western Christian rather than Yoruba origins. This remark in our view is suspect for implying that groups that have origins in western Christianity should not be considered syncretistic. According to Peel's definition, they are not when in fact they are. Therefore Beyer's approach is preferred because it applies 'syncretization' to both sides, including western Christianity. Anyone has the right to define syncretism. Peel decided to model the concept on the pluralistic system of Graeco-Roman paganism in late antiquity, a concept he uses considerably in his essay. However, the problem is that western Christianity is presented as non-syncretistic. Peel prefers to reserve the term 'syncretic' for individuals and movements which explicitly unite Christian and 'pagan' Yoruba ideas and practices into an integrative scheme, although he fails to demonstrate any clear distinction between 'Christian' ritual practices and 'African' cosmologies. Syncretism has mainly been used in theories of 'inculturation' or 'culture contact' that aim to classify religious expressions along a continuum whose poles are labelled 'traditional' and 'western'

(Meyer 1994: 45). This is what Peel himself aptly described as the 'mechanical assignation of cultural traits' (Peel 1968: 140).

The RCCG is a typical example of an African Pentecostal church, which has spread globally from Nigeria to about sixty countries and has over two million members throughout Africa, America, Europe, Asia, Australia, the Middle East and other parts of the world. Following a divine call to a special mission, Pa Josiah Akindayomi founded RCCG in Lagos (Nigeria) in 1952. He became popular for his charismatic qualities and healing activities, although the church he founded did not witness any large-scale expansion under his tutelage. The succession to the leadership as General Overseer in 1980 of Enoch Adejare Adeboye, a former University Professor of Applied Mathematics – Hydrodynamics, transformed the stature of RCCG and launched it into global religious maps. Through Adeboye's charismatic qualities and healing activities, coupled with modernization processes, the Church has sustained considerable organizational and numerical growth and geo-ethnic spread within Nigeria and beyond. It is believed to be the fastest growing and one of the most popular Pentecostal churches in Nigeria today, with a conservative estimate of over 5,000 parishes and a large membership spread across the globe (Adogame 2004a: 31).

The Living Faith Church, Nigeria, also known as the Winners Chapel (LFC), was founded about three decades later in the early 1980's in Kaduna, the commercial nerve centre of northern Nigeria. Islamic dominance of this area can be traced as far back to the Sokoto Caliphate and the Jihad of Usman Dan Fodio in the nineteenth century. David Oyedepo, a trained architect, founded the LFC. His spiritual life was greatly influenced by his grandmother, who was a staunch member of the Anglican Church. In 1981, Oyedepo claimed to have received a divine mandate to start a church ministry: 'The hour has come to liberate the world from all oppressions of the Devil through the preaching of the word of faith, and I am sending you.' He started the LFC as a house fellowship with about 48 members in Kaduna, and within six months the membership had risen to about five hundred. Today, the Church has relocated its international headquarters from Kaduna to Ota, a large expanse of land now called Canaan Land. Located in the international headquarters is a magnificent auditorium with a capacity of 54,000 worshippers, claimed to be the largest church auditorium in the world today. The church has over a thousand branches in Nigeria, over 36 missions in 28 African countries and several branches in Europe and America.

Spiritual Terrorism within Borders: The Winning People

One basic feature that reveals an affinity and continuity between African Pentecostal and Yoruba indigenous cosmologies is the belief in indiscernible spiritual forces. Linked to this is the tenacity with which ritual enactments take place (cf. Adogame 2004b: 503). We would argue that indigenous religious epistemology makes sense in terms of African Pentecostal ritual sensibilities. There is an observable resilience in the principles that lie behind the concept of spiritual power, a belief in the reality of and ritual attitude towards the supersensible powers. Members believe that the physical world is populated by a multiplicity of incorporeal entities. However, a remarkable change has taken place in the constitution of this spiritual repertoire, as well as in the agency and strategies through which ritual enactments are authenticated. Basically, African Pentecostals share a similar mentality in their belief tradition in that they employ an indigenous hermeneutic of spiritual power but cast it within new conceptual frames of reference (cf. Adogame 2004b: 504). The bedrock of the Pentecostal belief system is the pre-eminence of benevolent powers: God, Jesus Christ and the Holy Spirit. Within the indigenous religious worldview, the benevolent powers (the Supreme Being, Divinities and Ancestors) are propitiated through divination and sacrifice in order to ward off malevolent forces. Through elaborate rituals, they seek benevolent power and favour. This tendency has continued in the Pentecostal churches, although the medium and object have changed. The benevolent powers of the indigenous worldview become translated as malevolent forces in the new Pentecostal rhetoric. The RCCG and LFC contend that the Bible clearly portrays human life as lived in a context of continual warfare between the Kingdom of God and the Kingdom of Satan. The appropriation of the metaphorical language and imagery of warfare is rife in the Bible, pointing to the expediency and urgency for warfare on the part of God's forces to defeat the enemy – Satan and his demonic forces. African Pentecostals are very critical of western churches, which they claimed have been blinded by a western world view that ignores this facet of biblical teaching and social concern. Ostensibly, this is a case of anti-syncretism in which African churches lay claims to the 'purity' and 'authenticity' of their own Christian traditions.

The texture of spiritual terrorism that is ventilated in African Pentecostal movements shows a kind of adaptation of Christianity to the existential needs of Africans. Rituals in the Winners Chapel are packaged to handle spiritual terrorist attacks such as sickness, unemployment, social insecurity, death, emotional stress, hunger, poverty, barrenness and virtually all of life's vicissitudes. During my recent fieldwork and participant observation in a Badagry (Lagos) branch of the LFC, I (Kuponu) interviewed twenty-five members randomly selected. Of these, eighteen claimed to have joined after an 'encounter with Christ'. They claimed to have been 'born again' by accepting Jesus as their Lord and Saviour through spiritual baptism. Five interviewees claimed to have sought protection from traditional healers, but to no avail. Ten informants remarked that they had been tormented by the devil and therefore had come into the church in search of solutions to various existential problems. At the time of the interview, these ten informants were already university graduates in different disciplines and had been unemployed for a number of years. Seven respondents said the devil had denied them the fruit of the womb and and that they had thus been stimulated to seek a solution where 'the Living God dwells'. Others claimed to experience bad dreams periodically, in which they disclosed that strange things always occurred, like being chased by the devil for destruction. Twelve members were ready for marriage, but seven were yet to find their life partners. Five were having problems with pre-marital sex and pre-marital relationships. As another member testified:

> On the night of December 30, 2001, I woke up with a holy anger in me because I was in a bank with nothing to show for it. I told God in a prayer that I want a change and I was led to multiply my present monthly tithe by three. Also, in the month of November, when there was a call for sacrificial offering, I gave the whole of my November salary, and then during Shiloh in December, when the call for prayer request was made, I told God that I needed a job in an international oil company, and if not in an oil company, I want it in a reputable bank. To the Glory of God, between Shiloh and now, I've secured a job in an international oil company and two offers from two reputable banks. I give God all the Glory.

A cursory examination of these narratives above shows that, although the existential problems vary from one person to the other, the general interpretation links all the problems to one major actor, the devil. It is these enigmatic circumstances, consciously located within Satan's domain, that serve as stimuli of attraction and conversion. These members were attracted to the church due to their belief that the church is capable of dealing with the devil in the spiritual battle they are engaged in. The Winners Chapel is preoccupied with waging war against the terror, Satan and his cohorts. This is achieved through elaborate prayer rites, rituals of healing, deliverance, fasting, anointing, spiritual baptism and night vigils. As Bishop Oyedepo, the founder and leader of the Winners Chapel, remarked:

> Many people hate to hear the word 'battle' mentioned for any reason. Whether you like it or not, whether you are conscious

> of it or not, battles are a part of our existence. We are all involved in warfare; we are born into it...our victory in every battle is guaranteed in all ways and in every place. Interestingly, we are not the force behind this victory; God is. He causes the triumph. So, we are only instruments in His hands that He uses to fight against His arch enemy. We are called into warfare, and thank God, we are at the same time, called into triumph.... Battles are real to life, salvation notwithstanding. That you have battles does not mean that you have missed God; it only means you are on the path of destiny. (Oyedepo 1992: 99)

Oyedepo noted elsewhere, 'The devil is a mind-blocker. He organizes programmes to blind your mind, because he knows that when your mind is blinded, your destiny is blocked and your future becomes uncertain...the devil is very crafty! You can't catch him easily, except you are spiritually smart' (Oyedepo 2000: 140). And again: 'The end time army is a conglomeration of a strong people set in battle array – men who will run like horses, climb walls like men of war; men that if they fall on the sword cannot be wounded.... Sickness and disease will be so far from their dwelling places. They won't know the meaning of pain at all, but will enjoy heavy immunity by the presence of the Holy Ghost' (ibid.: 160). These discourses are vivid illustrations of what the Winners Church has come to represent for its members. They show that people are largely drawn to the Winners Chapel because they need answers to various existential problems believed to be caused by the devil. This explains why the Church is so much engaged in spiritual warfare: to deal with the problems confronting its members.

Witches Need No Visas for Europe: Deliverance Ritual beyond Borders

One informant's remark aptly summarizes the ritual attitude of most African Pentecostals, such as the RCCG and the LFC in the diaspora, when he stated: 'Witches do not require any visas to come to Europe from Africa. Some reside here, and others can come over as frequently as they have nocturnal assignments to accomplish. So as Christians, we must watch out for the red alert signal always' (Adogame 2004b: 505). Members of churches, such as the RCCG and LFC would claim that witches, wizards and sorcerers shuttle nocturnally and unrestrained across geographical boundaries. In other regards, many Africans find their sojourn in Europe rather more complicated than they had envisaged. Initial high hopes of 'making it' on arrival to Europe, to use Nigerian parlance for 'material success and upward social mobility', are soon dashed. In fact, the 'secularizing' Europe becomes personified as Satan's stronghold. Europe is further perceived as the 'Dark Continent' in dire need of spiritual regeneration. Life is particularly difficult for African migrants because of declining European economies, retrenched welfare systems, cultural gaps, xenophobia at the individual and institutional levels, acute unemployment, police harassment and brutality, dashed hopes, stress, loneliness, problems in bringing up children, extended family expectations from home, and mounting unpaid bills and mortgages. Many believe that specific demons are targeting children through variety of ways such as the media. Under these distressing conditions, many Africans find spiritual, psychological and material succour in the church. Through elaborate rituals, a sense of identity, security and protection is provided for members.

As opposed to divination and sacrifice in indigenous ritual praxis, RCCG and LFC members engage in deliverance rituals, healing rituals, night vigils, prayer and fasting rituals, and thanksgiving rituals in order to counteract Satan's evil machinations. They claim that the warfare motif in the Bible provides humans with ample instruments with which to thwart the enemy's plans. Prayer, fasting, repentance, forgiveness, righteousness and every other human attitude and form of behaviour that stands in obedience to God can be seen as acts of war and as means enabling God to achieve his

plans in the human realm. Their liturgical tradition is thus highly expressive and characterized by a heavy dose of rituals, which are enacted to solve individual and collective existential problems.
In the new Christian dispensation, this spiritual engagement and motif of warfare is legitimized with biblical authority in Ephesians 6: 10-17:

> Finally, be strong in the Lord and in his mighty power. Put on the full armor of God so that you can take your stand against the devil's schemes. For our struggle is not against flesh and blood, but against the rulers, against the authorities, against the powers of this dark world and against the spiritual forces of evil in the heavenly realms. Therefore put on the full armor of God, so that when the day of evil comes, you may be able to stand your ground, and after you have done everything, to stand. Stand firm then, with the belt of truth buckled round your waist, with the breastplate of righteousness in place, and with your feet fitted with the readiness that comes from the gospel of peace. In addition to all this, take up the shield of faith, with which you can extinguish all the flaming arrows of the evil one. (Holy Bible, trans. New International Version)
> Be strong with the Lord's mighty power. Put on all of God's armor so that you will be able to stand firm against all strategies and tricks of the Devil. For we are not fighting against people made of flesh and blood, but against the evil rulers and authorities of the unseen world, against those mighty powers of darkness who rule this world, and against wicked spirits in the heavenly realms. Use every piece of God's armor to resist the enemy in the time of evil, so that after the battle you will still be standing firm…In every battle you will need faith as your shield to stop the fiery arrows aimed at you by Satan. (Holy Bible, trans. New Living Translation)

Another passage often cited to give weight to the warfare motif is II Cor. 10: 3-4, which states: 'For though we walk in the flesh, we do not war after the flesh, for the weapons of our warfare are not carnal but mighty through God to the pulling down of strongholds...' There are several other biblical references that eulogize the rhetoric of the devil as enemy, thus highlighting the expediency of spiritual warfare (cf. 1 Pet. 5:8-9; John 10:10; 2 Kgs 6:18; James 4:7; Isa. 54: 17; Psa. 27: 1-3 and Lk. 10: 19). Adeboye (2002a: 76-8) isolates ten methods of warfare, various ways in which God fights the enemy on behalf of the Church's members. For the RCCG, this military-cum-spiritual offensive strategy can only be achieved through total dependence in God by faith. It is a form of warfare that can only be fought spiritually, not through any mundane means. Enoch Adeboye, the RCCG General Overseer, urges:

> Do not wait for the enemy to hit you first; hit the enemy first. Every true child of God must be a terror to the devil and his agents. You must learn to take an offensive stance. If you don't get rid of the agents of the devil in your life, they are likely to get rid of you... You are to resist the devil steadfastly in the faith. Go on the offensive as soon as you know the enemy is around. God says our defense is sure. This defense is impregnable, so we are supposed to be aggressive. Demons recognize and tremble at the name of Jesus Christ. (Adeboye 2002a: 68ff.)

Faith healing becomes a highly attractive alternative source of health. RCCG and LFC offer spiritual power to overcome and heal the maladies of poverty. Banners, personal testimonies, sermons, hymns and gifts of the Spirit give testament to the centrality of power in their spiritual discourse and praxis. This quest for spiritual fervour has led to the personification of certain illnesses as the outright manifestation of Satan, the devil or the demons. There are frequent references to the spirit or demon of disease, illness, barrenness, death, doubt, adultery, poverty, lying, drunkenness, etc. Adeboye writes further:

> Everyone has enemies. The enemy can be sickness, sorrow, failure, poverty, death, other people or whatever is warring against you. The enemy tries to put the cuffs on you and rob you of the joyful life God has intended for all His children to live.... Money is a defense. I pity those who say they don't want to hear about prosperity. I pity anybody who talks about nothing but prosperity. I pity anyone who preaches everything but prosperity. I am going to prosper. Poverty is a terrible thing. Your prayer should be that poverty should be a stranger to you. (Adeboye 2002a: 65, 93)

Adeboye explicates the elasticity of poverty in the discourse on barrenness. As he notes:

> Barrenness is an all-inclusive word and it affects virtually every area of life. A woman can be barren; a business venture can become barren; a pastor or a Christian worker can be barren spiritually, unable to bear fruits in Christian service. God has always intended that mankind should be fruitful in every way. We only have to obey Him.... However you view barrenness, it is a serious topic. As an experience in any aspect of life, it connotes a poignant deprivation. It is a terrible lack, and a painful bondage. The ingredients of life are missing. (Adeboye 2002b: 15-16)

The paraphernalia of the devil has become enlarged to include just anything that constitutes a roadblock to the attainment of good health and wealth. This lends credence to the multiple understanding and translations of poverty. It is also against this backdrop that the mechanics of the prosperity gospel can be better understood and interpreted. Thus, there is a remarkable difference in this conceptualization as compared to understandings of the prosperity gospel within American and European Pentecostalism.

The terrorism motif and theology assume a more complicated dimension, with the distinction being made between two interrelated plains of spiritual warfare. The horizontal axis, referred to as the 'ground-level warfare', involves dealing with the various spirits that inhabit people (demons), while the 'cosmic-level warfare' is the vertical axis dealing with different shades of higher-level spirits. In every society, the RCCG and LFC argue, the horizontal warfare contends with the issue of ground-level demonization. The indwelling spirits or demons may be of varying kinds, including family spirits, occult spirits, and 'ordinary' spirits such as those attached to fear, death and homosexuality. Demons are believed to work at ground level in ways appropriate to the society in which they operate. They adapt their approach to the problems and concerns that predominate in any given society. Vertical warfare includes territorial spirits presiding over cities, regions and nations; institutional spirits such as those assigned to churches, governments, educational institutions, occult organizations and non-Christian religions; and spirits assigned to oversee and encourage special functions, including vices such as prostitution, abortion, homosexuality, gambling, pornography and warfare. Other spirits are assigned to such things as objects, buildings and other spaces, as well as nonmaterial entities such as rituals and music. It is believed that people regularly become demonized through contact with non-material, 'demonically' infested entities. Ancestral spirits are also assigned to work with specific families. The cosmic spirits are apparently in charge of ground-level spirits, although both are tightly interconnected. In spiritual warfare, African Pentecostals engage the spiritual mapping technique in discerning and identifying cosmic-level spirits and the geographical areas, institutions, vices and objects over which they preside as a step toward developing strategies to oppose and defeat them. The confrontation of power that is central to the discourse of spiritual warfare is reminiscent of scriptural encounters such as those between Moses and Pharaoh (Exodus 7-12) or Elijah and the prophets of Baal (I Kings 18). Healing and deliverance from demons are perceived as encounters of power. Thus, any approach to Christianity and to spiritual warfare that neglects or ignores the three-dimensional balance of allegiance, truth and encounters of power is considered incomplete. While African Pentecostal and Charismatic Christians belief in the reality of these enigmatic forces that constitute terror, most western Christians would be sceptical not only about their actual existence, but most importantly what to do about them.

We shall illustrate this with reference to two remarkable incidents among African Pentecostal churches in Germany. An RCCG Pastor sent from the RCCG international headquarters in Lagos to head one of the parishes in Germany became very excited with the idea of building and strengthening ecumenical links with the German host churches. Through existing networks, he came across a number of local Pentecostal church leaders. At one of the meetings to further the network building process, he had pointed out to his German hosts the urgency of embarking on 'breaking strongholds of the devil in Germany'. His suggestion was that they engage in vertical warfare against institutional spirits. One of the demonic strongholds he identified was the famous Cologne cathedral, on the grounds that the historic demonic invasion of the edifice has largely turned it from a sacred space into a historical museum. His German colleagues, who not only saw this as a piece of effrontery but also described it as reflecting strange, syncretistic beliefs carried over from African culture, vehemently objected to this suggestion. Of course, this experience shattered any further attempts at local network building and led to the RCCG Pastor being demonized and blacklisted.

In another vein, the striking incident that occurred at a 'deliverance' (night-vigil) ritual will help illustrate the tenacity of ritual enactments against malevolent spiritual forces by African Pentecostals in diaspora. Secondly, through this we shall demonstrate how the public, 'the other', is often engaged in the politics of syncretism and diabolization. I (Adogame) was a participant observer at this ritual event in one of the RCCG parishes in Germany. The negotiation of ritual time is of symbolic significance to members. While deliverance rites are not limited in time-space, the preference for late evenings or night-times for such ritual enactments is based on the belief that prayers are more potent in the still of the night and during the small hours of the morning, since it is at this time that malevolent forces, witches, wizards, spirits are believed to be most active, mobile and dangerous as well. As a result, this space-time has been mapped as the instant when the fiercest spiritual wars are fought nocturnally on the spiritual battlefield. Members are encouraged to bring all their prayer petitions, supplications and all existential problems to this ritual forum, where 'prayer warriors' are on standby, fully equipped to terrorize the devil and his cohorts in the battlefield. This is analogous to the allocation of ritual time in the traditional African religious world view, since here too witches, wizards and spirits are believed to commute at night freely and unrestrained. This is when they are believed to attend their nocturnal conferences in covens, caves, on treetops, in groves and at road junctions and other strategic locations.

The deliverance service was attended by an average of 60-70 participants. Twenty percent were German, with five RCCG members and the rest as guests from the German host evangelical church. The German pastor and his congregation were specially invited to participate in this ritual worship. The event commenced with 'praise and worship', accompanied by drumming, loud music and dancing. This was followed by the exhortation (sermon) given by the local RCCG pastor. The carefully chosen theme, 'How to fight and win spiritual warfare in our world today', resonated with the specific nature and aim of the watch-night ritual service.

This climaxed in the 'altar call', in which the preacher gave open invitation to all those who wish to surrender their lives to Jesus Christ, to be 'born again'. Systematically, such volunteers are asked to signify by raising their hands while all the other members of the congregation are in prayer with their eyes firmly closed. They are again asked to take a 'bold step of faith' by standing on their feet and walking majestically to the rostrum towards the preacher. In a solemn state, this interregnum marks a liminal phase in the ritual lives of those members of the congregation or participants who intend 'to give their lives to Christ'. At this stage, they are neither 'here nor there' with their decision either to continue with their old 'sinful' lives or abandon them and start 'a new life in Christ'. The preacher engaged in a sustained spate of extemporized prayers facing the more than thirty congregants who had lined up at the bottom of the rostrum, while church elders and 'prayer warriors' stood behind like bodyguards waiting to protect or arrest any backsliders or any potential escapees. As the prayers intensified, the atmosphere became somewhat spiritually charged and tense. Suddenly, some of those standing started sobbing, screaming, weeping uncontrollably, jerking and moving their bodies indiscriminately. Some became 'slain in the Spirit' and fell over backwards to the floor, though quickly supported by the church elders. This is a feature characteristic of deliverance and healing rituals, particularly among African Pentecostals. One of the German female guests became 'slain in the spirit' as well, falling flat on the ground and muttering unintelligible sounds, to the chagrin and amazement of the German pastor and his co-guests from the Evangelical Church. Reacting to this very swiftly, though probably misreading the situation, the German pastor rushed to his office and telephoned the *Rettungsdienst* (emergency rescue team). The woman was assumed to have collapsed physically on grounds of ill health, physical exhaustion or some sort of manipulation. This threw the church into pandemonium, as virtually all the guests were scared stiff and sought immediately to escape from the scene. The African participants, on the other hand, remained unperturbed, as this was a regular occurrence in their ritual activities. All attempts by the church leaders and members to explain matters to the guests fell largely on deaf ears. Although the programme continued late into the night, several of the German guests left abruptly at this point.

Several interesting narratives emerged following this singular traumatic spiritual experience. A cursory analysis of these narratives illuminates an aspect of the political dimension of syncretization processes and discourse. It further demonstrates that anti-syncretic forms may also proceed from misinterpretations. I interviewed a number of participants after the programme to ascertain their assessment of the event. All the German guests concluded that what had occurred was not Christian at all but something to do with syncretic African religious culture. The African Christians were accused of promoting an entirely unprincipled jumbling together of different religions. The German guests doubted whether this practice was even biblical. They claimed that Africans are known for their association with voodoo and fetishes, which have been brought into Christianity. The sudden re-evaluation of this African congregation as 'sect-like' and 'cult-like' drew awe and skepticism from the Germans, some of who exerted pressure on the host German church administration to eject them from the building. Conversely, their African counterparts expressed some disgust about the ambiguity in their Christian belief. They could not comprehend any kind of Christians not believing and understanding such practices. They retorted: 'What we are doing is not new – we did not invent it. It is not African at all – it is in the Bible for all to see. However, you may not see it if you read the Bible upside down'. They queried further, 'Are these church goers or real Christians? Do they read their bibles? If they read them, do they read with understanding or a lack of understanding?'

The Enigma of a Concept: The Politics of Religious Syncretization

Stewart and Shaw (1994: 1) summarize syncretism aptly as the synthesis of different religious forms:

> It is a contentious and contested term which has undergone many historical transformations in meaning. Some see it as a disparaging, ethnocentric label for religious traditions (such as independent African churches), which are deemed 'impure' and 'inauthentic' because they are permeated by local ideas and practices. Yet in other contexts religious synthesis may have positive connotations as a form of resistance to cultural dominance, as a link with a lost history, or as a means of establishing a national unity in a multicultural state.

Syncretism was conceptualized as the study of acculturation, i.e. of contact between carriers of different cultures (Herskovits 1958), partly as a reaction to the evolutionist perspective that had shaped and dominated anthropological thinking previously. Syncretism originally was proposed as a dimension of reinterpretation in the acculturation process, conceptualized to picture what happened to a once isolated people and their culture when they entered into (prolonged) contact with another culture, usually a more powerful one, and often colonial or imperial in kind (Herskovits 1964). The mixing and the process, including the reinterpretation of form and meaning that led to the new merged form, came to be referred as syncretism (Greenfield and Droogers 2001: 26). Greenfield and Droogers (ibid.: 27) argue that the meaning and utility of syncretism as a concept and its value in analysing ethnographic data, like all concepts, was embedded in a paradigm, a particular view of what the world was like. Thus, reflections on culture-contact and change in anthropological research oscillated and reflected the shift between assimilation and multiculturalism. Syncretism was employed most often to indicate which specific aspects of the traditions of the different social groups had been incorporated into an emerging national culture.

More recently, it has been argued that notions like syncretism should be discarded because they are ideologically charged (Baird 1971, Adogame 1999). In spite of the inherent controversy associated with the usage, its resilience can be observed in both anthropology and religion itself (Droogers 1989; Stewart and Shaw 1994: 5; van der Veer 1994: 196; Aijmer 1995). Stewart and Shaw (ibid.: 2) stress that, in order to make the concept useful, any connotation of impurity or a lack of authenticity should be dispensed with. They argue that recasting a term that has attracted such pejorative connotations can result in a more challenging critique of the assumptions on which those meanings are based than can its mere avoidance. The attempt to whitewash this concept into a neutralizing, less nuanced term is useful in some respects. The authors suggest that it is perhaps less nuanced to focus upon processes of religious synthesis and discourses of syncretism than to treat syncretism as a category or -ism (ibid.: 7). In an effort to recast syncretism in religious studies, Droogers (1989: 17) suggests that we shift our view of power: 'to argue that power is a dimension of syncretism is one thing; interpreting relations of power is another'. He distinguishes two approaches to power, functionalist and Marxist, and makes another set of oppositions between what he calls the objective and subjective views of syncretism. This enables him to set off actors who may contest what scholars and others interpret objectively as syncretism. Stewart and Shaw (1994) have dealt interestingly with the ways in which power informs processes of religious synthesis by exploring issues of agency and power which are integral to the very process of syncretism, syncretization itself and the competing discourses which envelope them.

In our view, however, syncretism or the syncretization process as an 'othering' concept will remain highly contentious if we fail to sidestep the ideological flavour that has often characterized its usage and appropriation, particularly for African religious and cultural systems. The problem with syncretism is more in the very word itself and its history of application, than with any substantive objections to the semantics of the term. Consciously or unconsciously, the discourse on syncretism and syncretization continues to be informed by the charged notions of 'authenticity', 'originality' and 'purity'. Any serious engagement in these discourses on African religions and culture must come to grips with regionalized discourses and their trajectories of meaning and usage. Stewart and Shaw (1994: 13) argue that, in studies of syncretism, regional ethnography traditions intersect with disciplinary histories and religious discourses. Thus, syncretism in Africa, for instance, came to be defined primarily through studies of independent churches by missiologists. As they further state:

> Some of the consequences of these intersections of religious, disciplinary and regional discourses for studies of syncretism can be seen through the example of prevailing patterns of scholarship on syncretism in Africa...In this literature, particularly in studies of Independent churches in South Africa, the vocabulary of syncretism adopted is one of pathology, hazard, decline and loss: ominous references to 'the problem' or 'the dangers of syncretism', to 'syncretistic tendencies' and 'to forfeiting the essence of Christianity' recur. (ibid.)

For instance, Sundkler's (1961: 297) adoption of syncretism as an explanatory concept to characterize such degeneration is clear in his own words: 'The deepest cause of the emergence of Independent churches is a nativistic-syncretistic interpretation of the Christian religion...the syncretistic sect becomes the bridge over which Africans are brought back to heathenism – a viewpoint which stresses the seriousness of the whole situation'. Ostensibly taking a cue from Sundkler, Oosthuizen (1968: xi) further characterized Independent churches as types of 'post-Christianity' which 'form easy bridges back to nativism'. Chitando (2003: 243) argues that the image of AICs in Zimbabwe as a grouping of unlearned syncretists is a dominant one. Droogers (1989: 16) aptly argues that such evidently pejorative characterizations of syncretism are a powerful instance of a means 'used by religious elites to oppose unauthorized religious production'. As we have shown earlier, such tendencies often generate an anti-syncretic backlash.

Critical, negative appropriations of the syncretism concept still looms large in the works of scholars of religion, theologians, historians, anthropologists and other social scientists working without any particular religious affiliation or commitment. Even some who identify with a specific religious affiliation or work from within a particular religious tradition are prone to 'casting syncretistic stones' on other traditions. Thus, syncretism has remained a term of disapprobation and a polemically loaded concept denoting the confused mixing of religions (Stewart and Shaw 1994: 4). Who has the authority to describe a particular religious tradition, including their own, as syncretic? Who determines what is new? What is the *modus operandi* for realizing this? If syncretism is simply the synthesis of different religious forms, it presupposes that all religions, including European brands of Christianity, are syncretistic at various levels and in various shades. This makes more sense, as notions of 'pure religions' or 'pure Christianities' are highly contested and far from intelligible. Ongoing processes of synthesis and erasure have ensured religious reconstruction and reconstitution. If, therefore, we accept the claim that all religions are syncretistic in some sense, then to what extent does syncretism as an analytical tool enrich the discourse on a wider scale? On the one hand, it may simply be a way of underscoring the relative intensity of the process. Thus, religious boundaries are mapped showing how syncretization as a process is rapid and much more evident in one context than another. Although syncretism or syncretization processes exist everywhere, recognizing them is far from objective and automatic. Cases in which syncretism is denied, or left unnoticed, require attention just as much as those in which it is explicitly recognized (Stewart 1994: 127).

Shaw and Stewart (1994: 7) have moved this argument further by proposing the notion of 'anti-syncretism', through which they see human beings as actors constantly defining themselves symbolically and redefining themselves in respect to others in the social universe. They defined anti-syncretism as 'the antagonism to religious synthesis shown by the agents concerned with the defence of religious boundaries'. As the narratives above suggest, anti-syncretism is frequently bound up with the construction of 'authenticity', which is in turn often linked to notions of 'purity'. By introducing anti-syncretism while acknowledging that people always borrow, mix and redefine social meanings, syncretism becomes the study of the symbols people in groups use to defend their boundaries vis-à-vis other groups (Greenfield 1998: 12). As syncretism can be understood as a power tool or concept which strives towards both the adaptation and maintenance of identity, it raises further queries in relation to religion. Is the term reserved for conscious efforts to mix religious elements, or used also to refer to the unconscious merging of religious elements? Should it refer to the end result of mixing or to a continuing process of syncretization? Has it to do with the origin of religion or with later 'threats' to its integrity and identity? Does it indicate whether the two or more religions involved in the mixing process are influencing each other equally, or whether the process is asymmetric, with one dominating the other? Given some hindsight into these questions, the syncretization process in religious movements can take a variety of forms in terms of their intentions and functions. Groups could take in new elements and give them new meanings, drop some elements in the face of new considerations, or harmonize old and new elements in an overlapping form. Werbner (1994: 212) aptly summarizes this in his own definition: 'syncretism is delineated as the continually contested social action which, operating across cultures or traditions, appropriates, reproduces, or re-invents religious belief and practice'. The politics of syncretism and antisyncretism is a politics of interpretation, reinterpretation and misinterpretation. Since religious or cultural syncretism is not one but many processes, it is perhaps more useful to talk of processes of religious or cultural syncretization.

Conclusion

Scholars of African religions and cultures who continue to employ syncretism or syncretization as analytical tools, even in their revamped, recasted and neutralized state, must also cope with the issue of intentionality within the contours of the researcher and the researched. What intentions, either immediate or remote, lie behind our appropriation of the term? What is the heuristic value of its appropriation, and how does this help us in understanding the phenomenon in contradistinction to other similar phenomena? Those prone to describing a religious tradition or aspects of it as syncretistic can be understood within the political context of the insider and outsider (insider-insider, insider-outsider, outsider-insider and outsider-outsider). This insider-outsider dialectics may be broken down into four levels. First, there are those without any particular religious commitment and affiliation, perhaps including the self-acclaimed atheists and agnostics. Secondly, there are those who identify with religious traditions other than the one being described, who may be intra-connected, that is, members of one group within a larger religious tradition, or inter-connected, that is, belonging to a totally different religious tradition. Thirdly, there are those who are anti-establishment and inwardly critical of constituted religious authority, indeed, often self-critical about their own religious affiliations. The last category is an ex-affiliate of a religious group who no longer belongs to the group because of either formal expulsion or voluntary withdrawal. The narratives described above can best be located under the second level, which I have described as intra-connection and inter-connection. The castigation of the RCCG deliverance ritual as syncretic came from within a religious microcosmos rather than a macrocosmos. In this case, it was Christians, and even fellow Pentecostals, who branded one another as syncretic (cf. Chitando 1993).

Scholars should also take cognizance of the dimensions of official and popular religion in interpreting syncretization processes in relation to religions. The rationale is that what is often considered syncretic may be operating much more at the level of popular religiosity than of official religiosity. Thus, caution must be exercised in situating our interpretation along this ambivalent continuum. It may also be useful within our framework of analysis to counterbalance two levels in the syncretization process: the reflexive syncretism that is reactive, involuntary and unintentional; and conative syncretism, that is voluntary, spontaneous and discretionary. While some people may enact and reproduce 'popular' syntheses passively and unreflectingly (i.e. Rudolph 1979, cited in Droogers 1989), others may innovate syncretic strategies to further individual and collective interests. But if syncretic practices are not or no longer consciously syncretic, should they still be described as such? Religious synthesis does not always arise from intentional innovations, but may have unintended consequences too. For instance, Meyer (1994: 45-68) explores this unintended syncretism throughout the global dispersal of Christianity by means of translation, contrasting syncretism 'from above' and 'from below', each representing different poles in a 'field of power'. We must come to terms with the fluidity and political contingency of religious boundaries and recognize tropes of 'otherness' in discourses of syncretization. Scholars cannot always specify their field of study in advance, but they must remain sensitive to the ways in which people negotiate and redefine the boundaries of their ideas and practices. This becomes more expedient in geo-cultural milieus in which the demarcation between religion and other cultural spheres remains largely undefined.

Syncretism and anti-syncretism can both be paths to the construction and deconstruction of 'authenticity' and 'identity'. To realize this, however, we need to deal with the enigma of intentionality. The syncretic and anti-syncretic forms and dimensions to which we allude demonstrate that the processes of appropriation, 'globalization' and 'localization' are in themselves not unilateral. The terms 'syncretism' or 'syncretization' refer to a politics of difference and identity: as such the notion of power is quintessential in its conceptualization and contextualization. In further attempts at unmasking and whitewashing notions of syncretism and processes of syncretization, especially with reference to African religious cultures, it is hoped that scholars will escape being caught up once more in inventing 'another kind of intellectual imperialism' (cf. Stewart and Shaw 1994: 23).

Bibliography

Adeboye, Enoch A. (2002a): *Arresting the Arrester: Catching the Enemy in His Own Trap*, Largo: Christian Living Books.

Adeboye, Enoch A. (2002b): *Turning Point: From Bondage to Total Deliverance*, Dallas: One Hour Books.

Adogame, Afe (1999): *Celestial Church of Christ: The Politics of Cultural Identity in a West African Prophetic-Charismatic Movement*, Frankfurt am Main: Peter Lang.

Adogame, Afe (2004a): Contesting the Ambivalences of Modernity in a Global Context: The Redeemed Christian Church of God, North America, *Studies in World Christianity*, 10, 1: 25-48.

Adogame, Afe (2004b): Engaging the Rhetoric of Spiritual Warfare: The Public Face of Aladura in Diaspora, *Journal of Religion in Africa* 34, 4: 493-522.

Aijmer, Goran (ed.) (1995): *Syncretism and the Commerce of Symbols*, Goteborg: Institute for Advanced Studies in Social Anthropology.

Baird, R.D. (1971): *Category Formation and the History of Religions*, Mouton: The Hague.

Berner, Ulrich (1979): Der Begriff Synkretismus: ein Instrument historischer Erkenntnis?, *Saeculum* 30: 68-85.

Berner, Ulrich (1982): *Untersuchungen zur Verwendung des Synkretismus-Bergriffes*, Wiesbaden: Harrassowitz.

Berner, Ulrich (2004): The Concept of Syncretism: An Instrument of Historical Insight/Discovery?, in Leopold, A.M. and Jensen, J.S., (eds.): *Syncretism in Religion: A Reader*, London: Equinox, 295-315.

Chitando, Ezra (2000): Down with the Devil, Forward with Christ! A Study of the Interface between Religious and Political Discourses in Zimbabwe, *African Sociological Review* 6, 1: 1-16.

Chitando, Ezra (203): The Recreation of Africa: A Study of the Ideology of the African Apostolic Church of Zimbabwe, *Exchange* 32, 3: 239-49.

Droogers, Andre (1989): Syncretism: The Problem of Definition, the Definition of the Problem, in J. Gort et al. (eds.): *Dialogue and Syncretism: An Interdisciplinary Approach*, Grand Rapids, MI: William B. Eerdmans Publishing Co.

Greenfield, S.M.; Droogers, A., (eds.) (2001): *Reinventing Religions: Syncretism and Transformation in Africa and the Americas*, Oxford: Rowman & Littlefield.

Herskovits, Melville (1958): *The Myth of the Negro Past.* 2nd ed., Boston: Beacon Press.

Herskovits, Melville (1966): *The New World Negro: Selected Papers in Afroamerican Studies*, Bloomington: Indiana University Press.

Kiernan, Jim (1994): Variations on a Christian Theme: The Healing Synthesis of Zulu Zionism, in: Stewart, C.; Shaw, R. (eds.): *Syncretism/Anti-Syncretism: The Politics of Religious Synthesis*, London and New York: Routledge: 69-84.

Leopold, A.M.; Jensen, J.S., (eds.) (2004): *Syncretism in Religion: A Reader*, London: Equinox.

Meyer, Birgit (1992): 'If you are a devil, you are a witch and if you are a witch, you are a devil': the integration of pagan' ideas in the conceptual universe of Ewe Christians, *Journal of Religion in Africa* 22, 2: 98-132.

Meyer, Birgit (1994): Beyond Syncretism: Translation and Diabolization in the Appropriation of Protestantism in Africa, in: Stewart, C.; Shaw, R. (eds.): *Syncretism/Anti-Syncretism: The Politics of Religious Synthesis*, London and New York: Routledge: 45-68.

Oosthuizen, G.C. (1968): *Post-Christianity in Africa: A Theological and Anthropological Study*, London: C. Hurst and Co.

Oyedepo, David (1992): *Anointing for Breakthrough*, Lagos: Dominion Publishing House.

Oyedepo, David (2000): *Anointing for Exploits*, Lagos: Dominion Publishing House.

Pato, L. (1990): The Independent African Churches: A Socio-cultural Approach, *Journal of Theology for Southern Africa* 72: 24-35.

Peel, J.D.Y (1968): Syncretism and Religious Change, *Comparative Studies in Society and History* 10: 121-41.

Pye, Michael (1971): Syncretism and Ambiguity, *NUMEN* 19: 83-93.

Rudolph, Kurt (1979): Synkretismus: von theologischen Scheltwort zum religionswissenschaflichen Begriff, in: *Humanitas religiosa: Festschrift für Haralds Biezais zu seinem 70. Geburtstag*, Stockholm: Almqvist and Wiksell: 194-212.

Stewart, C.; Shaw, R. (eds.) (1994): *Syncretism/Anti-Syncretism: The Politics of Religious Synthesis*, London: Routledge.

Sundkler, B.G.M. (1961): *Bantu Prophets in South Africa*, London: Oxford University Press.

Van der Veer, Peter (1994): Syncretism, multiculturalism and the discourse of tolerance, in: Stewart, C.; Shaw, R. (eds.): *Syncretism/Anti-Syncretism: The Politics of Religious Synthesis*, London and New York: Routledge: 196-211.

Werbner, Richard (1994): Afterword, in: Stewart, C.; Shaw, R. (eds.): *Syncretism/Anti-Syncretism: The Politics of Religious Synthesis*, London and New York: Routledge: 212-15.

Creating a Transnational Public: The Faith Movement across Cultures

Simon Coleman

The re-emergence of syncretism as a topic of social scientific debate is perhaps not so surprising in a world increasingly described as both 'globalized' and 'creolized' (see Hannerz 1996). Yet, just as talking about 'the global' seems inevitably to attract equal and opposite talk of 'the local', so syncretism as a term seems to prompt its own theoretical antonyms. For instance, Shaw and Stewart (1994: 8) argue that depicting 'the pure' as authentic tends to be the dominant reading in anti-syncretic discourses of nationalist, ethnic, religious and regional identities.

As illustrated by Shaw and Stewart's example, the deployment of syncretism and anti-syncretism as labels for others can have deeply political implications – and here I am referring to more than just the politics of the academy. Meyer (1994: 45) notes that, in Christian contexts in Africa, the term 'syncretism' may suggest that a given cultural form is located somewhere along a continuum of development whose poles are the highly ideologically charged ones of 'traditional' and 'modern'. Or again, Adogame (2003) has traced the use of the term to level criticisms at African churches in Germany, and moreover to bundle together syncretism and sectarianism, since the two are assumed to go together in such contexts of worship.

Implicit in these debates over syncretism as a concept and a descriptive term is a wider question for my discipline, anthropology, relating to how we are to understand and characterize processes of cultural mixing. For Robbins (2003), syncretism belongs with terms such as 'localization' and 'indigenization' in the sense that they assert – as Robbins claims anthropologists tend to do – continuity in the face of change, in other words, focusing on the cultural structures underlying surface changes. However, he makes his point in the context of a study of global Pentecostalism, where he asserts that such faith simultaneously acknowledges the existence and importance of local ontologies while crucially changing their significance. For instance, spirits and other occult powers are typically perceived to exist rather than being dismissed out of hand, but are frequently redefined as enemies of the true faith. As a result, what often looks like continuity becomes, in due course, the harbinger of profound transformation rather than a stable or harmonious mix.

Robbins's argument is relevant to this chapter and this volume as a whole because it forces us not only to consider what 'new' cultural forms might be, but also to ask ourselves whether we would be equipped to recognize such forms even as we observed them. The point here is that anthropologists, in their 'knee-jerk' defence of the local, will tend, theoretically, methodologically and ethnographically, to privilege cultural forms that are perceived to be 'owned' by 'indigenous' populations. The argument also implicitly raises the question of temporality in the examination of cultural transformations – a constant issue for anthropological methodology. In other words, what might look like continuity in the short term (for instance, Pentecostalists accepting the existence of spirits) might in the longer term lead to profound change (radically altering the cultural significance of such spirits).

Bearing such worries about anthropology in mind, we might also want to reconsider our deployment of the terms 'syncretism' and 'anti-syncretism'. In common with debates over change, they seem to imply the possibility of recognizing the existence of some pre-syncretic cultural state, *after* which mixing occurs. Yet, as we know (despite our tendencies to emphasize continuity), such static models of culture are unconvincing. Similar concerns can be raised with regard to related debates over the 'global' and the 'local'. As many analysts have pointed out, anthropologists have tended to assume an isomorphism between place and culture, so that the idea of culture is itself built on the assumption of rupture – the intrinsic discontinuity between places as loci of meaning (Inda and Rosaldo 2002: 11). As Fardon points out (1995: 1-2), such assumptions themselves draw on the spatial images and metaphors central to much anthropological thought; yet, he continues (ibid.: 8): 'Globalization appears as a pervasive condition of transgression not only because it suggests culture to be fluid (a landscape become waterland), but because culture was conceptualized proprietarily. People possessed culture, but were also possessed by it so that nothing else could possess them without displacing, diluting or hybridizing inherited genius.' The language of transgression and dilution points to images of purity and holism that are inherent in debates over both syncretism and globalization, and equally problematic in both. In a curious sense, if we are not careful we will find ourselves returning to diffusionist assumptions (Strathern 1995: 24) as we attempt to redefine the contexts of knowledge in which we and our informants operate.

In this chapter, I want to examine these themes of continuity and discontinuity, as well as of cultural flow, from a slightly different angle. I am looking at a religious 'culture' – charismatic Christianity – many of whose adherents are themselves already oriented to the idea of communicative flows between people located in very different national contexts. I am interested in how such flows are managed between people who are located very far from each other, but who assume themselves to have fundamentally the same religious culture. In other words, and somewhat in common with many writings on syncretism, while I am concerned to examine the encounter between religious forms, my focus is actually on forms that belong to apparently similar rather than radically disjunct religious orientations. Robbins talks of Pentecostalism attacking its ideological opponents, but what of the encounters *between* Pentecostal or charismatic forms of worship as they mix with each other on translocal stages? Are there any ritual or other mechanisms that ease (or perhaps filter) the interactions among Christians who belong to the same faith, even in some cases the same self-identified movement, but who come from relatively different cultures in the wider sense?

My argument is going to be that such mechanisms exist, though whether they involve syncretic 'mixing' as opposed to mutual accommodation can perhaps be debated. Part of the point of such work is to see how charismatics themselves characterize the forms of cultural flow and blending that they consciously engage in, and this focus should allow me to examine one example of what Clarke (2004: xxii) has called 'the ritualisation of transnational religious practice'. Such an approach, then, is interested in the geographically and culturally expansive scales through which religious practices can seem to operate, as well as in 'the ways that globalization is producing culturally portable practices' (Clarke ibid.: 1).

In thinking about such portability, it will be useful to think about the distinction between the transnational and the cosmopolitan, since my chapter should also show how charismatics are able to manage the appearance of forms of cultural flow and interaction across great distances, without accommodating themselves very much to the cultural differences that cosmopolitanism might imply. Of course this is a huge topic, and here I can only deal with one example of how such a process might be managed. My focus will be on some of the dimensions of a very particular aspect of Pentecostal and charismatic practices of representing mutual global interconnections: the mass media, and especially the use of video technology. Although apparently limited, the concentration on such technology allows me to examine in some detail the ways in which a medium of cultural flow that is of very considerable importance to many contemporary charismatics is both conceptualized and used.

I start by giving a very brief introduction to the believers I shall be discussing and addressing the importance of media in forms of worship, not least in the promotion of interactions (or at least imaginaries) across temporal and geographical distances. I then examine a case study that illustrates how religious transmission is deemed to occur. While the main substantive focus in this chapter is not African material, I include a comparative perspective that deals with African ethnography, before finally reflecting on the usefulness (or otherwise) of the term 'syncretism' to my analysis.

The Faith Movement

Over the last three decades or so, conservative Protestantism, and in particular the loose association of people and charismatic ministries known as the Faith or 'Health and Wealth' Movement, has expanded hugely, spreading not only throughout the US and Europe, but also into the former Soviet bloc, West and Southern Africa, Latin America and parts of Asia. It consists largely of ministries, many but certainly not all American, closely connected with founding personalities who are famous in charismatic circles, such as Kenneth Hagin Sr. (now deceased), Kenneth and Gloria Copeland and Ray McCauley in South Africa and Ulf Ekman in Scandinavia. Ministries form a kind of internal if uneven market of charismatic goods and persons: preachers and their products circulate through workshops, websites, satellite television programmes, revival campaigns and bookshops, so that an informal and transnational star circuit of performers has emerged, explicitly playing on the sense that preachers traverse cultural distances in order to present what is apparently the same religious message to dispersed audiences.

In fact, from the very beginnings of radio broadcasting, conservative Protestants have been at the forefront of using the mass media to reach audiences far wider than those that can be contained in a pastor's office or even an open-air meeting. However, while the use of forms of mass communication may have helped convince these Christians that they are a part of mainstream public life, at least in the West audiences have usually been confined to small and already convinced sections of the population as a whole (Clark and Hoover 1997: 18-19). As a result, much contemporary charismatic talk in the US and Europe is actually talk to the *already* converted about reaching the unconverted. There is a sociological tension here between such Christians as constituting *a* public with its own conventions and modes of interaction and their having – or often not having – a missionary effect in the wider, often secular, public sphere.

Such tensions are deeply relevant to the Swedish Word of Life (*Livets Ord*) Faith Ministry that I have been studying since the mid to late 1980s. Based in Uppsala, this ministry embodies many of the characteristics of contemporary parachurch organizations. It is located on the outskirts of the city[1] in a huge modern building which contains many offices, a television studio and a hall seating several thousand. A congregation of over 2000 meets for worship there on Sunday and midweek, and to that extent the ministry does resemble a church – though many who attend the mass services also retain their membership in a more established denominational church as well. Despite the controversy surrounding the ministry – it is generally accused of being a conduit for American-style Moral Majority opinions in Social Democratic Sweden – it has proved popular with some younger Christians, particularly Pentecostalists, who are disillusioned with the staidness of the better established denominations in the country. There are other, smaller Word of Life-type congregations spread around the rest of Scandinavia, and the ministry helps to run Bible schools in countries such as Russia, Albania, Bulgaria and the Czech Republic. It also provides for more intimate gatherings in Uppsala: small Bible study groups meet in homes around the city during the week, bringing together people from the vicinity who may choose to missionize, study or watch videos together. Members can also join a monthly video club which exposes them to new ministries, either from Sweden or abroad.

[1] Uppsala, a medium-sized city containing one of Sweden's best-known universities, is located about an hour's drive to the north of Stockholm.

The Word of Life hosts regular open Bible schools bringing together people from all over the world, as well as two international conferences per year. In this respect, we can see the ministry as part of a much larger, global public, a public mesmerized by the loose group of extraordinarily mobile preachers who travel in an ever-widening spiral, ranging from the nationally known to the upper slopes of charismatic international stardom.[2] In common with many such centres, the Uppsala group possesses not only its great hall, but also a publishing and media business. Taped services are disseminated to potentially unlimited audiences, becoming important points of intersection and mutual gaze across the national cultures inhabited by Faith supporters. Satellite link-ups to distant sites are sometimes incorporated into local services (see Coleman 1996: 2000). Many Swedish believers are viewers of televangelism, such as the European channels on which the founder of the Word of Life, Ulf Ekman, regularly appears.

Swedish Faith Christians often assert that mediated religious occasions can be as much a conduit for the Word of God as any encounter in the flesh. Some offer a listener's and viewer's contract, which requires that videos, television link-ups and audio cassettes be 'received' in the proper state of mind. As a theory, this is rather akin to 'hypodermic' views of the mass media injecting messages into the brains of viewers and listeners: however, in this chapter, I am less concerned with measuring the actual sociological impact of the use of media than with how media images present visions of a religious public that acknowledge but transcend cultural difference. Thus Pastor Ekman appears at the beginning of some videos and says the following:

---

[2] Preachers valued by Faith Christians who do not come from the US include the South African Ray McCauley, the German-African Reinhard Bonnke, and Paul Yonggi Cho, a Pentecostal from Korea and pastor of reputedly the world's largest church. Ulf Ekman, the founder of the Word of Life, is himself becoming more prominent in global Faith circles.

> Before you go on I suggest you switch off the tape and take a moment, whether you're on your own, with your family, in a prayer-group or with your congregation, and pray that the Holy Spirit will lead you to the truth. It's important for you to expect that God will speak to you personally through His Word, that His Spirit will reveal itself to you.

Here, viewing is framed by prayer, being thus turned into a one-off event. The actual source of the personal Word from God is left unspecified, so whether the Lord speaks inwardly, through the Bible as recited by a televangelist, or through the mouth of a televised preacher is left open. However, what I want to emphasize is the apparently paradoxical, even Janus-faced aesthetic standard contained in these words. On the one hand there is the stress on the intimate personal indexicality of the occasion, in which 'God will speak to you personally', which is ideally achieved by a combination of personal prayer and viewing. At the same time, we see enacted what I call the Pentecostal process of 'reaching out' – an embodied notion of the Christian, wherever they happen to be, extending influence towards others who may be remote from the self. The significance of this practice of projecting the self outwards can hardly be over-emphasized for these Christians, as it applies not only to the classic stance of missionizing the unsaved other, but also to the ability to make contact with fellow believers across the globe. Intimacy is not believed to be compromised by such use of the media, and indeed the distance assumed to be travelled by the message may well give it extra enchantment in the minds of both the producer and receivers of the message.

It is this combination of intimacy and distance that I wish to explore in looking at the management of encounters across national cultures. If the video example I just mentioned deals with a Swedish preacher addressing a Swedish audience, how might such 'reaching out' be achieved in contexts where the audience is far less specified – indeed, where preaching may itself become a meta-commentary on the ways in which cultural and religious differences can be transcended? In the following, I address this question by looking in detail at just one example, a video produced by Morris Cerullo, an international charismatic figure who has been a regular visitor to the Word of Life. Cerullo, an American, has made his name not by pastoring a small, local congregation of tightly-knit believers, but by establishing a widely diffused reputation within a far-flung, sometimes even virtually articulated public of Christians. Interestingly, although he himself is an elderly white man, Cerullo has developed a particular following among black Pentecostal congregations in parts of Europe and the Caribbean (Schaefer 2004: 122). He is loosely affiliated with the Faith Movement, appearing with his colleagues in conferences and revival meetings around the globe, but is careful also to assert his independence from denominational ties. He has his own television ministry and distributes videos and other products throughout the world from his headquarters, Morris Cerullo World Evangelism, in San Diego. His tapes are markedly smooth products in which he experiments with a wide variety of television styles.

In the video I am examining here, *Morris Cerullo in Red Square* from the early 1990s, the hour-long programme has a television news magazine format, and each individual segment appears in a recognizable genre. In one such segment, Cerullo speaks directly to the camera as a talking head; in another, a blackboard talk to a 'seminar' in Florida, he mimics a training film; and there is even a section showing him leading a mass meeting in Moscow set out as journalistic reportage. Thus he starts the video in one place but moves easily between contexts and even continents. The likely consumers of the video are also likely to be far-flung, mostly American members of Cerullo's Video-Bible school, but also Swedish and indeed English supporters of the Faith movement.

Let us consider a brief extract from the tape in which Cerullo is being filmed while standing in the middle of the Square, and explaining that we are about to see a clip from Russian television. Within seconds we find ourselves watching Cerullo talking in a Moscow broadcasting studio. After some prefatory remarks, he addresses the camera directly and issues the following appeal to his remote audience:

> You repeat this prayer with my translator. / Dear God. / I come to you tonight / with all my heavy load. / Dear God, / take away my heavy load. / Lord Jesus, / I do not understand what this man Morris is saying. / But please, / I believe, you are the Son of God, / and I receive you / as my Lord, / as my Savior. / Please, Lord Jesus, / forgive all my sins, / and make me, / right now, / a child of God.[3]

Note how this passage compresses various voices, modes of address and narrative frames within a very short space. Cerullo is speaking, but he is not speaking as 'himself', a powerful charismatic personality – he is apparently adopting the voice of a bemused but engaged viewer. We are watching an American preacher narratively depicting, but also somehow embodying his Russian audience as they are transformed from listeners to speakers. Cerullo occupies the centre of the screen, but individual viewers are supposedly moving their attention away from him and towards God, while simultaneously shifting their allegiance away from communist atheism and Russian Orthodoxy towards charismatic Christianity.

Yet of course the audience for this tape is not primarily made up of Russian people. By being put into a video, the extract gains further significance through its double-framing. The original appeal was broadcast on national public television in Russia, but it has been edited into a product that can be marketed to a globally dispersed constituency of believers. The majority of viewers will probably be Western charismatics – in other words, those who are already converted – although the tape might also be used for evangelizing purposes in domestic contexts. The deictic 'right now' invoked by

[3] The forward slashes indicate the points of translation into Russian.

Cerullo's prayer can be reapplied to whichever temporal and cultural context video viewers happen to find themselves in.

Thus Cerullo's performance can ultimately be seen as being aimed at multiple audiences, containing groups of believers who come from slightly different Faith or 'Prosperity' traditions. His language is performative – he is, after all, trying to convert others – but in common with the quotation I supplied from Ulf Ekman, the agency of the words he uses has ambiguous origins and directions. The prayer Morris presents to his viewers is ultimately to be activated when *they* choose to speak the words themselves, when *they* take the decision not just to listen, but to repeat what he has said. It might seem, therefore, that Cerullo is removing himself from the picture, allowing himself to be present only in the act of embodying and therefore mediating a vision of the converted viewer who is turning to God. But the passage is also, as we have seen, a performance at yet another remove: once put into the video, the clip demonstrates Cerullo's proselytizing actions to his global audience of born-again consumers, and indeed much of the rest of this section of the video shows the effects of his missionary campaign in Moscow and beyond. Reframed, his appeal becomes both conversion narrative and metanarrative, both a form of witness and a charismatic commentary on the effects of such witness. Cerullo's apparent description of his travels in Russia is converted into the televisual equivalent of an altar call.

In the local context of Word of Life viewing practices Cerullo's prayer acts as a powerful catalyst of action, moving observers from watching to doing. Viewers often position themselves as the equivalent of Cerullo's studio audience, responding to his message with tongues and affirmative prayer.[4] For members of a much criticized

[4] The visual as well as verbal aspects of the video experience can be significant. As Meyer has noted (Meyer 2004: 101), despite its stereotype, vision plays a key role in Pentecostal practice more generally. Sermons, testimonies and prayers relate the spiritual things observed by the speaker, which are often invisible to the secular eye,

group such as the Word of Life, Cerullo – who has become an increasingly popular figure with Swedish charismatics over the past decade – also represents a further dimension of commitment: the confident presentation of the Word in the public sphere. In talking on Russian state television, he is occupying the Holy Grail of televangelism, the ultimate in secular mainstream programming, one that has very rarely been granted to Swedish Faith supporters. So the video – a private consumer good – is itself used to depict a very different kind of broadcasting, presenting a visual meta-narrative of the process of mediated charismatic representation. Cerullo's prayer enacts not merely the possibility of personal salvation, but also the merging of two wider contexts: the 'public' constituted by charismatics is shown in the act of occupying the public sphere of a contemporary state, and moreover one that has recently undergone its own political conversion.

In a recent article on Indonesian language and nation-building, Webb Keane (2003: 506), notes that language's general pragmatic capacities for self-abstraction and decontextualization make possible new and expansive modes of circulation. Indefinite and impersonal address can help to constitute a modern public (see Warner 2005), ideally remote (Keane 2003: 520) from deictics, and with specific topographical anchors or pronouns indexical of status. Keane's points help to highlight some of the ways in which Faith charismatics appear to construct publics through some rather surprising cultural

---

just as visions may be experienced in a dream or seen as coming from the spirit of discernment. Indeed, vision is seen as extension of the Holy Spirit, who grants the eye of God to his faithful servants, so that, even prior to the easy accessibility of the new visual technologies, vision was central to Pentecostal practices of mediation. Yet if sermons are confined to oral discourse emphasizing the necessity of vision, films are able to reproduce vision itself mimetically. In Meyer's case, this is significant in the fictional films produced for Ghanaian viewers, but it is also relevant to the more documentary style of video I discuss here, since the video provides a means of positioning the viewer in relation to speakers in ways that are not always evident even in one-to-one encounters.

materials. The liturgies of a video are simultaneously fixed and hyper-mobile, bound to repetition, though of course open to endless recontextualization and framing through prayer or other forms of charismatic discourse. In being appropriated properly, the words of the preacher become the basis of a further performance, which is made 'living' in charismatic terms (compare Engelke 2004: 77, 87). In addition, the characteristic mode of address of speakers is deeply personal yet ideally unconfined, with intimate personal indexicality oriented towards as wide a public as possible, aided by the fact that believers, and even many non-believers, are aware of a common set of characters and landscapes: those of the Bible. The rhetoric of much charismatic discourse, including that of some of the talk analysed in these videos, is conversionary in orientation. Yet to judge from observations in Sweden, such videos are rather more effective in introducing the already converted to practices of 'reaching out', thus helping to constitute a sense of believers being located in a landscape of charismatic agency that potentially has no limit.

One can therefore argue that, in its turn, the American preacher's rhetorical appropriation of Russian political and religious culture takes on a particular significance in the national circumstances surrounding the Word of Life. In Sweden, a broadly secular state and related interest groups (medical, academic, journalistic) permit groups such as the Word of Life to exist, but also regard them as a threat to national assumptions concerning tolerance and the degree to which religion and politics should mix. The charismatic public, in other words, is in considerable tension with the wider public sphere, so that a landscape of ideally unlimited agency is being represented by media products such as videos, whose circulation and production are, in practice, inevitably highly circumscribed.

Such a situation seems to contrast markedly with Birgit Meyer's recent depiction (2004: 92) of the ways in which the Ghanaian video-film industry has echoed the views and concerns of Pentecostal-charismatic (including Faith-oriented) churches and contributed to the emergence of a pentecostally infused – or 'pentecostalite' – public culture. With the term 'pentecostalite', Meyer is trying to capture a sense of the proliferation of Pentecostalist expressive forms through various channels in the sphere of entertainment – music, theatre, radio. Her argument (2004: 93) is that in Ghana, pentecostalite culture, as mediated by videos, provides an orientation geared more to global Christianity than to the national project. A new 'representational economy' (Keane 2002: 65) has emerged, and in Ghana it is one that challenges the Habermasian assumption that religion has been reduced to private sphere within the framework of the modern state. Thus, if in Ghana 'Pentecostalism and video-films come together and contribute to carving out a new public space for the articulation of alternative imaginations of modernity' (Meyer 2004: 96), in Sweden the situation appears rather different, with groups such as the Word of Life being able to gain access to privatized commercial media, but very rarely given access either to national broadcasting channels or mainstream cultural representations. But if the Swedish group's access to the public sphere in Meyer's sense is limited, at least its articulation of a public oriented beyond 'congregational particularities' (ibid.: 106) and towards a more global market of fellow believers is broadly similar to that of its Ghanaian equivalent.

Concluding Remarks

The Swedish Christians discussed in this chapter are often accused by the local press or church leaders of what one might call 'pejorative' and/or 'sectarian' syncretism. In other words, the group is sometimes seen as incorporating images of the pre-modern – shamanic rituals of excessive ecstasy – or alternatively those of the threatening hyper-modern, involving the Americanization of national culture as embodied in such figures as Cerullo. I have been talking about a rather different conceptualization of religious synthesis, however: one that focuses on the ways in which charismatics themselves represent the coming together of different strands of their own faith, given that Cerullo's depiction on video of an American's activities in Russia provides the ritual space for its appropriation by Word of Life members in Sweden, and indeed by Faith supporters elsewhere. In a sense, the 'coming together' I am describing has more to do with mutual encompassment in ritual and rhetorical terms than mixing per se.

We have seen how Cerullo's tape takes on specific local meanings in the light of the experience of the Word of Life. One further dimension of this experience should at least be mentioned here. The charismatic idioms deployed by the Word of Life have considerable resonance in the Swedish context in the sense that they parallel those of already established Christian churches in the country, and in particular those of older Pentecostalists. If the Word of Life can be said to be attacking certain local religionists, in the sense that it sees their power and influence as moribund, the force of such an attack depends on its ability to invoke a certain continuity with historically more established Pentecostal activities and ambitions in order to be seen to transcend them. One of the key distinctions between the Word of Life and such established Pentecostal Christians in Sweden lies less in the basic grammar of worship and much more in the extent to which the Word of Life locates itself on a self-consciously amplified, *global* sphere of operations, transcending geographical and cultural distance in order to spread salvation. Tongues, prophecy and so on are linked to a usually much more explicitly translocal spiritual landscape. As we have seen, images of preachers provide key depictions of mobility, expressed in a personal, quasi-intimate idiom.

Faith activities as I have described them therefore play a complex game of appropriation. On the one hand, charismatic culture as contained in Cerullo's video is shown to be 'dominating' national culture, in the form of the Russian social landscape that Cerullo bestrides. When deployed by Swedish believers, Cerullo's representation of the agency of charismatic culture can then be used not only to impart a sense of their 'taking over' Sweden in general, but also transforming – indeed, reviving – the Swedish religious landscape. Swedish believers use powerful metaphors to describe this sense of their religious commitment as a kind of juggernaut, for instance, when they talk of possessing faith 'that conquers all circumstances', including the parochial concerns of any given nation state or denomination.

Such ambition embodies both the attraction and the threat of the group in political and ecclesiastical circles in Sweden, just as it combines continuity and discontinuity with what is perceived to be local culture. What I have presented here may therefore not be a classic case of syncretism, but I hope it embodies those forms of affinity, repulsion and amplification that are usually involved in complex and ongoing processes of religious and cultural mixing. It also presents a variation on the situations described by Robbins (see above), in the sense that a form of charismatic Protestantism is simultaneously asserting kinship with, but also transforming the context of operation of, Pentecostal (as opposed to classically 'indigenous') idioms of worship. Many Faith Christians are open in their disdain for such 'syncretic' religions as the New Age, which they regard as a dangerous mixture of faiths and cultures. However, I have also tried to show how, in a less obvious but equally powerful way, commitment to the faith may involve the simultaneous acknowledgement of, but also highly regulated exposure to, the cultural differences of fellow believers.

Bibliography

Adogame, Afe (2003): From House Cells to Warehouse Churches? African Migrant Churches and the Politics of Religious Syncretism in Germany, Paper presented to 'Religion on the Margins' Conference, Halle: Max Planck Institute of Social Anthropology.

Clark, Lynn; Hoover, Stewart M. (1997): At the Intersection of Media, Culture and Religion: A Bibliographic Essay, in: Stewart, M. Hoover; Lundby, Knut (eds.): *Rethinking Media, Religion, and Culture*, Thousand Oaks: Sage: 15-36.

Clarke, Kamari Maxine (2004): *Mapping Yorùbá Networks: Power and Agency in the Making of Transnational Communities*, Durham and London: Duke University Press.

Coleman, Simon (1996): Words as Things: Language, Aesthetics and the Objectification of Protestant Evangelicalism, *Journal of Material Culture* 1: 107-28.

Coleman, Simon (2000): *The Globalisation of Charismatic Christianity: Spreading the Gospel of Prosperity*, Cambridge: Cambridge University Press.

Engelke, Matthew (2004): Text and Performance in an African Church: The Book 'Live and Direct', *American Ethnologist* 31, 1: 76-91.

Fardon, Richard (1995): *Counterworks: Managing the Diversity of Knowledge*, London: Routledge.

Hannerz, Ulf (1996): *Transnational Connections: Culture, People, Places*, London: Routledge.

Inda, Jonathan Xavier; Rosaldo, Renato (2002): A World in Motion, in: Inda, J.X; Rosaldo, R. (eds.): *The Anthropology of Globalization*, Oxford: Blackwell: 1-34.

Keane, Webb (2002): Sincerity, 'Modernity,' and the Protestants, *Cultural Anthropology* 17, 1: 65-92.

Keane, Webb (2003): Public Speaking: On Indonesian as the Language of the Nation, *Public Culture* 15, 3: 503-30.

Meyer, Birgit (1994): Beyond Syncretism: Translation and Diabolization in the Appropriation of Protestantism in Africa, in: Stewart, Charles; Shaw, Rosalind (eds.): *Syncretism/Anti-syncretism: The Politics of Religious Synthesis*, London: Routledge.

Meyer, Birgit (2004): 'Praise the Lord': Popular Cinema and Pentecostalite Style in Ghana's New Public Sphere, *American Ethnologist* 31, 1: 92-110.

Robbins, Joel (2003): On the Paradoxes of Global Pentecostalism and the Perils of Continuity Thinking, *Religion* 33: 221-31.

Schaefer, Nancy (2004): American-led Urban Revivals as Ethnic Identity Arenas in Britain, in: Coleman, Simon; Collins, Peter (eds.): *Religion, Identity and Change: Perspectives on Global Transformations*, Aldershot: Ashgate: 119-35.

Shaw, Rosalind; Stewart, Charles (1994): Introduction: Problematizing Syncretism, in: Stewart, Charles; Shaw, Rosalind (eds.): *Syncretism/Anti-syncretism: The Politics of Religious Synthesis*, London: Routledge: 1-26.

Strathern, Marilyn (1995): *The Relation Prickly Pear Pamphlet No. 6*, Cambridge: Prickly Pear Press.

Mwaka Koga: The Development of Syncretistic Rituals in a Globalising World

Ulrich Rinn

Introduction

Mwaka Koga is a New Year festival in an Islamic society which nowadays is predominantly secular. If one were to look at it only from the perspective of syncretism, its origins and development would be the aspects to analyse. However, the aim of this chapter is to consider its syncretistic aspects from the present perspective under the auspices of globalisation processes.

In the first part the historic and historiographic background to the festival will be described. In the following section, certain developments threatening the continuity of the Mwaka Koga festival in the twentieth century will be discussed.

The Mwaka Koga Tradition Before 1900

How old is the old? This is an important question in the analysis of the Swahili New Year festival which is the topic of the present discussion. The East African festival of Mwaka Koga appears to be very old, yet its actual origins are unknown. The feast of 'Bathing the Year' – as the Swahili expression can be translated – is believed to be pre-Islamic. It has been brought together with the Iranian Nou Roz festival, which marks the New Year of Zoroastrian religion and is also celebrated by Muslims as a secular festival. The alternative name of the Mwaka festival is Nairuzi. As the Swahili have many legends of state founders who originally came from Shiraz in the Fars province of Persia, and as there are also some eleventh-century ruins and artefacts – e.g. the Kizimkazi mosque and some ruins on Tumbatu Island – apparently in Persian style, many authors have come to the conclusion that the festival was introduced to East Africa by Shirazi immigrants.[1] In the nineteenth and early twentieth centuries, historians stressed the importance of foreign influences on Swahili society and culture. The Nairuzi festival seemed to be just one more proof of this among others, Islam and the Kiswahili language, with its wealth of Arabic loanwords, being the most prominent.[2] Since African countries gained independence, the focus of historical research has changes, the key questions now focusing on the African input into this mix. Some recent articles dealing with Mwaka Koga assume that the festival is basically an African development and not something borrowed from a foreign continent.[3] In both cases however, the present Mwaka celebrations are seen as the outcome of a syncretistic process: either a pre-Islamic Asiatic festival has been combined with African rituals and beliefs, followed by adaptation to Islam; or the Swahili New Year is the result of the fusion of an African festival with Islamic religious practices.

For centuries, Islam has shaped Swahili society and culture. Archaeological excavations in the Lamu archipelago, at Kilwa or on Pemba and Unguja show evidence of mosques in the earliest strata of the coastal settlements. In Shanga, Mark Horton discovered that the site of the mosque had been a place of Islamic prayer probably as early as the eighth century. Archaeology and oral traditions combined suggest that the festival has been part of Swahili culture right from the beginning, in the ninth to eleventh centuries AD. However, the earliest descriptions of the Mwaka Koga festival date from the nineteenth century, in the reports of European travellers, officers and missionaries.[4]

---

[1] E.g. Sheriff 2001: 35.

[2] Krapf, Burton, and Baumann are among nineteenth-century authors who stressed the Persian link, Gray (1955) being the most important writer in the mid-twentieth century.

[3] Racine 1994, 1998.

[4] Guillain, Burton, von der Decken, Velten and Mtoro.

The festival's main rituals will be summarised very briefly. There are some local variations, but basically the cultic acts are common right along the East African coast. The Mwaka Koga festival consists of a morning bath in the sea (*koga mwaka*), the procession around the village or town, and the subsequent slaughtering and cooking of a bull or goat or sheep (*kuzungusha ng'ombe*), which is shared and eaten by all participants as a communal sacrifice (*sadaka wa mji*). In some places offerings for local spirits are included, and in many places there is a ritual stick fight in the afternoon (*kirumbizi*). Usually in the evening there are dances and celebrations which continue over the following days.[5]

Such, in brief, are some of the main characteristics of the Swahili New Year. In relation to Islam, the predominant religion along the East African coast, the Swahili have found some ways to adjust their traditional Mwaka festival to Islamic rituals. When offering gifts at the dwellings of local spirits, the spirit priests use both Swahili prayers and recitations of the suras from the Koran. During the procession they sometimes sing local songs, but more common is the continuous declamation of the *takbira*, the prayer 'Allahu akbar'. In Tumbe, a place in the north of Pemba, participants in the procession use the call for prayer, the *adhan*, as their recitation whenever they reach a crossroads or a spirit's dwelling. While the *takbira* can be used in any context, the *adhan* is clearly being taken out of its regular context here, since normally it should be reserved for the five calls to daily prayers. The communal sacrifices after the procession around the villages and towns are accompanied by a collective recitation of the Koran.[6]

---

[5] Incomplete descriptions are found in Gray 1955, Racine 1994, 1998, and Frankl 2000. Two PhD dissertations on the Mwaka Koga festival are in preparation. I deal with the origins and history of the festival. M. Echtler focuses on the recent changes in Makunduchi's Mwaka Kogwa.

[6] This is based on research in Makunduchi and informants from Tumbe (on Pemba) and other places.

Clearly the Swahili have merged this traditional cult with the strictly monotheistic Islam. This syncretism has been part of Swahili life over the centuries so that for many Swahili it now forms part of their Islamic belief.

The Swahili have performed the Mwaka Koga festival for centuries for one main reason. The Nairuzi calendar has been necessary for agriculture and maritime occupations because it takes the solar year as its basis, thus keeping the seasons measurable. The Muslim lunar year, by contrast, is ten or eleven days shorter, which means that every month travels though all seasons once every 33 years. Yet the Swahili are not the only Muslim society to have kept an additional solar calendar together with the regular lunar one prescribed by Muhammad. In Iran and its neighbouring countries there is also a secular solar year. In Egypt the Muslims have celebrated the Coptic New Year, also called Nairuz, for a long time together with the Christians.

At the beginning of the twentieth century, Mwaka Koga still played a major part in the Swahili settlements along the East African coast. Yet by the end of that century it had disappeared almost everywhere. There are two questions to be answered here. First, why did it disappear in these places? And secondly, what has helped it survive elsewhere?

The End of a Syncretisation Process: One Part of the Swahili Experience

Why should one talk about the end of a syncretisation process and mention the Mwaka Koga festival of the Swahili, a festival that seems to be experiencing renewed prominence. Most of the travel guides for Zanzibar suggest that tourists should go to Makunduchi at the end of July to take part in a unique cultural heritage, the New Year festival, well covered by the local media, TV, radio and the press. Especially in advertising magazines aimed at guests from all over the world, the festival is praised as a must. The *Tanzanian Post* also issued a postage stamp in a series celebrating cultural heritage that featured Makunduchi as an important centre.

Yet the broad coverage of the Mwaka festival in Makunduchi is only a small part of the story of the syncretistic cultural elements in Swahili culture. The real picture is quite different. While the Swahili New Year had been celebrated all along the coast in every town and village up to the nineteenth century, it disappeared almost everywhere during the twentieth century. The main factors which let to the dwindling role of certain specific Swahili elements in East African coastal culture can be divided intothe political, the economic and the religious.

<u>The role of politics</u>

No one would deny that the political sphere can establish decisive frameworks for cultural changes, both fiscally and legislatively.

The Mwaka Koga festival came under threat while Europeans were the masters of East Africa. At the end of the nineteenth century, the British officers in the Zanzibar Protectorate interfered with the local Mwaka festival. Hitherto it had been the custom that, during New Year's Day, two groups of young people, representing the two groups of Swahili society which can be observed in all the towns along the coast, would meet at the creek between Stone Town and Ng'ambo and stage a ritual stick fight in the early afternoon. Regularly some participants got hurt, but blood was considered a sign of blessing, so bleeding wounds were a necessary part of the ritual fight. However, the British did not see the ritual significance: to them this was merely a sign of deliberate unrest, so they deployed the police to keep the two parties apart. In the 1930s the ban on fighting was extended to the town of Makunduchi, which had become famous as the original site of the New Year Festival. It began with the deployment of larger police forces to restrain the mood of the fighters. Then decrees were issued allowing only very thin sticks to be used in the fighting to reduce the number of wounded. Finally, in the last few years of colonial rule, the fights were forbidden completely, so that Sir John Gray, visiting Makunduchi during the Mwaka festivities in the early 1950s, did not witness any ritual stick fight.[7]

The First World War led to conflict in East Africa, including the Swahili coast. This meant that in many a town or village it was impossible to carry out the necessary rituals of transition in the annual festival. The disruption involved continued to be felt after the war. The calendar was a particular problem, since the necessary calculations depended on steadily counting the days. Also, the day of the week on which New Year's Day fell was important because a New Year on Monday was followed by one on Tuesday and so on. The towns and villages in the former German East Africa, now Tanganyika Territory, a League of Nations Mandate under British control, had to start the calendar calculation and the rituals of the festival again. Most places came to a tacit agreement about the proper date of the new start. In the village of Petukiza in Tanga Region called, however, the Mwalimu Suleiman had his own ideas about the proper time for the Mwaka day, which was earlier than the date of the festival in the surrounding area. The people in his village followed him, and he also gathered some supporters in other parts of Tanga region. Hence there were two Mwaka days, the regular Mwaka and the Mwaka wa Suleiman (Suleiman's New Year).[8] This is an example of politically created disruptions. Yet the implications did not go so deep that the celebrations were ended. In the twentieth century, there were other points on which politics had a deeper impact on the matters regarding the Swahili New Year festivals.

The nature of the political threat to the Mwaka festival in Zanzibar changed after the revolution. As is known, party politics in the Sultanate were combined with ethnic constructions of tradition and

[7] Zanzibar National Archives, BA 30: District Reports Zanzibar 1930s-50s; Gray 1955.
[8] Fieldwork, September 2001, in Tanga Region.

history, as well as with differential economic status. The ruling party coalition of the ZNP and ZPPP recruited its supporters from the Arab aristocracy and wealthy businessmen (ZNP) and the Shirazi, or Watumbatu and Wapemba (ZPPP). Together the two parties had the majority of seats in Parliament. The outright winner of the most votes, however, the ASP, received fewer mandates due to the unequal distribution of mandates and voters. Only four weeks after the Sultanate gained independence, the government was toppled by disaffected groups. After some confusion, the ASP was quickly able to gain the initiative. The party's leader, Karume, formed the new government and received support from abroad, especially from the German Democratic Republic and the Soviet Union. He was also joined by the local communists. The outcome was a clear swing to the left. To avoid a major crisis and to consolidate the government, Karume and President Nyerere of Tanganyika made a treaty to unite the two states to form the United Republic of Tanganyika and Zanzibar, later renamed Tanzania.

The Revolutionary Government of Zanzibar drew up plans for modernization. In its vague and crude communist ideology, old cultural traditions were banned as backward. This included the possession cults, the traditional healers' treatments and also the Mwaka festival in many places, especially where it was combined with a demonstration of 'Shiraziness'. In places like Pemba and Tumbatu, the Shirazi idea was very popular. As these places were bases for the ASP's opponents, they now faced difficulties.[9]

The ASP (Afro-Shirazi Party), although containing the name 'Shirazi', focused mainly on the idea of the Zanzibaris being 'African', with a strong connection to mainland Tanzania.

Especially in Pemba the Mwaka festival survived only in few places, and many traditions were given up due to the political repression and economic changes the ASP/CCM regime.

[9] Cf. Nisula 1999: 45f.

The role of the economy

Mainland Tanzania did not have to go through a revolution. This means that there was no stimulus to give up cultural habits such as the New Year festival. But there were two factors which diminished the importance of the festival gradually but effectively.

In 2001 in the village of Petukiza, which is halfway between Tanga and the Kenyan border, live a couple of old men who represent the last handful of those who are trying to keep the *siku ya Mwaka*, their New Year festival, alive. They tell a story about the difficulties their grandparents and parents had in continuing with this ancient festival after the disruption of World War One. The village became famous for the stubbornness of its Mwalimu Suleiman (see above).[10]

In 1978 Tanzania was drawn into a war with Uganda's dictator Idi Amin, who had tried to annex a small part of Tanzanian territory. The war ended with the ousting of Amin, who went into exile in Saudi Arabia, where he died last year. Tanzania was the victor, but at almost too great a cost. The territory of the Republic was now secure, but the costs of the war had been tremendous. Tanzania was bankrupt. A sharp economic crisis followed the war, ending in the liberalisation of the economy and orientation towards market capitalism in the mid-1980s, when Nyerere resigned as President and his successor Ali Hassan Mwinyi launched an economic reform programme.

The end of the 1970s and the 1980s was a period of great problems for the whole population. In 2001, the old men of Petukiza recalled that, around that time, the younger people in the village refused to donate their share of the money required to buy the animal to be sacrificed as a communal offering after the New Year's procession of blessing around the village. The main reason was the general lack of money, the men said, but the young people had also argued

[10] Interviews, September 2001.

that in Islam there was no Mwaka festival. So in the years that followed it became increasingly difficult for the few traditionalists to carry on with the New Year rituals. They continued it by buying goats instead of a bull. Later they could only afford a chicken as sacrifice, and since the late 1990s they have not been able to afford any sacrifice at all, so they reduced the rituals again. They merely continued with the New Year's bath which gives the festival its Kiswahili name (*mwaka koga*), as well as surrounding the village in the procession of blessing, in which they continually recited verses from the Koran, one of the syncretistic features which has helped the pre-Islamic festival to survive for so long.

It will only be a few years before the rituals of this ancient festival will have disappeared in Petukiza too, as it has in so many other places along the coast.

In many cases the lack of money led to the old cultural elements being abandoned. The Mwaka was too expensive because it meant buying an animal for the communal sacrifice and wearing new clothes, as well as providing plenty of food for the guests one might expect during New Year's holiday.

The role of religion

The example of Petukiza shows that religious motives have been cited for abandoning the festival, even though the old men claim this was purely for lack of money.

In another village in the Tanga region, the refusal of the younger generations to pay for the sacrifice meant that Mwaka Koga could not be maintained because the older people, who would have liked to continue with their customs, were too weak to sustain the economic burden. Here too, however, the main argument was that Islam only has two religious festivals, Nairuzi not being one of them, so there was no need to celebrate a heterodox festival at all.[11]

---

[11] Interviews, Kimavu 11.9.2001.

The debate over whether or not the Mwaka Koga festival is opposed to Islam has been fiercely pursued for some time in Mombasa as well.[12] The present situation will be discussed in a separate paragraph.

The Lamu archipelago on the Kenyan coast also offers some examples of the role played by religious movements with regards to the Mwaka festival.[13] Lamu has been a renowned centre of Swahili and Islamic scholarship for a long time and in recent decades the place has fallen under the influence of various religious reform movements.

Preachers have been very successful in propagating the necessity for a pure form of Islam, without pagan elements. Since Lamu has many competing mosques, a kind of competition over purity soon developed, and Mwaka Koga soon lost public support as a result. For the locals the main discussion is nowadays whether the very popular Maulidi festival can be considered orthodox enough.

In the small town of Shela near to Lamu, one informant explained the religious situation. He said that almost everybody was a follower of the local movement of puristic Islam, so that only two or three families were left who still counted the solar year and had a private Mwaka celebration. In Lamu also, only a few people maintained their private New Year celebrations due to the public pressure against 'paganism'.[14] In the remoter areas of the Lamu archipelago there are still some relics of Mwaka celebrations, but given the values of modern Islam, people no longer consider the old traditional rites necessary.[15]

[12] Cf. Frankl and Omar 2000: 18, 24.
[13] Information gathered in summer 2001.
[14] Interview, 27.8.2001.
[15] E.g. in Matondoni or Pate.

Maintaining Syncretistic Rituals: Examples of Survival

In the first part of this chapter, the factors causing the decline and disappearance of Mwaka Koga in almost every part of the Swahili coast have been discussed. The following section deals with examples that show the vitality of the festival in other places. It is divided into three parts, each taking one particular town or village as a case study. All three have their specific characteristics, which are the cause of their particular method of maintaining ancient cult practices.

Case study 1: Kojani

In the list of 'positive' examples of surviving New Year festivals, Kojani is somehow outstanding, the place where one could say that the traditions have survived in their purest form until today. The festival is still pursued with all the rituals over three successive days, the full amount of offerings and sacrifices, and the participation of almost the whole population.[16]

One possible reason for the strong preservation of tradition here is the remoteness of the place: Kojani is the sole settlement on a small islet off the east coast of Pemba that is divided by a small creek from the main island. The population has not received much influence from outsiders for a long time period but has developed in relative isolation. The effect is felt by the distinctiveness of the dialect spoken in the village, which is also renowned for its mighty spirits and spirit mediums, as well as its traditional healers. Many people fear Kojani people and the place as a whole. Although the revolutionary government in Zanzibar tried to suppress traditional religious and cultural habits such as spirit possession cults, local medicine and festivals in many different ways, the people of Kojani managed to maintain their heritage. This helps explain the conservatism of Kojani people and their ability to stick to this heritage.

---

[16] Interviews, 2002; cf. Racine 1998.

Case study 2: Mombasa

Mombasa is a very interesting example of the difficulties facing the Mwaka festival. At one point it looked as if the Swahili New Year was doomed in this old centre of East African coastal culture. Then, after the mid-1990s, a process of refreshing Swahili culture started with the help of donors from abroad. A Swahili committee was established to take care of the city's cultural heritage. One effect of this has been the establishment of an arts and crafts school where young Mombasans can learn coastal-style woodcarving or Swahili-style poetry.[17]

Another project has been the re-popularisation of Mwaka Koga.[18] The committee has started printing leaflets and posters, which have been distributed throughout the town.[19] Some rituals have been given up, such as the procession with the bull through Stone Town. The festival now starts where the procession formerly ended, in the school grounds of Alidina Visram, where there is a grave said to be the resting place of Shee Mvita, the pre-Portuguese ruler of the nine tribes of Mvita, which, together with the three tribes of Kilindini, formed the Mombasa 'nation'. At the grave the bull is slaughtered and cooked, and different dances take place, e.g. the *gungu* or 'sword dance'. Bathing early in the morning of New Year's Day is still done by some people, but as a private decision no longer with any connection to the feast at Shee Mvita's grave.[20]

The motives for the revival of Mwaka Koga should be considered carefully. The explanation involves taking into account a whole complex of political, religious and social factors. Until 1963 the coastal strip was part of the Zanzibar Sultanate under the British Protectorate Administration, while the hinterland was ruled directly

---

[17] Interview with H.M. Hassan, member of the Swahili Committee, 18.8.2001.

[18] Cf. Frankl and Omar 2000: 23ff.

[19] Interview with H.M. Hassan, member of the Swahili Committee, 18.8.2001.

[20] Cf. Frankl and Omar 2000; interviews with A.S. Nabhany, 12.8.2001, H.M. Hassan, 18.8.2001.

by the British as a colony. Kenya is largely Christianised, but there are also still groups of adherents of traditional religions. In recent decades, the Christianity has been strongly influenced by Pentecostal movements. Popular culture and mass media are also shaping culture and social habits. It is different on the coast. The traditional Swahili towns have been open to Islam for centuries. Mombasa is by far the most important port along the East African coast, the starting point for the Uganda Railway and an industrial centre of modern Kenya. Also tourism is very developed in the region, where there are many beach resorts etc. In present-day Kenya, this ancient Swahili port city plays a part in all the social movements.

Muslims from the Swahili coast have never played a major role in Kenyan politics, so politically Mombasa belongs to the periphery. Nonetheless the growing economic power of the port city has attracted masses of people to move there in the hope of finding work. Some Swahili Mombasans have therefore come to feel marginalized in their own environment. Local Muslims are more and more faced with people of different cultural and religious backgrounds. In the past they were proudly conscious of being members of what was perceived as a high-status coastal society. Now everything seems to be dominated by a new life-style, with Nairobi and the west as its role models, and with radio, newspapers and television as its media. The revival of the Mwaka Koga festival can be seen as a means to demonstrate 'Swahiliness', to demonstrate one's claims to authenticity and autochthony by maintaining distinctive cultural festivals and customs. Yet there are others who would rather take their orientation from the so-called Islamic reformist movements. At present no one can say what developments the Mombasan Mwaka festival will undergo.[21]

[21] Cf. Frankl and Omar 2000: 27.

Case study 3: Makunduchi

The third example of surviving Mwaka Koga festivals is the most complex one. It concerns a village in southern Unguja (Zanzibar). The area has been settled by the Kae people, formerly called Hadimu, a name rejected by the people themselves because of its derogatory connotations of 'servile peoples' almost equal to the slaves. *Kae* means old, authentic and original, and the people use it also as a term for their dialect, Kihadimu, a very rural variety of Kiswahili with fewer loanwords.[22] Nowadays it seems that Mwaka and Makunduchi are one and the same festival. One can easily take one of the travel handbooks on Zanzibar and find the suggestion that, during the last weeks of July, one should not miss the opportunity to visit this village at the southern end of the island and witness the ancient cultural New Year festival. Even the local press mentions the Mwaka festival in Makunduchi and sends radio, TV and newspaper reporters to cover it. The *Tanzanian Post* also produced a postage stamp featuring the Mwaka festival at Makunduchi's in a series for collectors on the national cultural heritage. There is some sense in focusing on this village in southern Unguja. In the past the festival was ubiquitous on the island and all along the Swahili coast, but during the twentieth century it disappeared from almost all villages and towns. In Zanzibar Town the Mwaka seems to have been celebrated for the last time in the 1960s.[23] Today only Makunduchi seems to be left. But in the forgotten north of the island, the other ancient people of Zanzibar, the Tumbatu, still celebrate their New Year in the traditional manner in the Nungwi area and on Tumbatu Island.[24]

The festival of Makunduchi has only been able to survive with various difficulties. Files in the Zanzibar National Archives and

---

[22] Many contemporary authors still call the people of southern and central Unguja 'Hadimu', while a modern dictionary uses the term 'Kae'.

[23] Information gathered in summer 2002.

[24] Information gathered in Jongowe and Gomani on Tumbatu, August 2002.

eyewitness reports show that British colonial rule had a direct influence on the proceedings of the Mwaka festival in the Zanzibar Protectorate, as it banned the 'violence', in the form of the stick fight which took place between the youth groups of the northern and southern halves of the village while the ceremonial hut was being burnt. After the First World War the British successfully suppressed the stick fight dances in Zanzibar Town as part of the Mwaka day, these fights being reported in the *Zanzibar Gazette* from 1895. In Makunduchi, this fight-dance, which was in British eyes a mere act of violence, had been given up after World War 2 due to administrative pressure on the local *mudir* and the massive presence of police forces at the festival in some years.[25] When Sir John Gray, who wrote the most important scholarly article about the Nairuzi festival, visited the Mwaka celebrations in Makunduchi, he found that the people had replaced the stick fights with certain dances which originally had a different place in the spirit possession cult.[26] Yet history does not necessarily develop all in one direction. After independence the people of Makunduchi renewed the traditional ritual stick fight between the two parties. This shows that features formerly perceived as important and necessary can be revived in more favourable circumstances. It also shows the persistent power of traditions and rituals deeply rooted in local culture.

One might have thought that after the revolution – i.e. under Karume's regime – Mwaka Koga would disappear as it had in most other places because of the ban on traditional medicine, spirit cults and 'Shirazi' communal rituals. But Makunduchi had the advantage that the majority of its inhabitants were stout followers of the ruling Afro-Shirazi Party and always had good contacts with important members of the government.

---

[25] Zanzibar National Archives BA 104: Zanzibar Gazette; BA 30: District Reports Zanzibar 1930s-50s.

[26] Gray 1955: 15f.

The group of elders who dealt with the Nairuzi ritual were also quite inventive. They created a committee for Mwaka Kogwa (the new spelling used in Makunduchi) and invited the government to share responsibilities for holding the festival. The new local and regional commissioners were invited on to the board or committee dealing with publicaffairs. Every year a guest of honour was invited who was a member of parliament or of the government or a leading party politician from ASP, TANU and later CCM. In fact, the revolutionary government of Zanzibar used the Mwaka festival as a platform to gain access to the masses and secure popular support.

Ritual affairs were kept apart from this public and more political role. There was a separate committee, the Kamati wa Wazee wa Mwaka Kogwa, that is, 'the Committee of the Elders of the New Year'.[27]

In order to accommodate the political guests of honour, some adjustments had to be made to the plan of the festival. This provides an opportunity to witness certain new syncretistic features which have not been fully included in the original rituals, but have been kept separate as far as possible from the religious sphere consisting of the traditional rituals: the blessing of the community, repentance, and accommodation of the local spirits, the genii loci, who are believed to be the original owners of the place and who only accept humans living there as guests who must pay them tribute in the form of various offerings.

These modern, politically motivated syncretistic additions have not changed Mwaka's core rituals. What has changed is that, before the ceremonies are conducted, step by step the guest of honour is shown around and explained the meaning and symbolism of everything he witnesses, though in a very superficial way. But the deeper structure of what happens during Mwaka Kogwa in Makunduchi is

---

[27] Interviews, 2001, 2002, 2004; Racine 1994: 172f.

kept secret by the ritual's elders, those who actually perform the liturgical duties.

However, there is a risk that in future the Mwaka festival in Makunduchi may lose what is still left of its cultural significance and become a merely popular and folkloristic event. The Nairuzi follows a solar calendar of 365 days which is difficult to calculate. Since there is no intercalation of the sort which keeps the Gregorian calendar in step with the actual seasons, the date of the Mwaka celebrations keeps wandering through the months. The calendar has been used for maritime and agricultural purposes, through which certain features of pre-Islamic religion have been able to survive up to the present day. Nowadays pupils in school learn the Gregorian calendar in use by the government and the administration, which is now as widespread as the lunar calendar, which is religiously important for the Muslim population. This more accurate calendar enables one to follow the seasons better than the old Nairuzi calendar. Farmers, fishermen and even the teachers in the Koranic schools have already replaced their ancient calendar with the western style of reckoning time.[28] Without its own calendar, the New Year's Day will soon lose its reason to exist. All that will be left are folkloristic reminiscences.

Concluding Remarks

The Mwaka Koga festival is first and foremost an example of cultural heritage under threat from the impacts of modern society and both local and world politics;. in other words, it is affected by a changing world and faces transformations in the present globalisation process.

In most parts of the Swahili world, the rituals have already disappeared after the loss of many of their functions. Modern religious

[28] Interviews with people of different professions in Makunduchi carried out in 2001, 2002, and 2004.

politics and the attraction of Islamic reformist thought have undermined the original ritual function of the New Year. The Nairuzi festival is no longer important in fighting the odds of nature and evil spirits. In Lamu it has been replaced by the Maulidi, the festival in honour of the Prophet Muhammad's birth. In agriculture and sailing, the old Swahili solar calendar no longer is needed for the calculation of the seasons and monsoon winds because the western Gregorian calendar fulfils this purpose more accurately, having been in use in schools and administration since the colonial era. Economic reasons have been mentioned as well. lasting recent decades the situation for ordinary people has been declining continuously, so that they have been less and less able to afford to maintain a festival which required them to contribute financially for public sacrifices. Apart from these factors, Zanzibar politics has also played a minor role in the disappearance of Mwaka Koga.

The situation in those areas where the festival has survived is also difficult. The economic situation is grave for most people. The influence of Islamic reformist movements cannot be assessed fully. Only in Makunduchi does the situation not look critical at first glance. Using globalisation, which is bringing mass tourism to East Africa, as a means of promoting the festival internationally fetches the organizing Mwaka committee additional money. The invitation to a high-ranking politician each year as a guest of honour creates political goodwill and local media coverage. But behind the scenes there are also critics from among both religious performers, who wish to abandon the 'pagan' cult, and traditionalists, who wish there were fewer visitors to disturb the rituals, as they frequently do out of ignorance.

Bibliography

Frankl, P.J.L. and Y.A. Omar (2000): Siku ya Mwaka: The Swahili New Year, *AAP 64, Swahili Forum VII*: 5-31.

Gray, John (1955): Nairuzi or Siku ya Mwaka, *Tanganyika Notes and Records* 38: 1-22.

Nisula, Tapio (1999): *Everyday Spirits and Medical Interventions: Ethnographic and Historical Notes on Therapeutic Conventions in Zanzibar Town.* Saarijärvi: Gummerus Kirjapaino Oy.

Racine, Odile (1994): The Mwaka of Makunduchi, Zanzibar, in: Parkin, David J. (ed.): *Continuity and Autonomy in Swahili Communities: Inland Influences and Strategies of Self Determination*, Vienna: Afro Pub: 167-75.

Racine-Issa, Odile (1998): Le Mwaka de Kojani (Pemba), *General Linguistics* 38,1: 199-229.

Sheriff, Abdul (2001): The Historicity of the Shirazi Tradition along the East African Coast, in: Cultural Council of the Embassy of I.R. Iran, Nairobi (ed.): *Historical Role of Iranians (Shirazis) in the East African Coast*, Nairobi: Aquapet Printers: 21-41.

Authors:

Afe **Adogame** received his PhD in the History of Religions from the University of Bayreuth, Germany. Until his appointment to the facultuy at the University of Edinburgh in 2005, he was Senior Research and Teaching Fellow at the Department for the Study of Religion and Institute of African Studies, University of Bayreuth from 1995-1998 and 2000-2005. He was part of the SFB/FK 560 Project (B1).

Peter **Beyer** is Professor of Religious Studies at the University of Ottawa, Canada. He studied and lectured at the University of Toronto till 1995. His publications include *Religion and Globalisation*. He is also known for his American edition of Niklas Luhmann (*Religious Dogmatics*).

Astrid **Bochow** is a Research Fellow and Ph.D. student in the Ethno-Sociological Department at the University of Bayreuth. . Her field of research is Ghana. Her main research interest is marriage, love and family change in African contexts.

Simon **Coleman** is Professor of Anthropology at the University of Sussex. He came to the University in September 2004, having spent eleven years at Durham University as Lecturer and then Reader in Anthropology and Deputy Dean of the Faculty of Social Sciences and Health. He obtained his PhD from Cambridge. His interests include conservative Protestantism, pilgrimage and aesthetics.

André **Droogers** is Professor Emieritus of Cultural Anthropology at the Department of Social and Cultural Anthropology, Faculty of Social Sciences, Free University of Amsterdam. He has done field-work in Congo and Brazil, and has also held academic positions in both countries.

Magnus **Echtler** studied social anthropology, philosophy and religious studies at Bayreuth and Berlin. He has conducted research on the Swahili New Year festival in Zanzibar and Tanzania, and more recently on the Nazareth Baptist Church in Durban, South Africa. Currently he teaches African Religions at the University of Bayreuth.

Peter **Gottschligg** was a member of of the linguistic SFB-project B6 on contrastive cognitive semantics in Northern Nigeria. His main research fields are Fula language, ethnolinguistics and dialectology. He has been doing research since 1982 in Senegal, Mali, Burkina Faso, Côte-d'Ivoire, Niger, Togo, Benin, Nigeria and Cameroun. He held several appointments as a lecturer, visiting senior lecturer and visiting professor at the Universities of Vienna, Maiduguri and Hamburg.

Hans Peter **Hahn** studied ethnology, prehistory, early history and botany at the Johann Wolfgang Goethe-University in Frankfurt am Main from 1984 till 1994. He was member of SFB 268 at the University of Frankfurt till 1995. Since then he has worked as research and teaching fellow at the University of Bayreuth. His areas of research are Togo and Burkina Faso, and his main fields of research material culture, cultivating, crafts and trade.

Dymitr **Ibriszimow** holds the chair of African Studies II (African languages beyond Niger-Congo) at the University of Bayreuth. His research foci are Chadic, Berber and the other Afro-Asiatic languages, comparative and historical linguistics, ethnolinguistics, linguistic geography and cognitive semantics. Dymitr Ibriszimow is Director of the Institute of African Studies (Institut für Afrika-Studien) at the University of Bayreuth.

Said A.M. **Khamis** is Professor of the Literature of African languages at Bayreuth University. He was founder of the units for Kiswahili in Moi University, Eldoret, Kenya, and the University of Nairobi, Kenya. From 1990 to 1997 he was a Visiting Professor at Osaka University of Foreign Studies in Japan. He is also a well-known writer of Swahili literature, having published six novels, three collections of poems, four stage plays and three collections of short stories.

Karina **Kopatsch** was previously Lecturer in African language studies at the University at Bayreuth and a member of the linguistic project B6 within the SFB-FK 560 researching contrastive cognitive semantics and conceptual structures of everyday lexemes in regional Nigerian languages and Nigerian English in relation to language and social context in northern Nigeria.

Selome **Kuponu** recently completed his PhD program at the University of Bayreuth in July 2007 with a thesis on the Living Faith Church (Winners Chapel) in Nigeria. He was part of the SFB/FK 560 (B1). He is a Lecturer in the Department of Religions, Lagos State University, Nigeria.

Roman **Loimeier** was perviously research and teaching fellow at Bayreuth University. He has been doing research in Senegal, Nigeria and Zanzibar since 1981. Currently he is working at the Centre for Modern Oriental Studies in Berlin, where he has a project on 'Plural Concepts of Time in (Trans)local Contexts'.

Elísio **Macamo** is Assistant Professor in the Cultural Studies Faculty at Bayreuth University. His main research interests are on Risk, Crisis and Disasters, the political sociology of Portuguese-speaking countries in Africa, the sociology of religion in Africa, and the sociology of knowledge. He is the author of several books and articles.

Dieter **Neubert** holds a chair of development-sociology at the University of Bayreuth. His main research interests are the political sociology of Africa (democratization, civil society, patron-client relations and decentralization), the sociology of violent conflicts, local knowledge and participatory research, the sociology of development policy (particularly non-governmental organisations) and the social-structure of Africa.

Jonathan **Owens** is Professor of Arab Studies at the University of Bayreuth. His fields of research are Nigeria, Libya, Chad, Sudan, East Africa and the Arabic world in general. His main research areas are Arabic Hausa, Creole-Arabic, Glavda, socio-linguistics, the Arabic history of speech, etc.

Ulrich **Rinn** was a Research Fellow in African History at the University of Bayreuth until 2006. As part of the SFB project, he carried out research into ancient globalisation. Today he is Lecturer in the Institute of Ethnology and African Studies, University of Mainz.

Dana **Rush** is Assistant Professor in Art History in the Department of Art and Design at the University of Illinois at Urbana Champaign. Among other things she has been doing research on 'African Art in the Museum: Problems of Presentation and Representation'.

Hans-Jörg **Schmid** studied English and physical education at the University of Munich, Munich Technical University and the University of Exeter (UK). He was full-time research assistant in English linguistics, University of Munich from 1989 to 1999 and spent one year in London and one year in Oxford. Schmid held the chair of English Linguistics at Bayreuth University from 2000 to 2005, when he moved to Munich University to take over the chair of Modern English Linguistics.

Farouk **Topan** taught at the School of African and Oriental Studies in London where he was Senior Lecturer and Chair of the Department of Africa. His publications are on various aspects of Swahili written and oral literature, spirit possession, religion and identity in East Africa. His latest volume is a co-edited book, with Pat Caplan: *Swahili Modernities. Culture, politics and identity of the East Coast of Africa.* Topan was a founding member of the Department of Swahili, University of Dar es Salaam, in 1970. He introduced the teaching of Swahili literature at Dar and also at the University of Nairobi. Topan is also a playwright: one of his plays (*Mfalme Juha*, 'The Idiot King') is a set text on the Tanzanian school curriculum.

Ulf **Vierke** has studied social anthropology, European folklore, Islamic studies and law. He wrote his dissertation on the trade in glass beads from central Europe to East Africa. Currently he is lecturer at Iwalewa House, the centre for contemporary African art at the University of Bayreuth. Since 2005 his research has focused on art in lusophone Africa, especially on contemporary art and photography in Angola.

Beiträge zur Afrikaforschung

hrsg. vom Institut für Afrika-Studien der Universität Bayreuth

Peter Probst; Gerd Spittler (eds.)
Between Resistance and Expansion
Explorations of Local Vitality in Africa
Be it the vitality of African popular culture, the vitality of religious ideas or the vitality of artistic forms of expressions – invoking the notion of vitality has become a common practice in Africanist discourses. Most often, the purpose of invoking this notion is to emphasize the unexpected and astonishing power and strength of certain cultural fields in Africa. But what is really meant with the notion of local vitality beyond its metaphorical usage, beyond the underrated and unforeseen? The present volume brings together a number of essays exploring the answers to these questions from different perspectives and disciplines. Based upon an international conference on Local Vitality and the Globalization of the Local organized by the Humanities Collaborative Research Centre at the University of Bayreuth, Germany, the contributions discuss the various dimensions of vitality in the context of debates about identity and self-assertion, locality and appropriation, and rivalry and resistance.
Bd. 18, 2. Aufl. 2006, 480 S., 29,90 €, br., ISBN 3-8258-6980-6

Peter Probst
Kalumbas Fest
Lokalität, Geschichte und Rituelle Praxis in Malawi
Bd. 19, 2005, 376 S., 24,90 €, br., ISBN 3-8258-6981-4

Roman Loimeier; Dieter Neubert; Cordula Weißköppel (Hg.)
Globalisierung im lokalen Kontext
Perspektiven und Konzepte von Handeln in Afrika
Bd. 20, 2005, 360 S., 34,90 €, br., ISBN 3-8258-6983-0

Gordon R. Woodman; Ulrike Wanitzek; Harald Sippel (Eds.)
Local Land Law and Globalization
A comparative study of peri-urban areas in Benin, Ghana and Tanzania
Bd. 21, 2004, 392 S., 29,90 €, br., ISBN 3-8258-7843-0

Jeannett Martin
Been-To, Burger, Transmigranten?
Zur Bildungsmigration von Ghanaern und ihrer Rückkehr aus der Bundesrepublik Deutschland
Bd. 22, 2005, 336 S., 24,90 €, br., ISBN 3-8258-8079-6

Hauke Dorsch
Globale Griots
Performanz in der afrikanischen Diaspora
Bd. 23, 2006, 384 S., 29,90 €, br., ISBN 3-8258-8977-7

Mohamed Pakia
African Traditional Plant Knowledge Today
An ethnobotanical study of the Digo at the Kenya Coast
Bd. 24, 2006, 224 S., 29,90 €, br., ISBN 3-8258-9056-2

LIT Verlag Berlin – Hamburg – London – Münster – Wien – Zürich
Fresnostr. 2 48159 Münster
Tel.: 0251 / 620 32 22 – Fax: 0251 / 922 60 99
e-Mail: vertrieb@lit-verlag.de – http://www.lit-verlag.de